Field Guide to
MEDICINAL
WILD PLANTS

Field Guide to
MEDICINAL WILD PLANTS

BRADFORD ANGIER

Illustrations by Arthur J. Anderson

STACKPOLE BOOKS

FIELD GUIDE TO MEDICINAL WILD PLANTS

First printing, December 1978
Second printing, March 1981

Published by
STACKPOLE BOOKS
Cameron and Kelker Streets
P.O. Box 1831
Harrisburg, Pa. 17105

Published simultaneously in Don Mills, Ontario, Canada
by Thomas Nelson & Sons, Ltd.

The identification, selection, and processing of any wild plant for use as a
medicinal requires reasonable care and attention to details. As indicated in the
text, certain parts of some plants are wholly unsuitable for use and, in some
instances, are even toxic. Consistent with the capabilities of modern printing
technology, every effort has been made to illustrate each plant with utmost
fidelity of color and hue; nevertheless, some variations in their actual
appearance may be encountered in the field as a result of seasonal and/or
geographic factors. Because attempts to use any wild plants as medicinals
depend on various factors controllable only by the reader, the publisher
assumes no responsibility whatsoever for adverse health effects of such failures
as might be encountered in the individual case.

LIBRARY OF CONGRESS CATALOGING IN PUBLICATION DATA
Angier, Bradford
    Field guide to medicinal wild plants
    Includes index.
    1. Botany, Medical—North America.   2. Materia medica,
Vegetable—North America.   3. Indians of North
America—Medicine.   I. Title.
QK99.N67A53   1978   581.6'34'097   78-19112
ISBN 0-8117-2076-4

Printed in the United States of America.

For the talented
Fred and Paula Penney,
our friends

OTHER BOOKS BY BRADFORD ANGIER

The Master Outdoorsman
Ask for Love and They Give You Rice Pudding
  with Barbara Corcoran
Wilderness Wife
  with Vena Angier
Looking for Gold: The Modern Prospector's Handbook
Field Guide to Edible Wild Plants
The Freighter Travel Manual
The Home Book of Cooking Venison and Other Natural Meats
Introduction to Canoeing
  with Zack Taylor
Survival with Style
Wilderness Gear You Can Make Yourself
One Acre and Security
Feasting Free on Wild Edibles
How to Live in the Woods on Pennies a Day
The Art and Science of Taking to the Woods
  with C. B. Colby
A Star to the North
  with Barbara Corcoran
Home Medical Handbook
  with E. Russel Kodet, M.D.
More Free-for-the-Eating Wild Foods
Being Your Own Wilderness Doctor
  with E. Russel Kodet, M.D.
Gourmet Cooking for Free
The Ghost of Spirit River
  with Jeanne Dixon
Skills for Taming the Wilds
Free for the Eating
Home in Your Pack
Mister Rifleman
  with Colonel Townsend Whelen
We Like It Wild
Wilderness Cookery
On Your Own in the Wilderness
  with Colonel Townsend Whelen
Living Off the Country
How to Build Your Home in the Woods
At Home in the Woods
  with Vena Angier

DIRECTORY OF
WILD MEDICINALS

* All names in boldface type indicate major sections of this book.

7

H

Hackberry, 254
Hackmatack, 47, 193
Hackmatick, 152
Hack Tree, 254
Hagthorn, 132
Hairy Balm-of-Gilead, 45
Hairy Sumac, 240
Hamamelia, 311
Happy-Major, 96
Hard Maple, 165
Hard Pine, 193
Hare's Beard, 179
Haw, 132
Hawthorn, 132
Hawthorne, 132
Heartease, 158
Heartroot, 140
Heart Snakeroot, 140
Heartweed, 158
Hedge Maple, 165
Hedge Taper, 179
Herb Robert, 283
Herb Wickopy, 130
Heron's Bill, 283
High Angelica, 41
High Blueberry, 66
Highbush Blackberry, 62
Highbush Blueberry, 66
Highbush Cranberry, 238
High Cranberry, 238
High Cranberry Bush, 238
Hillberry, 81
Hindheal, 261
Hind Heal, 261
Hive Vine, 266
Hogapple, 99
Hog Apple, 99
Hogbrake, 69
Hog Brake, 69
Hog Cranberry, 52
Hog Plum, 295
Honeyberry, 254
Hoofs, 93
Hooker Evening Primrose, 118
Hoop Ash, 254

Hop Clover, 281
Horehound, 172
Horsefoot, 93
Horse Foot, 93
Horse Gentium, 63
Horsemint, 172
Horse Plum, 295
Horseradish, 286
Horse-Radish, 286
Horse Savin, 152
Horsetail, 135
Horsetail Grass, 135
Horseweed, 89
Hot Potato, 140
Huckleberry, 66
Hudson Bay Currant, 124
Hudson's Bay Tea, 161
Hurts, 66
Husk Tomato, 252
Hybrid Amaranth, 33

I

Iceland Lichen, 76
Iceland Moss, 76
Ice Leaf, 179
Indian Apple, 99
Indian Cherry, 295
Indian Chickweed, 84
Indian Elm, 232
Indian Fig, 137
Indian Ginger, 140
Indian Grape, 127
Indian Jack-in-the-Pulpit, 143
Indian Lettuce, 146
Indian Mozemize, 111
Indian Mustard, 182
Indian Nosy, 228
Indian Paint, 250
Indian Pear, 215
Indian Plantago, 235
Indian Psyllium, 235
Indian Rice, 148
Indian Root, 228
Indian Strawberry, 250
Indian Tobacco, 179
Indian Turnip, 143

Lodgepole Pine, 193
Lombardy Poplar, 45
Long Boughs, 311
Longleaf Pine, 193
Longstalk Clover, 281
Lords and Ladies, 143
Love-Lies-Bleeding, 33
Low Birch, 58
Lowbush Blueberry, 66
Lowbush Cranberry, 106
Low Hop-Clover, 281
Low Oak, 185
Low Pigweed, 200
Low Sweet Blueberry, 66

M

Mackerel Mint, 170
Mahogany, 35
Mahogany Birch, 56
Mahonia, 188
Mandrake, 99
Manroot, 38
Man's Health, 38
Manzanita, 52
Maple, 165
March Turnip, 143
Mare-Blobs, 168
Marigold of Peru, 256
Marsh Cinquefoil, 91
Marsh Fivefinger, 91
Marsh Marigold, 168
Marsh Onion, 292
Marsh Pine, 193
Marsh Potato, 43
Marsh Tea, 161
Masse-Misse, 111
Masterwort, 41
Masterwort Aromatic, 41
May, 132
Mayapple, 99
May Apple, 99
May Apple Rhizome, 99
May Apple Root, 99
May Blossom, 132
Mayflower, 132
May Haw, 132

Meadow Bouts, 168
Meadowbright, 168
Meadow Clover, 281
Meadow Fern, 305
Meadow Garlic, 292
Meadownut, 91
Meadow Sage, 210
Meadow Salsify, 122
Meadow Turnip, 143
Mealberry, 52
Mealyberry, 52
Mealy Plum Vine, 52
Memory Root, 143
Mexican Dock, 108
Mexican Ground Cherry, 252
Mexican Juniper, 152
Michigan Banana, 102
Milfoil, 314
Milfoil Thousand-Leaf, 314
Milkweed, 228
Miner's Lettuce, 146
Minor Birch, 58
Mint, 170
Missey-Moosey, 111
Mississippi Hackberry, 254
Missouri Currant, 124
Missouri Gooseberry, 124
Missy-Massy, 111
Mitten Tree, 217
Montpelier Maple, 165
Monterey Pine, 193
Moon Mint, 172
Moor Grass, 91
Mooseberry, 238
Moose Elm, 232
Moose Maple, 165
Moosewood, 165
Morning Primrose, 118
Moss Rose, 298
Mossycup Oak, 185
Mother's Heart, 78
Moth Herb, 161
Mountain Ash, 111
Mountain Berry, 81
Mountain Bilberry, 66
Mountain Blackberry, 62
Mountain Blue Elderberry, 113

Silver Poplar, 45
Silver Saltbush, 213
Silver Scale, 213
Silver-Sheathed Knotweed, 158
Silverweed, 91
Skoka, 197
Skunk Currant, 124
Skunk Grape, 127
Slash Pine, 193
Sleek Sumac, 240
Sleek Sumach, 240
Slender Gooseberry, 124
Slender Nettle, 245
Slender Pigweed, 33
Slim Amaranth, 33
Slim-Flowered Scurvy Pea, 41
Slipper Thorn, 137
Slippery Elm, 232
Sloe, 295
Sloe Plum, 295
Slum Bloom, 283
Slum Root, 283
Small Cranberry, 106
Smaller Hop-Clover, 281
Small Grape, 127
Small Houseleak, 248
Small Jack-in-the-Pulpit, 143
Small Soapweed, 318
Small-Toothed Aspen, 47
Small Wood Sunflower, 256
Smartweed, 158
Smelling Stick, 217
Smooth Pigweed, 191
Smooth Sumac, 240
Smooth Wild Gooseberry, 124
Snakeberry, 266
Snakeroot, 140
Snakeweed, 158, 235
Snapping Hazel, 311
Snapping Hazel-Nut, 311
Snowball Tree, 238
Snow Willow, 308
Soapweed, 318
Soap Weed, 318
Soft Elm, 232
Soft Maple, 165
Soft Yellow Poplar, 47

Soldiers Herb, 235
Soldier's Woundwort, 314
Soldier's Wound-Wort, 314
Sourberry, 190
Sour Cherry, 215
Sour Dock, 108
Sour-Top Blueberry, 66
Souther, 272
Southern Bayberry, 49
Southern Crab Apple, 274
Southern Fox Grape, 127
Southern Hackberry, 254
Southern Lewisia, 60
Southern Poplar, 47
Southern Red Oak, 185
Southern Snakeroot, 140
Southern Witch Hazel, 311
Sowberry, 190
Sowfoot, 93
Spanish Bayonet, 318
Spanish Dagger, 318
Spanish Lettuce, 146
Spanish Oak, 185
Spanish Psyllium, 235
Spatlum, 60
Spearmint, 170
Spear Orach, 213
Spiceberry, 81, 272
Spice Berry, 81
Spicewood, 272
Spicebush, 272
Spicy Birch, 58
Spicy Wintergreen, 81
Spiked Maple, 165
Spiked Willow-Herb, 130
Spleen Amaranth, 33
Spleen Fern, 305
Spleenwort Bush, 305
Spleenwort Fern, 305
Spoonwort, 233
Spotted Alder, 311
Spotted Crane's Bill, 283
Spotted Geranium, 283
Spotted Knotweed, 158
Spotted Saxifrage, 221
Spring Wintergreen, 81
Spurry Knotweed, 158

INTRODUCTION

When the aurora borealis was abroad and the timber wolves were howling throughout much of the savagely bitter winter of 1535–36, the second voyage of Jacques Cartier, the French navigator and explorer who had discovered the St. Lawrence River, was at a standstill, with his trio of small ships frozen in solidly near the present site of Montreal and the crew shut off from the rest of the world not only by ice but by nearly shoulder-high snow and forced to exist on the dwindling stores stowed in the holds.

No more than 10 men out of a crew of 110 were fit for duty by February 1536, and none escaped entirely the ravages of the then unknown disease that had already killed 25. At first no cure could be found, although postmortem dissections were painstakingly conducted.

Then Cartier, able leader that he was, fortunately discovered that similarly affected Indians were being rapidly cured by a decoction made from the sap and juice of a certain evergreen which has now been generally accepted to be the juniper. The Indian women were stripping the branches from this tree, which he called the *annedda,* boiling the needles and bark, and applying the results to the legs of their stricken people. No one knew of vitamin C then, and of course the external applications accomplished nothing. But what was later to be known as spruce beer smelled so good that some of it was drunk. That accomplished the miracle. The French hurriedly tore and cut a whole tree bare, drank the decoction with its inviting Christmas-treelike aroma, and within a week all were cured.

This was all the more remarkable because scurvy, as it was later called, remained a debilitator and killer until well into this century, even after the discovery of vitamins and antiscorbutics. During the California gold strike of 1849 the forty-niners were dropping with the disease until the Indians, and the Spanish who had been informed by them, told these prospectors and miners of miner's lettuce. Then hundreds more weakened, lost their teeth, and even their lives farther north during the Klondike stampede at the turn of the century until Indians showed them the virtues of such remedies as a number of greens that came to be known as scurvy grass and of spruce tea steeped from the needles of that tree.

The long-continuing error of the seafaring English in treating scurvy was their dependence on such things as lime juice, which became a daily issue in the navy in 1793, the accepted thought being that the sourer it was the better; whereas the fact is that no matter how sour a lime, lemon, orange, or onion, or anything else may be, it all goes for naught unless that particular article is fresh. The fresher an edible is, and the less it is subjected to heat, the better it will prevent and cure scurvy; although, of course, wild medicinals vary widely in their content of vitamin C, which the body needs regularly as the human system cannot store it.

The impact of American Indian medical practices, abetted by those of the pioneers, was considerable in its influence on the medicine, healing, and pharmacology of today's world. Drugs such as the antibiotics, insulin, and even aspirin were anticipated in their basic forms by our Indians.

Some 150 wild medicinal plants, and about 40 more from the natives of the Caribbean and Latin America, were given to the civilized world's pharmacopoeia by the Indians of North America. In other words, the influence of American Indian healing practices has been inestimable in present-day medical lore. As a matter of fact, animal bladders and hollow-bone syringes were utilized by the Indians of this country for enemas, douches, and for irrigating wounds long before the first Europeans reached this continent.

Perhaps the most obvious manifestation of Indian prestige in American medicine is evidenced in the fact that more than 200 native drugs which were being utilized by one or more Indian nations have been official in the *Pharmacopoeia of the United States of America* for differing periods since the first edition appeared in 1820, and in the *National Formulary* since it was started in 1888. So absolute was the aboriginal knowledge of our native flora that Indian usage and therapeutic practices can be traced for all but a scant five or so of the aboriginal uses of these wild medicines, paralleled, moreover, by those approved in the *U.S. Dispensatory*. There are also several hundred native reliefs and cures which have been used in domestic medicine by qualified doctors despite the fact that they have not gained official recognition.

Time brings about changes. Thousands of pounds of the lowly little wintergreen, especially interesting to me as it was the first wild plant I ever gathered and used, were once sought and sold for commercial purposes. These were later replaced by the oil of the birch tree, as the latter, botanically similar, was more easily and inexpensively procured. Today the still very widely used wintergreen is synthetically manufactured. The same is true with penicillin and other antibiotics, with the fever-reducing and arthritis-prescribed aspirin which is also found in willow and poplar bark, and with many other pharmaceuticals.

Because of prudent common sense, and because of the completely reasonable code of the qualified M.D., nothing in this book proposes to be other than interesting, valuable, and engrossing history. Nowhere is the reader advised to attempt self-diagnosis or self-medication. In fact, he is most strongly advised against it.

"Self-diagnosis and self-medication may be extremely hazardous to one's health" is the way my friend Thomas J. Gray, M.D., long distinguished Director of Student Health at sprawling San Jose State College, puts it. "This is particularly true with regard to dosing one's self with unstandardized substances, the potency of which has not been carefully calibrated."

AMARANTH (*Amaranthus*)

Family: Amaranth (Amaranthaceae)

Common Names: Spleen Amaranth, Palmer's Amaranth, Red Amaranth, Redroot, Wild Beet, Red Cockscomb, Green Amaranth, Green-Opened Amaranth, Prostrait Amaranth, Prostrate Amaranth, Slim Amaranth, Hybrid Amaranthus, Prince's Feather, Pigweed, Slender Pigweed, Prostrate Pigweed, Keerless, Careless, Careless Weed, Love-Lies-Bleeding, Floramor, Flower Gentle, Velvet Flower, Flower Velure.

Characteristics: Amaranth is an erect annual, some 1 to 6 feet high, and branched above. The stemmed leaves, about 3 to 6 inches long, are dully green, rough, hairy, ovate or rhombic, with wavy rims. The small flower clusters end in pyramidiçal, loosely branched, reddish or greenish inflorescences. The fleshy taproots, lengthy and pinkish to red in color, give the medicinal some of its local names.

It is an easy thing to mistake amaranth for pigweed (*Chenopodium*), which makes little difference to the food gatherer, as both are about equally delicious. But the leaves and stalks of the amaranth are ordinarily softly fuzzy, whereas those of the *Chenopodium* are smooth with a loosely attached whitish bloom. Also, the *Amaranthus* has noticeably strong veins. It has picked up its deceptive common name of pigweed in some locales because it likes the rich soil found in and about pigpens.

The Zunis believed the rain gods brought the bright and shiny black seeds from the underworld and dispersed them over their lands. Minute, these seeds are numerous—some 28,000 per ounce—and are widely distributed by the wind. They emerge as plants within fourteen to twenty-one days at temperatures from 65 to 75°F. Department of Agriculture scientists have found that if water does not reach them, those of the *A. retroflexus* are still living and capable of reproduction after forty, but not fifty, years in the soil.

Area: Except where thwarted by frozen ground and too much cold, the amaranth thrives throughout most of the United States and Canada where there is enough dampness.

Uses: Containing, despite a water content of nearly 90 percent, 3.9 milligrams of iron per 100 grams (more than any green vegetable except parsley listed in the U.S.D.A. *Composition of Foods*), amaranth is extremely important to anyone with a deficiency in this mineral, including most women. It is also a vital antiscorbutic, the same 100-

Amaranth (*Amaranthus*)

gram portion boasting 80 milligrams of vitamin C. Yet countless tons of this unusually nutritious and delectable vegetable, considered by most to be just another weed, go to waste annually.

Amaranth used to be considered helpful in treating mouth and throat inflammations and sores, and in quelling dysentery and diarrhea; one dose was a teaspoonful of dried leaves steeped in a cup of bubbling water, although stronger dosages were considered more valuable. It was also thought to stem abnormally profuse menstrual flows as well as internal hemorrhaging. Taken internally, too, it was supposed to help quiet and eventually cure ulcers in the digestive tract.

Flowers, leaves, and roots were sought because of their astringent quality for external wounds, sores, and ulcers. They were simmered to make a mouthwash for cankers, sore throats, ulcerated gums and to strengthen gums that bled too freely after ordinary tooth brushing. Amaranth was even said to be useful in the care of venereal diseases. At the other extreme, it was one of the remedies for a nosebleed.

Because of its ability to produce a soapy lather, the leaf of the *A. retroflexus* was used in the washing of bandages and other fabrics from the sickroom.

Indians made poultices from it to reduce ordinary swellings and to soothe aching teeth. A tea made from the leaves by some of the tribes to allay stomachache was also used to wash arthritic parts of the body. Strong decoctions were thought to kill and expel intestinal worms.

AMERICAN COFFEE BEAN (*Gymnocladus*)

Family: Pulse (Leguminosae)

Common Names: Kentucky Coffee Tree, Kentucky Coffeetree, Coffee Nut, Chicot, Mahogany.

Characteristics: The American coffeee bean tree has such attraction that few, once they look for it and find it, will forget it, especially as it is widely used for landscaping. Its French-Canadian name, heard in Quebec, is *Chicot,* which translates as "stump." The generic name *Gymnocladus* refers to "nude branch." Both names recognize the fact that this tree is without its doubly compound, almost 3-foot-long and 2-foot-wide leaves a great part of each year, being one of the last trees to leaf in the late spring and among the first to defoliate in the early fall.

American Coffee Bean (*Gymnocladus*)

It is then that the big seedpods on their robust stems, ordinarily remaining on the tree all winter if not picked, gain attention. They come from verdant white blossoms, flowering in terminal racemes— simple inflorescences in which the elongated stalks bear their flowers on short stems successively toward the tips. The flattish and rather heavy pods, dark and leathery and mahogany-colored with a grayish and powdery covering, grow some 4 to 18 inches in length and a rugged inch or 2 inches wide. Each encases in a dark sweetish mass of tissue some half dozen to a dozen seeds. These are more like beans; they are hard, somewhat ovoid and flattish, nearly an inch long (although usually shorter), chocolate to grayish brown entities, not likely to be mistaken.

About 240 of these well-known native, macrobiotic seeds make a pound. The flowering is generally in June, so that, on those trees whose pods open, the seeds are normally dispersed from September to March. Having impermeable seed coats, they weigh on the average of 1,649.45 grams per 1,000 cleaned seeds, according to the U.S. Department of Agriculture, which has made a study of them.

Area: The American coffee bean, liking rich damp land, is usually found, where it is growing naturally, in lowlands by running water. Although it is capable of existing outdoors during New England winters when introduced for landscaping, the American coffee bean ranges naturally from as far north as Minnesota and New York south to Tennessee and Oklahoma.

Uses: At about the time Daniel Boone was helping to settle Kentucky, the early pioneers found that the seeds of what they came to call the Kentucky coffee tree resembled coffee beans; so they roasted and ground them for making a substitute coffee, which proved to be nutritious, refreshing, and stimulating after an especially wet day in the forest. It was so utilized widely in the interior of the budding colonies by the settlers from the Old World, even on exploration trips that reached as far as the Missouri River, where it was found growing wild. The Pawnees were among the Indians roasting the seeds around their campfires, not then pulverizing them for beverage uses but eating them like chestnuts for nutritious and healthful reasons.

The pods with their pulpy fillings were put up as preserves by the pioneer women, who found that they had a gentle laxative effect. They were also crushed, sweetened, and used on the spot for the same purpose.

The roots of this *Gymnocladus dioica* were dried, pulverized by rubbing them between two smooth stones, and used in an enema for internal disorders, such as constipation, diarrhea, and hemorrhoids; the American Indians had independently discovered the bulb syringe and the enema tube.

Whereas the ladies of Europe used smelling salts to revive those in a faint, their relations in this New World found that the powdered American coffee bean has an even more drastic effect. Causing uncontrollable sneezing, it quickly revived such a patient, being so powerful that it was also so used as an extreme remedy to bring more than one individual out of the torpor of a coma.

AMERICAN GINSENG (*Panax quinquefolium*)

Family: Ginseng (Araliaceae)

Common Names: Ginseng, Gensang, Sang, Jinshard, Grantogen, Garantogen, Garantogere, Garentoquere, Ninsin, Manroot, Man's Health, Tartar Root, Redberry.

Characteristics: American ginseng is a native of this continent, its favorite habitat being rich moist soil in shaded hardwood forests. The name *Panax* comes from the Greek, a panacea—a reference to the multitudinous virtues attributed to the plant.

It is an erect perennial, growing some 8 to 15 inches high and usually bearing three leaves at its summit, each consisting of five thin, stalked, ovate leaflets. These have long points at the tip, are narrow or rounded at the bottom. With toothed margins, the three upper leaflets are the largest.

From six to ten small greenish yellow flowers grow in an inconspicuous manner during July and August, followed later in the season by shiny, bright, crimson berries.

American ginseng has a thick, spindle-shaped root, at least 2 to 3 inches long, and sometimes more, and about ½ to 1 inch thick, the outside being prominently marked with circles or wrinkles. After the second year it usually becomes forked, and it is the branched root, particularly if it resembles the human form, that finds favor in the eyes of the Chinese, who are the main consumers and purchasers from the various herb companies.

Ginseng root has thick, pale yellowish white or brownish white bark, conspicuously wrinkled traversely, the whole root being fleshy and somewhat flexible. It has a slight aromatic odor, and the taste is

American Ginseng (*Panax quinquefolium*)

sweetish and mucilaginous. The proper time for digging the root is in the autumn, when it should be carefully washed, sorted, and dried. If collected at any other season, it will shrink more and will not have its prime, plump appearance. If not thoroughly dried, it will mold.

Indians gather the root only after the fruit has ripened, and it is generally their practice to bend down and cover the stem and the ripened berries to provide for continued propagation, since they claim that a large percentage of the seeds thus treated do germinate.

Area: American ginseng grows mainly and naturally from Maine to Minnesota, south to Oklahoma and the mountains of Georgia and Arkansas.

Uses: A tea made from the root is used in Appalachia today as a tonic and stimulant and, hopefully, as an aphrodisiac. The Indians believed it prevented conception. On the other hand, the French Canadians credited it with increasing fertility. Some powdered it and added it to other medicines in an effort to increase the latter's potency.

On its own the tea was given to stop vomiting and convulsions. It was another of the sought-for arthritic aids. The Indians and the settlers tried it in the treatment of nervous disorders, dizziness, shortness of breath, fevers, and even headaches. It was used to help stanch the flow of blood from gashes, cuts, and other wounds.

The root was chopped, boiled, and given to babies for colic. Infants were also treated by it for croup. The ground root was utilized for asthma and for queasy stomachs. Old-time doctors sometimes believed that externally the root helped stop bleeding and that internally it was good for the urinary system, even to the point of ridding the urinary system of stones and gravel. They utilized it for coughs and to promote perspiring, which thus lowered fever.

Chewed, the root was credited by the Indians with aiding digestion. They also made a tea of the leaves for chronic coughs. This was also resorted to as a demulcent. Indians in the South rubbed the milky juice from the roots on bothersome sores. The roots were crushed to provide a poultice for earache and for sore eyes. The Cherokees turned to decoctions of the root for feminine cramps and related disorders.

ANGELICA (*Angelica*)

Family: Parsley (Umbelliferae)

Common Names: American Angelica, Great Angelica, High Angelica, Common Angelica, Seacoast Angelica, Purplestem Angelica, Purple-Stem Angelica, Purplestemmed Angelica, Alexander's Angelica, Masterwort, Masterwort Aromatic, Scurvy Pea, Slim-Flowered Scurvy Pea, Bellyache Root, Alexanders, Archangel, Dead Nettle, Aunt Jericos.

Characteristics: The stout, hollow, purplish stalks of this shrub, also known as wild celery because of its similarity to this garden vegetable which many believe it exceeds in tastiness and juiceness, grow erectly up to some 7 or 8 feet high, often rough with oil veins.

The *Angelica archangelica,* for example, has three coarsely toothed leaves at the end of each leaf stalk. The leaflets are ovoid to oblong, 1 to some 3 or 4 inches long, with wide, leathery, enwrapping bases. The tiny, white or greenish blossoms are borne in nearly globe-shaped terminal assemblages 2 to 6 inches wide. The entire medicinal is agreeably aromatic, similar to store celery.

Area: Angelica thrives by the sea and streams, preferring low rich loam and detrital soil deposited by running or flowing water. It is found in marshes, swamps, ditches, water-fed ravines, moist meadows, and by mountain brooks, from farthest Alaska to Labrador, south to Illinois, Delaware, and West Virginia.

Uses: In Appalachia the root is harvested in the fall for immediate and winter use. Its volatile oil is still used there to treat colic and digestive gas.

The Indians used it to help discharge mucus from the respiratory tract. A strong, warm solution made by steeping the root in water was sometimes resorted to to induce vomiting. The root was also given for consumption and tuberculosis. The leaves and stalks are an antiscorbutic.

One of the oldest poultices on this continent was made by mashing the roots of the *A. archangelica,* blending them with the pounded leaves of one of the northern sagebrushes (*Artemisia canadensis*), heating the whole pulpy mass, and applying it to the side of the body opposite a pain. The pasty mash was also turned to for bringing down swelling.

Root tea was resorted to in lingering illnesses, particularly those

Angelica (*Angelica*)

of children. It was believed useful for irregular menstruation, to stimulate it, and for sharp cramps.

A decoction made by simmering the root was drunk as a tonic morning, noon, and at bedtime by some of the Rocky Mountain Indian bands. A strong tea thus made was imbibed several times daily by Indians and pioneers to build up strength after sickness. It was also sipped in small amounts to combat venereal diseases and as a wash for sores resulting from them.

A white physician of early days asserted that eating 15 to 60 grains of dried angelica root would break the drinking habit. Others claimed that taking small quantities of the powdered dried root in wine would abate sexual desire.

The Creeks used it for digestive difficulties, colic, hysteria, to kill and expel worms, and for back distress.

For kidney difficulties, including scantiness of urination, root tea was used. It was also given for heartburn, sour stomach, fever, and for cold and flu symptoms. It was believed by some to be effective in bringing epidemics to an end and for making the heart stronger. The tea was thought to be an effective cleanser and healer of lingering ulcers. The dried root, powdered, was similarly used.

Poultices of the mashed roots were applied for arthritis, chest discomfort, and pneumonia. Small scrapings of the root were used for coughing and sore throat, as well as for bronchitis. To clear the head, as during colds, scrapings of the dried roots were smoked. The roots were also crushed and spread over sores and wounds. The tea was even used as a mouthwash to make the breath more agreeable.

ARROWHEAD (*Sagittaria*)

Family: Water Plantain (Alismaceae)

Common Names: Arrowhead, Broad-Leaf Arrowhead, Duck Potato, Swan Potato, Swamp Potato, Tule Potato, Marsh Potato, Wapato, Wapatoo, Katniss.

Characteristics: The arrowhead, as its name suggests, has a pointed arrowheadlike leaf with the two barblike continuations, one on either side, as well as a stout green stem which might well be the shaft of the medicinal replica of this part of the Indians' arsenal—which also included bows, tomahawks, and lances. Just as they used the bow and arrow, Indians from one coast to the other relied on this wild vegeta-

Arrowhead (*Sagittaria*)

ble as food and medicine. All leaves are not the same, especially when the plants grow submerged and ribbonlike foliage is formed, but there are generally enough in a group for sure identification.

Three-petaled white flowers, with numerous pistils and yellow clusters of stamens, grow on their own single stems from June to September. Papery thin leaves extend directly below in the form of attractive clusters of subtending bracts. They mature into fruits with two-winged, round-topped, generally flattish seeds.

The tubers are the important parts, and those on the nearly three dozen different species of arrowhead in North America are all edible. Inasmuch as none is harmful, there is little need to try to segregate them botanically, although only about half a dozen produce the big, starchy corms which wading squaws ordinarily located with their toes, then loosened so that they would float. Long sticks can also be used to release them from mud and roots.

Area: Growing commonly in wet places, the arrowhead can be seen in damp locations throughout the southern parts of Canada and where it is damp enough in the original forty-eight states.

Uses: In addition to being considered a valuable and easily digestible food for invalids and convalescents, the corms were used as a diuretic. Juice pressed from them by the Indians, later by the newcomers from the Old World, was thought both to increase the flow of urine and to multiply the amount of the discharge of other waste ingredients in the process. The quickest action was found to take place when this juice, or the concentrated liquid from boiled tubers, was drunk on an empty stomach, preferably while the patient remained inactive and particularly if he stayed lying down in a comfortable place.

BALM-OF-GILEAD (*Populus candicens*)

Family: Willow (Salicaceae)

Common Names: Balm-of-Gilead, Hairy Balm-of-Gilead, Poplar, Balm Buds, Cottonwood, Eastern Cottonwood, Black Cottonwood, Swamp Cottonwood, River Cottonwood, Whitewood, Canoewood, Cucumberwood, Canary-Yellow Wood, Balsamroot, Balsam Poplar, Poplar Balsam, Poplar Tree, Lombardy Poplar, White Poplar, Bolles Poplar, Tacamahac Poplar, Silver-Leaf Poplar, Silver Poplar, Blue

©AJA

Balm-of-Gilead (*Populus candicens*)

Poplar, Yellow Poplar, Soft Yellow Poplar, Black Poplar, Southern Poplar, Carolina Poplar, Swamp Poplar, Downy Poplar, Sap Poplar, Tulip Poplar, Popple, Tulip Tree, Saddletree, Saddleleaf, Tackamahac, Tacamahac, Taccamahac, Hackmatack, Old Wife's Shirt Tree, Aspen, Quaking Aspen, Trembling Aspen, Small-Toothed Aspen, Large-Toothed Aspen, Big-Toothed Aspen, American Aspen.

Characteristics: Many of these trees are slim, small, or medium-sized, but they also reach heights of 100 feet with trunk diameters of about 6 feet. They are often the first trees to thrust up after fire and logging operations. They have a distinctive medicinal odor, especially when the large, sticky, frequently reddish brown, fragrant, and very resinous buds are present.

Some forest trees develop mature seeds in no more than two months after flowering, and certain of the balm-of-Gileads are examples. The blossoms burst forth before the leaves in the early spring, the trees boasting either male or female blooms that droop in catkinate clusters, petalless but surviving in tight circular rows on slim stems. Soon maturing, they break open to release tightly packed seeds that, bearing long fluffy hairs which waft them about with the breezes, give some of the species their cottonwood names.

The bark of many of the trees, darkly ridged when mature, are notably smooth when young and floured with a greenish white powdery coating that brushes off on hands and clothing.

Area: Reaching from Newfoundland to Alaska, the balm-of-Gilead family extends south to Pennsylvania and throughout the mountains to Kentucky, west through the Rocky Mountains to New Mexico and California.

Uses: The fragrant, very sticky leaf buds of the balm-of-Gilead were mashed in lard to make a soothing salve that was spread on sunburned areas, scalds, scratches, inflamed skin, and wounds. They were also simmered in lard for the same use as an ointment for easing pain and for antiseptic purposes. Olive oil, cocoa fat, and even rendered grizzly bear oil and pure white black bear lard were also used as the base.

Besides such use as a vulnerary, the bud salves were also rubbed on the chest for coughs, colds, flu, and pneumonia. Soaked in a little honey, they were believed to be helpful for dull sight.

The medicinal-smelling, resinous properties of the clammy buds before they burst into leaves were also extracted by alcohol for salves and ointments, and for sparing internal use for stomach and kidney troubles, colds, coughs, as an expectorant, and as an antiseptic gargle. In some sections of the New World a skin lotion was prepared by soaking the buds in some high-proof alcoholic beverage, such as brandy, for two days.

The resin of the often pesky buds, which adhere to everything as they fall, was also used for scurvy and as a stimulating and blood-purifying spring tonic. A tea made by steeping a teaspoon of the buds in a cup of boiling water was believed to be even more soothing and stimulating than Oriental teas. It was certainly aromatically pleasant.

Some colonists collected the leaf buds in the springtime, dried them in closed containers during the summer and fall, then later made them into a salve to treat long-enduring ulcers and sores on the skin.

The mashed leaves were made into compresses to alleviate headaches and are still so enjoyed today in some areas. Their juice was injected into the ears to treat earache. Applying bandages soaked in vinegar in which the new young leaves had been crushed was believed to help in treating parts of the body affected by gout.

Colonists from Europe introduced the practice of steeping the fresh blossoms in cold water, straining, and then drinking the liquid to purify the blood.

Some Indians and settlers praised what they believed to be the effectiveness of chewing the root bark for relieving sore throats. The roots, both raw and boiled, were used as poultices for sprains and bruises. The water from the simmered roots was believed especially effective for treating sprains. It was applied, warm, to infections and to rheumatic parts to ease pain. It was taken internally in small amounts to help malaria and hysteria.

Dissolved or held in suspension by alcohol, the chopped bark was recommended by a number of old-time settlers for such varying purposes as infections of the kidneys, chest, digestive system, and for scurvy, arthritis, and gout.

The water that gathers in the hollows in these trees was once considered helpful in removing warts and allaying wheals—those suddenly burning or itching elevations of the skin surface.

The bark was once believed to be a substitute for quinine and useful as a generally stimulating and invigorating tonic, as well as for a more specific aid in cases of weakness, fever, stomach disturbances, sciatica, and for liver and kidney troubles.

Both the leaves and barks of the quaking aspen in particular were steeped in water to make a tea for internal use to help arthritis, cold symptoms, and acute allergic nasal catarrh and conjunctivitis, more commonly known as hay fever, and for the various so-called influenzas.

BAY (*Myrica*)

Family: Bayberry (Myricaceae)

Common Names: Bayberry, Black Bayberry, Bayberry Tallow, Tallow Bayberry, Southern Bayberry, Myrtle, Myrtle Tree, Wax Myrtle, Waxberry, Waxtree, Common Wax Myrtle, Dwarf Wax Myrtle, Bayberry Waxtree, Bearing Myrica, Candleberry Myrtle, Candleberry, Tallow Shrub, American Vegetable Tallow, Tallow, American Vegetable Wax, Cirier, Puckerbush.

Characteristics: The bay is a perennial shrub that soars to the treelike height of some 30 feet. The leaves, pleasingly evergreen and growing from about 1 to 4 inches long, are narrow, tapering at each end. The stems are short and the leaves themselves many times delicately toothed.

The trunks, from several to 30 inches thick, have a grayish bark. The fruit is gray, too. Inasmuch as the female and male flowers thrive on separate shrubs, only some of these produce fruit. The male catkins are prominent in the spring, particularly when the dusty pollen is borne aloft by the wind.

The charming fruit is coated with the whitish green of dry wax with a grainy texture. Once you have appreciated its attractively persistent odor, you'll never forget it. Many smell it in widely distributed waxberry candles before ever seeing its source. The abraded leaves, too, have a never-to-be-forgotten scent. Really a nutlet, the fruit is actually a delicately coated stone, directly covered with memorable grains resembling gunpowder, inside of which is a twin-seeded kernel.

Area: The bay is essentially a waterside shrub, abounding in moist and sandy, never muddy, soil. It tends to form clumps and thickets, and its distribution has been widened by the practice of planting it as a decorative shrub. Originally largely a small seaboard tree and a relatively thick and compact shrub, the bay's native range also extends along the St. Lawrence River to the start of the Great Lakes, which provide part of the United States and Canadian northeastern

Bay (*Myrica*)

boundary. One species thrives along the Pacific Ocean down into Mexico, while half a dozen others grow in the East from Canada to Florida and the Gulf of Mexico.

Uses: The base of the bark, best secured during the later part of autumn, was often gathered by bringing in the entire root, washing and scrubbing it diligently, and then, while it was still fresh, separating the bark with a hammer or by pounding and grinding the whole between two smooth stones. Others went to the trouble of stripping it in small shreds from the still-growing roots. The bark, in any event, was kept in a dry place and, when dehydrated, was pulverized. The resulting powder was thoroughly dried and kept in a dark place in a sealed jar or bottle.

The powdered bark was then steeped or boiled—the former process by stirring a teaspoonful of the ingredient into a cup of steaming hot water, allowing this to cool, and then, when it was cold, drinking 1 or 2 cupfuls a day—the latter procedure by simmering an ounce of the powdered bark in 2 cups of bubbling water and imbibing it while it was still warm.

The outstanding characteristic of both infusions was a marked astringency. It was used in cases of diarrhea and dysentery, both as an enema and as a drink. In larger doses it was sometimes employed as an emetic. Particularly since it has an agreeably aromatic scent and a spirited medicinal taste, it was favored as a mouthwash, especially when cankers were present and the gums were sore and bleeding, and as a gargle for sore throats. The tea was also deemed efficacious in cases of jaundice. It was sometimes used, too, to treat uterine hemorrhaging.

The powder, used as a snuff, was adjudged excellent for catarrh and for clearing nasal congestion. This powder was also used to treat boils, carbuncles, and milder sores, being applied directly to the afflicted parts. It was used in poultices for cuts and even bruises, troublesome scratches, and insect bites.

The leaves and stems of the bay were boiled in water and drunk both to allay fever and, in stronger doses, to eliminate worms in the intestinal tract. The leaves, with their vitamin C, cured and prevented scurvy. The berries were used to relieve flatulence and to ease cold symptoms.

BEARBERRY (*Arctostaphylos uvaursi*)

Family: Heath (Ericaceae)

Common Names: Arberry, Bear's Grape, Bearberry, Alpine Bearberry, Red Bearberry, Uva Ursi, Bear's Bilberry, Bear's Whortleberry, Red Bearberry, Foxberry, Crowberry, Mealyberry, Mealberry, Rockberry, Upland Cranberry, Hog Cranberry, Mountain Box, Mealy Plum Vine, Universe Vine, Barren Myrtle, Manzanita, Coralillo, Brawline.

Characteristics: Usually growing in dry, sandy, gravelly, sunny, poor soils, and where limestone is predominant, this perennial evergreen is especially noticeable in northern areas when its encouraging verdency becomes bright amid melting snowdrifts.

This member of the heath family is an attractive, creeping, ground-covering shrub with stems seldom much more than 3 inches long. It has reddish bark and long, sinewy roots. Small pink-marked, white blossoms cluster into view in the summer, as inconspicuously as do the later smooth, generally orange to reddish berries with their dry, seedy, rather tasteless mealiness.

Growing in thick carpets, the bearberry has numerous, short-stemmed, odorless, shiny, vein-skeined, small but thickish, ovate, green leaves which brown and toughen as they remain on the trailing branches from season to season. The white to pinkish flowers, each with five segments and formed like tiny narrow-mouthed urns, mature into small fruits with five seeds.

Area: Because bearberries also grow in the northern parts of Europe and Asia, their medicinal properties were observed by Kublai Khan, founder of the Mongol dynasty in China, and by Italian traveler Marco Polo. On this continent they thrive from the Arctic and northern reaches, south in the East to Virginia and in the West to California, where the aborigines early used them, passing along their lore to those of the earliest pioneers who were not aware of it all.

Uses: For later use, as to increase the flow of urine and generally to cleanse the urinary tract, Indians and pioneers commonly gathered basketfuls of the younger, more perfect leaves about August, the more particular waiting until the dew and any rain was off them, as the practice was to dry them at living-quarter temperatures for later use as a tea, steeping a rounded tablespoon in a quart pot of boiling water until cool enough to sip by the cupful.

A pioneer innovation was soaking the dried and powdered leaves

Bearberry (*Arctostaphylos uvaursi*)

in an alcoholic beverage and imbibing a small amount of this in a cup of hot water for chronic inflammations of the kidneys or bladder, as well as for gravel and kidney stones. Such tea was sometimes given mothers hemorrhaging from childbirth. The stronger teas in both instances were used as astringents.

When an Indian or mountain man was parched, he often reached down for several of the bitterish leaves to chew to start his saliva flowing again. On this continent the leaves were many times mixed with dwindling supplies of regular tobacco and even smoked by themselves.

The leaves were also boiled with water, allowed to cool, and the decoction relied upon to stop the itching and spread of poison oak and poison ivy. The same infusion was also drunk for widely different ailments, from stomachache to sprains. The extract made from the leaves was believed to help catarrh and chronic bronchitis, as well as menstrual difficulties.

Furthermore, a tea made by soaking bearberry leaves and those from the beebalm or horsemint in water (elsewhere discussed in this book) was drunk to help complications arising from the common cold.

The powdered leaves, tan in color, tinted with a greenish yellow, were also soaked in rum and brandies and used like the leaf extract and sparingly as a spring tonic.

The orangish red berries, still enjoyed today as a food by many an Indian and backwoodsman, were considered to be helpful for those unfortunates suffering with kidney stones.

BEECH (*Fagus*)

Family: Beech (Fagaceae)

Common Names: American Beech, White Beech, Red Beech, Ridge Beech, Winter Beech, Stone Beech.

Characteristics: This continent's sole native beech, one of the quartet of recognized species throughout the world, is a large, magnificent tree, with a 3- or 4-foot diameter, reaching in some instances more than 100 feet into the sky. Its green leaves, 2 to 5 inches long, turn brightly silky before they mature, beautifully yellow in the fall. Its closely clasping, bluish or light gray bark, frequently blotched in the fall, is smooth. During winters our beech cannot be mistaken for any

Beech (*Fagus*)

other native tree because of its slim, distinctively conelike, scaly buds, about 1 inch long.

Both the pollen-rich male flowers and the pistillate female blossoms grow on the same tree, the latter in pairs where the upper leaves lift from the twigs. These mature in the autumn into small, hairy, four-part burrs, readily opened by the thumbnail to reveal two little, brown, triangular, concave nuts eagerly sought by birds, animals, and hungry human beings. Deer, among other big game, eat the buds, twigs, foliage, and bark as well.

Area: Choosing moist, rich, and shadily cool uplands and bottom surfaces whenever possible, beeches thrive naturally from Wisconsin and Ontario to New Brunswick and Nova Scotia, southward to the Gulf of Mexico. It is also a favorite shade and ornamental tree, which widens its range.

Uses: About an ounce of fresh or dried beech leaves were covered with 2 cups of boiling water and simmered for half an hour or more by the Indians and frontiersmen, strained, cooled, and then lightly washed over scalds and burns. Frostbitten parts, such as fingers, were held in it as soon as it was cool enough.

The Rappahannocks cut bits of the bark from the north sides of the trees, which, if the beeches got much sunlight, were darker, and steeped it in 2 cups of slightly salted, hot water until the liquid was well colored. They then used this to bathe parts of the body afflicted with the rash or the inflamed sores of poison ivy and poison oak, to alleviate the itch and to dry up the eruptions.

Some tribes applied the fresh green leaves of the tree to cool and alleviate swellings. These leaves were also boiled to make poultices and ointments. The bark was considered to be astringent and stimulating. Eating the nuts themselves, besides being pleasantly nourishing, was believed to ease kidney pain.

BIRCH (*Betula*)

Family: Birch (Betulaceae)

Common Names: Silver Birch, Golden Birch, Yellow Birch, Red Birch, Black Birch, Gray Birch, White Birch, American White Birch, European White Birch, Blueleaf Birch, Mahogany Birch, Mountain Mahogany Birch, Paper Birch, Mountain Paper Birch, Canoe Birch,

Birch (*Betula*)

Lady Birch, Swamp Birch, River Birch, Tundra Dwarf Birch, New foundland Dwarf Birch, European Weeping Birch, Northern Birch, Virginian Birch, Cherry Birch, Spicy Birch, Sweet Birch, Oldfield Birch, Minor Birch, Water Birch, Poverty Birch, Wirefield Birch, Poplar Birch, Low Birch.

Characteristics: Historically, the birch probably derives its name from a somewhat similar Sanskrit word translated as "that which is written upon." Numerous letters and journals have been inscribed on thin sheets of the multilayered bark of the white birches, so durable and pliable that many an Indian canoe was made of it.

There are two distinct types of birches growing on this continent—the well-known white birches and the so-called black birches with their black to reddish brown bark. The former grow up to about 100 feet high, with papery bark, flutters of which can be pulled off without disfiguring the trunks for easily and quickly starting campfires, even in the rain. The black birches can be differentiated from some of the wild cherries in that the broken twigs of the former have the smell of wintergreen, whereas those of the cherries are characterized by a bitter-almond odor.

Area: The familiar white birches, both trees and shrubs, thrive over the majority of Canada and the United States with the exception of a wide band down the central western portion of this country, along the lower Pacific Coast except where they have been transplanted as bright and cheerful decorations, and in the Southwest in general.

The black birches grow largely in higher, chillier, and not so fertile eastern regions of this country, where they became historically important when their nutritious bark was credited with saving the lives of numerous Confederate soldiers at the time of Garnett's retreat across the mountains before regrouping at Monterey, Virginia. For decades the path of the soldiers could be traced by the peeled birch trees. Black birches grow from Ontario to New England, south to Delaware and Ohio, and along the Appalachian range to Alabama and Georgia.

Uses: Before the commercial oil of wintergreen was manufactured synthetically, it was distilled from the bark and twigs of the black birch, this process being easier and less expensive than obtaining it from the spicy little wintergreen plant (*Gaultheria procumbens*), as was done previously on a large scale for such uses as a flavoring agent for toothpastes and other medicinals. The active principle here is methyl salicylate. Wintergreen tea, made by steeping a large handful of the freshly gathered, green leaves, was drunk, 1 or 2 cups a day, by the Indians and pioneers as a remedy for rheumatism and for headaches, its inherent salicylic acid being the prime ingredient of the aspirin that doctors prescribe today.

Some tribes, passing their lore along to frontiersmen, made a tea of the dried bark and leaves of the birches by steeping a teaspoonful to a cup of boiling water until the infusion cooled and then drinking it, strained, for the above and for a fever reducer to a stimulant and for relief from the pain of kidney stones. It was also used to relieve the cramps and discomfort caused by gas in the digestive system. The early Americans utilized it as a disinfectant and as a mouthwash, especially for sour mouths.

This infusion was also thought to be useful in stimulating the flow of urine, in purifying blood after the long cold winters, in expelling worms from the alimentary canal, and as a treatment for gout.

The maple-syruplike sap of the white birch—obtained in the spring as I have done by boring an inch or two into the lower tree trunk with an auger, fashioning a spout from a hollowed elderberry branch from which the pith has been poked or from a bent top of a tin can, and catching the drippings in a clean can whose wire bail is hung from a twig—may be boiled down in an uncovered pot for the hours needed to thicken it to a syrup which may then be mixed with cough syrup or drunk as is to relieve stomach cramps. (The hole in the tree was later plugged with wood.)

Some Indians brewed a tea from the leaves of the white birches, and made a poultice of the boiled bark for the treatment of burns, wounds, and bruises. The ashes they utilized to soften and eventually remove scabs.

The sap secured from the black birch was applied externally to help heal sores and boils or carbuncles.

Skin troubles such as eczema sometimes seemed to respond to an oil secured from white birches by boiling the wood and bark in water, leaving enough moisture to make an ointment which was rubbed onto the afflicted part.

The small conelike structures formed by the maturing of the fruits of the low birch (Betula pumila), long central spikes to which innumerable tiny dry scales adhere, were steeped in boiling water to make a tea which women sipped during painful menstruation and as a tonic following childbirth. The cones of this birch were also roasted on the coals of an almost expired campfire and the fumes inhaled for chronic nasal infections such as catarrh, an inflammation of the mucous membranes of the nose and air passages.

The Catawbas simmered the buds of the black birch to make a syrup to which sulphur was added to provide a salve for ringworm and for sores in general. Indians in Texas boiled the bark of this tree for use in healing sore hooves on their horses.

Many early Americans recognized the efficacy of the vitamin C in the sap of the white birch in preventing and curing scurvy. In writing of the use of the enema among aboriginal North Americans, Robert F. Heizer said in 1686 that the Ojibwas used steeped paper birch bark for this.

The sweet black smoke given off by burning white birch bark was believed efficacious in fumigating the air in dwellings where patients with contagious diseases had been confined.

The sap of the white birches was also credited with being laxative and diuretic. The bark and leaves of these widespread trees were applied externally by some of the tribes to cleanse ulcers and carbuncles, to combat gangrene, and to act as a general disinfectant in skin diseases.

BITTER-ROOT (*Lewisia rediviva*)

Family: Purslane (Portulacaceae)

Common Names: Sand Rose, Rock Rose, *Rediviva*, Redhead Louisa, Lewisia, Southern Lewisia, Tweedy's Lewisia, Tobacco Root, Spatlum.

Characteristics: The thick, linear rosettes of the sometimes 2-inch-long leaves of the bitter-root often fall off and are blown away by the time the bright rose, pink to whitish flowers appear nudely from March to July terminally on 1- to 3-inch single stems.

The blossoms of the perennial, up to about 2 inches in diameter, have twelve to eighteen showy oblong petals and six to eight petallike rose to white sepals comprising a cuplike calyx. Numerous golden to pinkish stamens enhance the middle of each blossom, often accompanied by pink-topped, conelike buds nodding on nearby stalks. The large, white-cored, starchy roots, the most important part of the plant to Indians, are best uncovered when revealed by the leaves as the ground first thaws.

Bitter-Root (*Lewisia rediviva*)

Area: The medicinal, named genetically after Captain Meriwether Lewis of the Lewis and Clark Expedition and adopted as the state flower of Montana, grows in and about that region and in the evergreen forests of northern California to British Columbia.

Uses: Early dried and stored for later use by the Indians, the mucilaginous substances given off by the roots when they were boiled in water served to bring up phlegm from the lungs and throat. The finely ground dried roots were particularly resorted to by the older members of the tribes for chewing when one had a sore throat.

Also called bitter-root—as well as feverroot, feverwort, tinker's weed, horse gentian, and wild coffee—was the eastern *Triosteum perfoliatum,* found southward from the Maritimes, Quebec, Ontario, and Nebraska with rough, opposite, leaves narrowing at their bases and many times uniting about the rather hairy 3- or 4-foot-high, unbranched stems with up to about eight egg-shaped to roundish, dark red to golden fruits—maturing from large, fragrant, scarlet flowers—crowned blueberrylike by five puckered sepals, each holding a trio of big, bony seeds.

Although these were sometimes roasted for use as a wild coffee, they were said to have a sedative effect. Root tea of this particular bitter-root was claimed to be either emetic or purgative, depending on the dosages. It was brewed mildly for those recovering from fevers and was believed to be a body-cleansing spring tonic. Mashed for use as a poultice, it was sought for the treatment of open wounds and sores.

BLACKBERRY—RASPBERRY (*Rubus*)

Family: Rose (Rosaceae)

Common Names: Highbush Blackberry, Running Blackberry, Tall Blackberry, Sand Blackberry, Creeping Blackberry, Mountain Blackberry, Swamp Blackberry, California Blackberry, Blackcap, Black Raspberry, Purple Raspberry, Purple-Flowering Raspberry, White-Flowering Raspberry, American Red Raspberry, Wild Red Raspberry, Virginia Raspberry, Western Raspberry, Arctic Raspberry, Flowering Raspberry, Rocky Mountain Raspberry, Salmonberry, White-Flowered Salmonberry, Cloudberry, Wineberry, Nagoonberry, Red Nagoonberry, Dewberry, Thimbleberry, Western Thimbleberry, Baked-Apple Berry, Bake-Apple, Plumboy, Flymboy, Gout Berry.

Top: Raspberry (*Rubus*); *Bottom:* Blackberry (*Rubus*)

Characteristics: Being the most valuable wild fruit in North America, both because of the money made from it and because of its eminence as a summer food for birds and animals, the blackberry-raspberry family is known to all. The facts that some plants are thorny and others thornless, that a few grow only a couple of inches and others taller than a man can reach, and that there is a wide variation in color and even taste makes little difference in their worth as a wild medicine.

The simplest method of identifying them is their likeness to market varieties. Rapidly gathered in heartening amounts, the ripe berries—each made up of innumerable tiny, fleshy, and juice-rich little globes, in the middle of each of which is a seed—detach readily from their light-colored, stem-attached centers and five-petaled hulls, coming off in the hand in a fragile, hollow completeness in which each part has rounded from its own ovule.

Area: At the very least, fifty distinct species of blackberries and raspberries thrive throughout all fifty states. They also abound in Canada.

Uses: Juice and wine made from the berries is still used in Appalachia to combat diarrhea. The berries and their juice were long used by many Indian tribes to rid their members of chronic stomach trouble and to allay vomiting and retching. It was considered effective in preventing miscarriage. It is astringent and believed generally beneficial to digestion, being thought mild enough to control diarrhea and dysentery even among infants and young children. In fact, early Americans sometimes combined it with honey and alum to tighten loose teeth. The settlers also came to use the juice to dissolve tartar on the teeth. It was turned to by numerous tribes to cure cankers of the mouth, gums, and tongue.

A few of the berries, or their strained juices, were added to other wild medicines to make them less disagreeable. The juice, held to be extremely soothing and tension-relieving, was turned to by many of the Indians and pioneers to lessen the menstrual flow without suddenly ending it entirely. When the bowels were loose, it was drunk instead of tea or coffee. It was thought to ease nausea, to be an antacid, and to act as a parturient.

Many a colonial deemed his medicine chest incomplete if it did not contain blackberry brandy or cordial. Not only were mixtures of the juice and sugar fermented, but juice boiled down with a few spices for flavor was bottled with regular brandy to make a thick, sweet cordial, handy for unexpected digestive upsets. Too, blackberry brandy was considered to be a rapidly acting remedy for diarrhea. So, in fact, was the eating of a large quantity of the ripe berries.

The young leaves of these plants were gathered after the dew was off them on a dry morning, dried at no more than ordinary room temperature—not in the sun—and stored throughout the fall and winter in tightly capped jars in dark, dry cupboards for use like the regular Chinese tea whose taste the resulting beverage resembles, especially when served with a little sugar but no cream or milk. Like commercial tea, it is rich in tannin and similar substances and is therefore astringent, being considered in Appalachia and other places useful in controlling diarrhea.

The amount of dry leaves easily pinched by the fingertips of one hand, dropped into a warmed teapot, then covered with a quart of boiling water, and steeped for up to ten minutes, depending on individual tastes, was used to make four pleasantly steaming cups that were held to be an enjoyable blood purifier and spring tonic. A more precise measurement, recommended by many, was and is a level teaspoon of the dried leaves to a cup of bubbling water, steeped until it cools, and then drunk cold, 2 cups a day. It was thought to help mothers in childbirth and was given as a refreshing drink during delivery. The leaf tea, brewed so as to be particularly potent, was also applied to severe sores. Used as a gargle and mouthwash, it was also recommended for bad breath.

Such a tea was similarly made from the roots and rhizomes. This was also held to be effective against diarrhea and, in strong doses, even as an antidote against some poisons. The root tea was thought to be useful for drying up runny noses. The astringency and apparent healing properties of the roots resulted in their flavor as a gargle for sore throats and mouths, for cankers, and as a medication for bleeding cuts and wounds.

There are reports that some 500 Oneida Indians, beset by dysentery in one season, all recovered when treated with blackberry root, at the same time when many of their white neighbors, not using this primitive native medicine, fell before the ailment.

Other Indians used blackberry roots and vines for a tea taken internally by members of the tribe who were vomiting and expelling blood. Others utilized a solution made by soaking blackberry roots for bathing sore eyes and also for moistening compresses for use as poultices. Ojibwas simmered the branches for increasing the flow of urine and steeped the roots to make an infusion for stopping trouble with loose bowels.

The dried bark of the roots and rhizomes of the species were long officially recognized by the medical world both as an astringent and as a tonic. They were marketed as a diarrhea cure well before the Civil War. One prescription was for an ounce of blackberry roots boiled down from 6 cups to 4 cups, then drunk by the half cup about every two hours as long as the trouble persisted. A bigger dosage of this astringent tea was said to be useful in helping those suffering from whooping cough.

A tea made of the bark of these plants was used to control dysentery.

Raspberry stems powdered between two smooth rocks, or with mortars and pestles which the Indians also used, were applied dry to cuts.

The leaves were steeped in water, without boiling, and given to pregnant women to ease delivery. This infusion, the subject of later experiments in its ability to relieve labor pains, seemed to act principally to relieve muscular tension about the uterus.

In the desert and on the dusty plains, often when such expanses were scoured by savage winter winds, the Indian use of tea steeped from *Rubus* leaves to increase the flow of urine was adopted gratefully by the white newcomers. Bark scraped from the branches and vines of these species was also favored in a decoction for upset stomachs.

BLUEBERRY—HUCKLEBERRY (*Vaccinium*) (*Gaylussacia*)

Family: Heath (Ericaceae)

Common Names: Lowbush Blueberry, Highbush Blueberry, High Blueberry, Low Sweet Blueberry, Early Sweet Blueberry, Late Low Blueberry, Sugar Blueberry, Swamp Blueberry, Bog Blueberry, Box Blueberry, Blueridge Blueberry, Sour-Top Blueberry, Early Blueberry, Velvet-Leaf Blueberry, Dwarf Blueberry, Thin-Leaf Blueberry, Western Blueberry, Alaska Blueberry, Huckleberry, Twin-Leaved Huckleberry, Dwarf Huckleberry, Blue Huckleberry, Evergreen Huckleberry, Mountain Huckleberry, Squaw Huckleberry, Whortleberry, Oval-Leaf Whortleberry, Big Whortleberry, Whorts, Bilberry, Dwarf Bilberry, Great Bilberry, Bog Bilberry, Mountain Bilberry, Sierra Bilberry, Farkleberry, Deerberry, California Black Buckleberry, Dangleberry, Hurts, Tangleberry, Blue Tangle.

Blueberry (*Vaccinium*)

Characteristics: None of the blueberry-huckleberry genus, with their unmistakable puckery tops, is inedible. The difference between this duo of extremely similar fruits? The blueberry (*Vaccinium*) is full of innumerable soft seeds. The huckleberry (*Gaylussacia*) has exactly ten, hard-shelled, dry seeds with a separable rind or shell and interior kernel. Also, the huckleberry has tiny quantities of wax on its foliage and new shoots. The two berries are so similar that they are usually gathered and used together.

As may be inferred by the various names, these toothsome members of the heath family thrive thickly, many times by the acre, on an assortment of several-stemmed woody plants from small low shrubs to dense growths of thick high bushes, all of them pleasantly without thorns. Because these plants thrive on acid soil and sunshine, Indians set fires to clear land for this rapidly spreading fruit, so sought by squaws and game. The settlers soon followed suit—a practice that continues today.

In most instances, bluish to blackish when ripe, usually with a lighter bloom that, not at all detrimental, comes off on the hands, the mature fruit is occasionally reddish, yellowish, and greenish.

Area: Some thirty-five members of this family grow on this continent, from Arctic Alaska and Canada southward.

Uses: The juice of the berries, especially when boiled down to a syrup, was considered to be one of the best and certainly most agreeable medicines for diarrhea.

The astringent and bitterish mature leaves were also steeped in boiling water, a heaping teaspoon to a cup, for this same purpose, 1 or 2 cupfuls being drunk cold in a day.

This tea was also considered to be a blood purifier and was widely turned to as a spring tonic. Too, it was believed to increase the flow of urine and was sometimes resorted to for inflammation of the kidneys. The bark of the roots was boiled to make drinks for the treatment of both sore throats and abnormal frequency of intestinal discharges.

Laboratory tests were credited with finding bark extracts effectual against disease organisms and germs.

BRACKEN FERN (*Pteridium aquilinum*)

Family: Fern (Polypodiaceae)

Common Names: Brake Fern, Brake, Pasture Brake, Hogbrake, Hog Brake, Western Brake, Western Bracken, Western Brake Fern, Eastern Brake, Eastern Bracken.

Characteristics: Its vigor, fertility, and coarse ruggedness make the bracken fern the most familiar of North America's ferns, especially as it is among the first to poke its way up through the ground in the springtime and as it continues to produce new fronds until freezing temperatures interfere.

The rugged, stiff, darkly green fronds, reddish at their bases, vary from about 1 to 4 feet tall; unlike most of this continent's usually shade- and moisture-seeking ferns, they reach across many a sunny, dry stretch.

When they expire in the autumn, their wind-rattling brown expanses, when not flattened by heavy snows, stay to pinpoint the whereabouts of the highly edible fiddleheads when they arise the next growing season. These peculiar entities—each coming into being singly from the usually long, prolific root which extends horizontally underground, where it tends to branch over a sometimes considerable area—curl in such a way that they look something like the tuning end of a violin. After some 4 to 10 inches of edibility, depending on the region, they uncoil in a tough, stiff, toxic—darkening into the familiar, broadly triangular, erect, some 1 to 4 inches tall—fanlike verdancies that spring up to green many a burnt area.

The brown fruiting bodies are grown on the undersurface of the fronds. The ferns are among the first great group of plants that develop an independent sporophyte—the asexual phase of the plant's life circle, whereby the fertilized egg with true roots, stems, and leaves is retained for some time in the female sex organs. This happens to be one of the most important steps in the evolution of the plant kingdom. The development of a vessel system, which allows water and food to be conducted rapidly through stems, roots, and leaves, was mainly responsible for this advance in the earth's destiny.

Area: There is only one species of the bracken fern (*Pteridium aquilinum*), and this grows widely across this continent, from Labrador to Alaska southward.

Uses: Although poisonous in large-enough amounts, especially to grazing cattle, the fronds of the bracken fern boiled with water and

Bracken Fern (*Pteridium aquilinum*)

sugar were adjudged to be a good medicine, especially for those with lung ailments. The fronds were also boiled with a syrup of this sort, in small proportions, for liver troubles.

The roots or actually rhizomes, when boiled into a stronger tea than usual, were used for worms, for the relief of digestive gas, and to quell diarrhea. Root tea was also advocated to soften caked breasts, although that brewed from the fronds was widely held to be dangerous for this purpose.

Ojibwa squaws were among those using the tea prepared from rhizomes for cramps, while the Delawares recommended it as a diuretic to increase the flow of urine.

Inhalation of smoke from dried fronds laid on the ebbing coals of a campfire—perhaps a few embers moved away from the main fire and covered with ashes so that the vegetation would fume instead of flame—was thought to help headache.

BULRUSH (*Typha*)

Family: Cat-tail (Typhaceae)

Common Names: Rushes, Flags, Cat-tail, Cat-tail Flag, Narrow-Leaved Cat-tail, Broadleaf Cat-tail, Reed Mace, Cossack Asparagus, Cat-o'-Nine-Tails.

Characteristics: Although our ancestors used these favored tall, strap-leaved plants for floor coverings, woven mats and rugs, and seats and backs for chairs, they are now largely neglected except for the wild food seekers and the birds. They are easily recognizable both for their long, tapering, pointed, ribbonlike green leaves and for the wienielike plumpnesses which grow on separate, substantial, round stalks. These hot-dog-shaped protuberances are crowded with initially green feminine flowers. Above these later are shriveling, microspore-crammed tops which, when maturing, drop their male cells of their own accord to fertilize their sisters, eventually producing golden pollen and hoards of tiny, white-tufted seeds that the winds disperse over the landscape.

Almost every part of the bulrush, from the large starchy roots to the cornlike buds and later the flourlike pollen, is healthfully edible.

Area: Except in the permafrost of the Far North, bulrushes grow almost everywhere where there is fresh water and dampness in Canada and the United States.

71

Bulrush (*Typha*)

Uses: The mature brown bulrush cobs used to be kept in closed dry places during the winter and their soft, alleviating down was spread antiseptically over burned, scalded, and chafed portions of the body. The roots were also crushed into a pulp, mixed with some wholesome fat such as black bear lard, and applied as a salve in such instances.

The cut, sliced, and chopped stems were spread upon wounds, burns, and sores. They were also hopefully taken internally to quell diarrhea, kill and expel worms, and for gonorrhea.

BUTTERNUT (*Juglans cinerea*)

Family: Walnut (Juglandaceae)

Common Names: Oilnut, White Walnut, Filnut, Lemonnut.

Characteristics: The butternut, a slightly smaller relative of the black walnut, is ordinarily a 40- to 60-foot-high tree with a diameter of about 2½ feet, some lone specimens soaring to nearly 100 feet. The light grayish bark is segmented into broad, flat ridges by moderately deep grooves.

The branches, with a lone leaf at the tip of most, have compound leaves with from about ten to sixteen other leaflets arranged opposite one another. Having extremely short stems, these average about 2 to 6 inches long and approximately half as wide.

After blossoming with short flower spikes and catkins from April to June in most localities, usually in fertile woods or along streams on well-drained ground, these develop single nuts or clusters of about two to five nuts, pointed and elliptic. The hard, horny, hairy, green shells, some 2 to 2½ inches long, are sticky and strong-smelling.

You'll need to wear waterproof gloves when gathering and husking them or you'll color your hands with an almost indelible stain. Once this thin husk is broken, however, the sweetish and delectably edible kernels are relatively easy to separate. They are very oily and, when gathered in large numbers, are usually dried in a dark warm place before using them.

Area: Butternuts thrive from southern Ontario to New Brunswick, Nova Scotia, and Prince Edward Island, south to Arkansas, Mississippi, Alabama, and Georgia and west to North and South Dakota and Kansas.

Butternut (*Juglans cinerea*)

Uses: The oil from the ripe nuts, still so used in some parts of the country, was believed to be valuable in treating tapeworms as well as fungus infections and other skin diseases. This oil was also thought to be highly valuable for ensuring healthy hair and scalps. It was obtained by the Indians by boiling the nuts in water, which they afterward dried and ate, then skimming off the oil which rose to the surface.

Shredded bits of the inner bark of the tree, one teaspoonful to a cup of boiling water, were steeped until cool and then drunk a cupful a day as a laxative by the colonists as far back as the Revolutionary years. As a matter of fact, the nuts eaten in large quantities were also found to be slightly laxative.

Because of its action as a laxative, the tea was considered to be an effective treatment of dysentery. In Appalachia today many of the inhabitants consider the bitter, faintly aromatic inner bark of the root to be a good cathartic. The sap of the butternut, too, was boiled down to a syrup for a physic.

The root and nuts of the butternut were boiled in water to make an emetic.

The bark decoction was believed to be a mild stimulant for the liver. For use throughout the year, the bark of the butternut root was dried and powdered, and a brew was composed by stirring a teaspoon of the bark to a cup of boiling water. This was drunk, a few sips at a time, throughout the day. It was also sometimes used in cases of malaria. At one time the nut kernels themselves were a favored prescription for mental patients. Today such nerve-strengthening minerals as phosphorus, magnesium, silicon, and calcium, which they contain, are often said to be stabilizing for the blood and brain.

During the Civil War, besides being taken internally for dysentery and diarrhea, a strong decoction made by simmering and steeping the bark and leaves in water was used as an external wash for ulcers, open sores, and other skin troubles. It was also thought to be an effective gargle and mouthwash for sore throats, cankers, and other mouth irritations such as those caused by the rubbing of artificial teeth, like George Washington's wooden set.

The outer bark, the cambium of the trunk and roots, and the leaves were usually harvested during the growing weeks; the nuts, as they were ripening in the early fall.

CARIBOU MOSS (*Cetraria*)

Family: Iceland Moss (Parmeliaceae)

Common Names: Iceland Moss, Iceland Lichen, Lichen, Cetratia, Eryngo-Leaved Liverwort.

Characteristics: This lichen, which has saved virtually thousands of people from starvation, is composed of an alga and a fungus that combined to make one of the oldest medicinals in the world. In fact, the 3,000- to 4,000-year-old sequoias and the even older bristlecone pines were mere infants centuries and centuries after these and the other lichens were ancient. Their organic acids, with the help of light and of the rains and fogs and other moisture in the atmosphere, draw health-giving minerals from the rocks they conspire to decompose.

Caribou moss, whose importance cannot be overemphasized, is a ground-clinging, mosslike plant which, with dividing stems in place of leaves, lifts but several inches high, branching spontaneously in mats with innumerable stalks that are paperlike thin, flattish, and extremely narrow. Brownish and grayish white to somewhat reddish, the medicinal lives in masses that are free of smell.

The top parts of the numerous tubelike uprights are ordinarily smooth, creasing, furrowing, and guttering toward the base. Rolling inward at the rims, they make canal-like, hollow, elongated ducts which end in relatively smooth projections with minutely serrated rims. What seeds there are exist principally along the lips of the lobes.

Caribou moss loses hydrogen and oxygen in the windiness and the coldness of winter, when it becomes brittle. Upon immersion in water, however, it regains the elasticity that is so prevalent during the warm months, when it exists in rubbery bodies and tangled and twisted masses along the surfaces of the areas where it grows.

Area: Caribou moss prospers in the Arctic regions of the United States and Canada, where the only growth harmful to mankind is one type of toadstool. It also exists on mountains above the upper limits of arboreal growth, often being the only plantlike food living higher than timberline. Growing through Canada and our northernmost states, its range extends down into Pennsylvania, New Jersey, and the mountains of North Carolina.

Uses: One of our naturally growing antibiotics, caribou moss was among the more important Indian so-called blood purifiers and spring tonics for the settlers after the long winters. Bitter, it is still regarded in some regions as an agent that restores, invigorates, refreshes, and stimulates the human system.

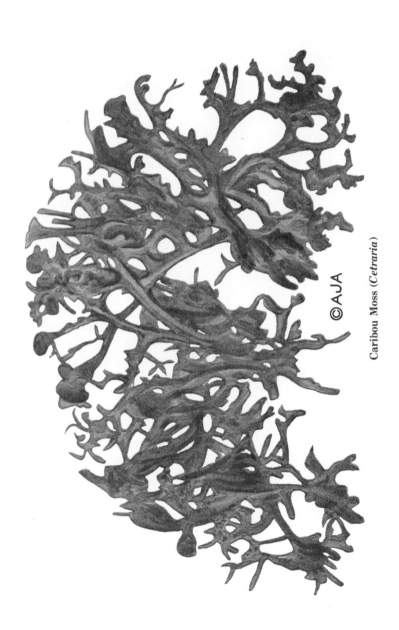

©AJA

Caribou Moss (*Cetraria*)

Iceland moss, as it is also known, was scraped from stone, rocks, and ledges, soaked overnight in unheated water, then drunk to control diarrhea. Dry, it is acrid, astringent, crisp, cartilaginous, and leathery. It can then be rubbed and pounded into a more easily handled powder.

The rock-dissolving acids in this lichen, although not poisonous, will cause severe digestive upsets in most individuals. Before the plant is taken internally, these acids should be removed by soaking it in cold water at least overnight, then preferably in a second bath of cold water for an additional eight hours or so, before straining and draining it. The result is so easily digested that it is used—flavored to taste and, if this is wanted, simmered to what will cool into a firm, quivering, jellylike gruel—for invalids and convalescents. It is also supposed to be tonic as well as soothing—a hearty combination.

An ounce of the caribou moss, washed of all sandy and rock-fragmented materials and then boiled in 2 cups of water, was not only used to ease coughing but also as a medicine for long-enduring bronchitis and inflammation of the mucous membranes chronically affecting the air and nose passages.

The taking of the soaked and nonbitter decoction was believed to assist in both better digestion and better appetite.

The powdered preparation, after the bitterness had been soaked out, was dusted on mouth sores and was considered so mild that it was also used with children for the purpose of healing cankers.

A tea made of the medicinal was taken internally for lung troubles, consumption, and general weakness.

CASEWEED (*Capsella*)

Family: Mustard (Cruciferae)

Common Names: Shepherd's Bag, Shepherd's Purse, Pick Purse, Lady's Purse, Pickpocket, Pepper and Salt, Pepper and Shot, Pepper Grass, St. Anthony's Fire, St. James, St. James' Wort, Toywort, Cocowort, Mother's Heart, Shovelweed, Poor Man's Pharmacetty.

Characteristics: Caseweed is a white-flowered, weedy, annual herb. A member of the widespread mustard family, its tiny blossoms grow in the form of a four-armed cross. Clustering close together near the tips of the stalks, those at the bottom open first, so that in the spring there are often still unflowered buds at the tops of the stems. Small yellow stamens thrust up in the center of each quartet of petals, below each of

Caseweed (*Capsella*)

which is a minute green sepal. These together produce triangular notched pods which upon maturity open to reveal peppery little seeds.

The basal leaves of the caseweed are long, deeply notched, strongly spined, and dandelionlike. Higher on the flower stalks are more green leaves, these shaped like narrow arrowheads.

Area: This wild medicinal—and, incidentally, food—grows throughout almost every part of the United States and Canada, even in the Arctic.

Uses: Indians, pioneers, frontiersmen, settlers, and colonists in the New World used for medicine every part of the caseweed, known by a host of different names in various localities. For one thing, it was regarded as a simple cure for troublesome diarrhea.

Pungent and bitterish, it was valued for its astringent properties. Cotton moistened with its juice was stuffed into the nostrils to quell nosebleeds. In fact, it was widely used to stop both external bleeding as well as internal bleeding of all kinds. The common preparation for this was made by simmering 3 ounces of the entire plant in a quart of bubbling water.

For internal use, 2 teaspoons of this fresh solution were sipped every four hours. Externally, the cooled solution was applied directly to the wound with saturated compresses or by holding wet cotton balls firmly against the wound until, ideally, the bleeding stopped. Scratches, ulcers, and the like were also so treated. An ointment, too, was made for such uses by simmering the herb, regarded to be strongest in the fall, in unsalted lard of one sort or another.

In this connection, it was regarded as one of the best remedies in cases of hemorrhaging after childbirth, as well as to check what was regarded as excessive menstruation. A heaping teaspoon of the chopped plant was mixed into a cup of boiling water, allowed to steep half an hour, and then drunk to relieve bleeding hemorrhoids.

Such solutions were also thought to be fine remedies for diarrhea and for bloody urine, as well as to clear the urine of mucous matter. When necessary, it was also imbibed to increase the flow of urine, since it was effective in checking inflammation of the mucous membranes. For obstruction of the bowels, it was given as an enema. Individuals also utilized it to clear phlegm from the lungs.

Even with all those uses, caseweed was also considered to be helpful in checking intermittent fever. Being rich in vitamin C, the fresh green plant can be eaten raw; when it is boiled until barely tender, it may be used to cure or to prevent scurvy.

CHECKERBERRY (*Gaultheria procumbens*)

Family: Heath (Ericaceae)

Common Names: Chequerberry, Wintergreen, Creeping Wintergreen, Western Wintergreen, Spicy Wintergreen, Aromatic Wintergreen, Spring Wintergreen, Three-Leaved Wintergreen, Checkerberry Wintergreen, Winterberry, Teaberry, Hillberry, Berried Tea, Canadian Tea, Woodsman's Tea, Mountain Tea, Mountain Teaberry, Mountain Berry, Red-Berry Tea, Box Berry, Boxberry, Chickerberry, Dewberry, Deerberry, Grouse Berry, Partridge Berry, Partridgeberry, Pigeonberry, Roxberry, Spice Berry, Spiceberry, Ground Berry, Ground Ivy, Ground Holly, Trailing Gaultheria, Salal, Wax Cluster, Clink, Red Pollom, Ivory Plum.

Characteristics: When crushed or tasted fresh, the shiny and waxy evergreen leaves of the checkerberry and its winter-clinging little red berries give off the familiar wintergreen aroma.

The small trailing perennial creeps through and under the woodland humus, moss, and ground, thrusting up separate blooming and leafing clusters. The frosty flowers appear like chaste, white, miniature bells, with their unions of five petals, growing between stems and leaves about summertime, maturing into solid red fruits in fall and winter, each with a distinctive pucker on top. The leaves, which become leathery and ruddy with age, have tiny teeth, each with bristlelike tips.

The salal (*Gaultheria shallon*), the western variety, also widely used medicinally although not so spicy, is an evergreen shrub growing up to several feet tall with nodding flowers, each boasting a yellowish five-cleft calyx and urnlike corolla which have five tiny recurved lobes and eight to ten stamens, and which mature into black spicy berries. The leaves are roundish to oval, glossy dark green, and finely toothed. The western medicinal is taller and not so delicate as its eastern cousin.

Area: Checkerberries grow in the East from the Great Lakes to Newfoundland, south through New England to Mississippi across to Georgia. *G. shallon* lives, particularly along the coast, from Alaska and British Columbia to California.

Uses: The still very familiar wintergreen flavor, now produced synthetically, was once the reason for gathering huge amounts of the checkerberry plants approximately each October, drying them, and shipping them in great bales to where the volatile oil, incidentally

Checkerberry (*Gaultheria procumbens*)

poisonous when concentrated, could be distilled. Later the cambium and twigs of the black birch, being easier to collect in quantity and giving forth the same oil, replaced this industry until the chemists stepped in.

The Indians, passing along their pre-Columbian lore to the settlers, long considered the leaves to be an important remedy for arthritis and overexerted muscles and joints—perhaps a reason you still smell it in locker-rooms and training quarters. Steeped into a tea, it was drunk for this purpose and also used as a gargle for sore throats. Crushed into poultices, it was applied externally to aching and painful parts, including those arising from lumbago.

Such poultices were also placed on swellings, boils, carbuncles, felons, wounds, rashes, eruptions, and inflammations—even on aching teeth. The oil was used externally as a counterirritant and antiseptic, as well as a means of bringing down ordinary swelling from a bruise or contusion.

The Penobscots believed wintergreen (*G. procumbens*), as it was also commonly known, to be helpful in treating gonorrhea. The tea and mildly delectable and nourishing berries were resorted to for increasing the flow of milk in nursing mothers. Also, it sometimes seemed effective in starting delayed menstruation. It was used for dysentery.

The Sioux, Nez Percé, and other leading Indian tribes were cognizant of the fact that infusions of checkerberry leaves, although they did not realize it was from their salicin content, lowered fevers and eased the pain of arthritis, lumbago, or just overexerted joints and muscles.

Individuals turned to it for alleviating hoarse sore throats, as well as other cold symptoms. It was thought to be a coagulant, one of the reasons for its wide use for wounds and for stanching bleeding. The tea, being astringent, was taken internally both for hemorrhages and for ulcers, particularly those of the bladder and kidneys. It was believed helpful for dropsy. It was in some places relied upon to clear up obstructions in the alimentary canal. The tea was used for astringent douches, as well as for just plain antiseptic washes.

A conservative way of making checkerberry tea was to immerse a teaspoonful of the chopped plant in a cup of boiling water, let this steep until cold, and then sip one cupful during each day. The woodsman, however, more usually dropped a handful of the leaves into his suspended can of boiling water, set this beside his campfire to steep for five minutes, and then drank it both as an antiscorbutic and stimulant by narrowing his lips on whatever receptacle he was using and thus straining away the leaves. The tea is ruddy. It was widely resorted to during the American Revolution in the place of imported teas contaminated with a British tax.

No matter how used, the leaves and berries have to be freshly picked, as they quickly lose their aromatic qualities.

Resorting to them also as a diuretic when the flow of urine was scanty, many of the Indians also automatically reached down for the leaves and berries when they were experiencing stomach upsets. They also drank the tea for gas, colic, and for stimulating the appetite.

Steaming solutions made by steeping the plant in hot water were sought by the Indians and later by some of the pioneers to bring on sweating in the treatment of typhus. It was so relied on to induce perspiration in an effort to bring down fevers in general.

It was an early ingredient in commercial sarsaparillas and in some of the brews concocted by traveling medicine salesmen with their whoopla and minstrel shows.

CHICKWEED (*Alsine*) (*Stellaria media*)

Family: Pink (Caryophyllaceae)

Common Names: Common Chickweed, Indian Chickweed, Star Chickweed, Great Chickweed, Starwort, Scarwort, Starwirt, Stitchwort, Adder's Mouth, Tongue Grass, Satin Flower, White Bird's Eye, Pamplinas, *Mouron des Oiseaux.*

Characteristics: As the meekest sometimes turn out to be the strongest, so is it with chickweed, which is an apparently feeble member of the pink group but is actually a lusty annual with matted to upright green stems that take over many an area. Commencing its growth in the fall, it vigorously thrives through the sleet and snowstorms of winter even in the Far North, survives most weed killers, starts blooming while the snow is often still on the ground, and many times finishes its seed production in the springtime. It is so abundantly fruitful, however, that it flowers throughout most of the country every month of the year.

Growing to a foot high in matted to upright trailing stems, it has egg-shaped lower and median leaves and stemless and highly variable upper leaves. In the star chickweed or great chickweed (*Stellaria pubera*), the characteristic blossoms, brightly white and about ½

84

Chickweed (*Alsine*) (*Stellaria media*)

inch across, have such deeply notched petals that their five appear more like ten, the number of the stamens. Usually gathering themselves together at night and on cloudy or foggy days, they unfurl under the brilliant sun.

Area: Growing the year around from Alaska to Greenland southward, chickweed is generally blooming in some area in every state, province, and territory in the United States and Canada throughout the year.

Uses: Far from being just a troublesome weed, chickweed is a valuable antiscorbutic and medicinal, as well as a low-calory spinach-treated food more tender than the majority of wild greens.

Gathered fresh and dropped into enough bubbling water to cover, it is still regarded in numerous regions as an excellent warm poultice for inflammations and otherwise irritated skin, abscesses, swellings, wounds, cuts, sores, and even erysipelas, infections, hemorrhoids, inflamed eyes, ulcers that have been difficult to heal, boils, and carbuncles. Used on loose bandages, it was renewed at short intervals, the cooled water in which it had been steeped often being utilized on the trouble spot as a wash.

In fact, there were not many such troubles for which chickweed was not used, including swollen testicles and venereal diseases. It was also so utilized fresh, dried, powdered, and made into salves.

Believed to soothe and heal anything it came in contact with, it was taken internally for bronchitis, coughs, cold symptoms, hoarseness, arthritis, and such.

For blood poisoning, the affected part was treated by the usual poultice, and the chickweed also taken internally. For severe constipation, one prescription was for 3 tablespoonfuls of the fresh plant to be boiled in a quart of water until only 2 cups remained; then a warm cupful of this was taken at least every three hours—in badly blocked cases oftener—until evacuation was successful.

Chickweed was also credited with being a refrigerant, an alternative, and an expectorant.

It was considered to be rich in potash salts and therefore fine for the undernourished, especially children, whom it was claimed it rapidly strengthened—all this with a weed now considered merely pesky by many gardeners and enthusiastic lawn growers.

CHICORY (*Chichorium intybus*)

Family: Composite (Compositae)

Common Names: Blue Dandelion, Blue Daisy, Blue Sailors, Ragged Sailors, Blowball, Succory, Wild Succory, Wild Endive, *Barbe de Capuchin,* Wild Bachelor Button, Witloof.

Characteristics: Chicory blues roadsides and fields with its large prominent flowers, usually blooming from May to October and also occasionally showing white or pink. Although on cloudy days the flowers often remain open, they ordinarily close in the noontime sun and then resemble small blue stalks. The daisylike rays have five square-rimmed straps at their tips. Many times in clusters but usually twins, the blooms are generally about 1 to 1½ inches wide.

As it had accompanied the Roman legions, the chicory came to the New World with the first settlers and was quickly adopted by the Indians. The perennial, resembling the dandelion except in color, forms a similar rosette of multifariously lobed, indented, and toothed leaves that taper into lengthy stalks. Those growing upward on the stem have clasping bases and are not so big.

Chicory grows from a large, deep taproot, erectly and rigidly angular, up to about a yard high, resembling the dandelion most when young, although it always remains bitter and exudes an acrid white juice when broken, cut, or bruised like its cousin, likewise a member of the extensive composite family.

It is now produced commercially in the western states, particularly in California and Idaho. With the *Cichorium intybus,* which tolerates cool soil, there are approximately 27,000 seeds per ounce, each requiring some five to fourteen days to germinate at temperatures from 68 to 86°F.

Area: The alien chicory has spread from the Maritime Provinces and New England west to the plains, then in the West from British Columbia to California.

Uses: A pound of chicory leaves, despite being a bit more than 95 percent water, contains 82 milligrams of calcium, 95 of phosphorus, 2.3 of iron, 32 of sodium, and 826 of potassium, plus vitamins A and C, thiamine, riboflavin, and niacin. The roots for centuries have been roasted and ground for making into a coffeelike beverage and as a stretcher, flavorer, and adulterant of the familiar coffee bean.

A medicinal infusion for upset or overacid stomachs was made by adding a teaspoonful of the dried, chopped root to 2 cups of boiling

Chicory (*Cichorium intybus*)

water, sipped cold several times a day. It has also been brought to a boil like regular coffee, in smaller amounts since it is stronger, set off the heat to steep, strained, and then drunk like coffee to increase the flow of urine, as a mild laxative, and as a tonic. An ounce of the powdered root to 2 cups of water was sometimes tried for the allaying of yellowish pigmentation of the skin, tissues, and body fluids caused by the deposition of bile pigments.

Being one of the first greens of spring, it was used raw when young, simmered when older, as a bitterish source of vitamin C to prevent and to cure scurvy. A reputedly healthful tea was steeped from the dried leaves.

Crushed chicory leaves were turned to as poultices for ordinary swellings, inflammations, irritations, rashes, and even for smarting and inflamed eyes, the patient lying down in the latter case with moist and cooling bruised leaves laid over the ailing eyes.

The root beverage was used by some for difficulties with the liver, spleen, gallbladder, and urinary system.

CHICORY LETTUCE (*Lactuca*)

Family: Composite (Compositae)

Common Names: Wild Lettuce, Canada Wild Lettuce, Tall Lettuce, Blue-Flowered Lettuce, Blue Lettuce, Larkspur Lettuce, Horseweed.

Characteristics: The chicory lettuce family, when its small ½-inch or so broad ray flowers are not bluish or pale purple as in the *Lactuca pulchella,* has numerous little, pallid, yellowish blossoms which look like those of an undistinguished and miniaturized dandelion except that they grow in lengthy, slim clusters at the top of the medicinal, with only a few open at a time. The smoothly hollow-stemmed annual or biennial grows 3 or 4 to about 10 feet high, the latter in uncrowded, sunny, and moist situations. Like its cousin, the dandelion, also a member of the huge composite family, this wild lettuce, as it is also called, has a bitterish milky sap.

The lower leaves, also like those of the dandelion, are deeply indented, nearly to their centers, and likewise toothed; but instead of growing in rosettes from the roots, they climb and clasp the usually single stems. The upper leaves, though, only undulate and tooth slightly and are more lanceolate, tapering to a tip at their apexes. The

89

Chicory Lettuce (*Lactuca*)

leaves are bright green, although those at the lower part of the medicinal have a somewhat milky bloom to them, as does the stalk.

Area: The chicory lettuce family grows from the Pacific to the Atlantic in southern Canada, down through the United States from coast to coast.

Uses: Used as an antiscorbutic raw when young, then when tougher simmered briefly until the flowering stage, the species with its milky white juice had the reputation of being gently sedative. The sap was formerly gathered, kept by drying, and used to increase the flow of urine and as a so-called hypnotic, as well as being considered relaxing and a help to those with nervous indigestion or intestinal spasms. Gum concocted from it became the basis of widely used cough syrups.

The sap was also applied directly to areas irritated, itching, and perhaps blistering from exposure to poison ivy and poison oak. It was also used to soothe less severe rashes, as well as sore, chapped, and sunburned skin.

The entire annual or biennial is still being used in parts of Appalachia as a diuretic, emollient, and antispasmodic. Be wary, however, of applying the milky sap around the eyes, as it is extremely irritating to them.

CINQUEFOIL (*Potentilla*)

Family: Rose (Rosaceae)

Common Names: Cinque-Foil, Silver Cinquefoil, Shrubby Cinquefoil, Glaucous Cinquefoil, One-Flower Cinquefoil, Rough Cinquefoil, Sticky Cinquefoil, Marsh Cinquefoil, Purple Cinquefoil, Purple Marshlock, Purplewort, Silverweed, Argentina, Goose Tansy, Good Tansy, Wild Tansy, Five-Leaves, Fivefingers, Marsh Five-Finger, Five-Finger Grass, Goose Grass, Moor Grass, Cramp Weed, Wild Sweet Potato, Meadownut, Cowberry, Purple Marshwort.

Characteristics: These members of the important rose family are divided into a number of different species, some of which might be mistaken for the buttercup if it were not for the distinguishing stipules at the base of the leaves, as well as the enlarged end of the stalk of the flower stems on which the floral organs are borne.

There are other differences among the species found in North America, one being that in the so-called one-flower cinquefoil, *Poten-*

Cinquefoil (*Potentilla*)

tilla uniflora, two blossoms are sometimes found. This typical mountain species has stalks only a couple of inches long which thrive in crowded, compact clusters. The tops of the green leaves are distinctively silky. On the other hand, their undersides are a woolly white. They grow at altitudes up to more than one mile.

Area: Cinquefoil in North America, liking damp to wet habitats, grows from the Aleutians all the way past Hudson Bay to Newfoundland, south to New Mexico and Arizona in the West and to New Jersey in the East.

Uses: Historically famous because in times of famine cinquefoil roots have kept whole groups from starving for extended periods of time, the perennials were widely valued among the Indians and the pioneers.

The name *Potentilla* was won because of its supposed powers as medicine. For those distressed with cramps in the stomach either the scrubbed roots of the *P. palustria*—known in various regions as the purple marshlock, marsh five-finger, purple marshwort, purplewort, purple cinquefoil, meadownut, cowberry, et cetera—could be steeped, or the entire plant of the rough cinquefoil (*P. norvegica*) similarly treated.

The bitterish, astringent root of the cinquefoil family's *P. canadensis* was regarded as efficacious as a mouthwash and gargle after a teaspoonful of the chopped plant had been covered with a cup of boiling water and steeped for half an hour.

The cinquefoils as a whole were also utilized as teas for various purposes for which an astringent was called for, as in diarrhea.

The entire top of the plant was also used to control fever, as well as a wash for the mouth, sore throat, piles and as a general lotion.

COLTSFOOT (*Tussilago farfara*)

Family: Composite (Compositae)

Common Names: Colts'-Foot, Coltfoot, Foalfoot, Foal's Foot, Folesfoot, Horsefoot, Horse Foot, Hoofs, Cleats, Colt-Herb, Bullsfoot, Bull's Foot, Sowfoot, Dove-Dock, Ginger, Gingerroot, Ginger Root, Faafara, *Filius Ante Patrem,* Gowan, British Tobacco, Flower Velure, Butter, Clayweed, Dummyweed, Cough Herb, Coughwort.

Coltsfoot (*Tussilago farfara*)

Characteristics: The white, woolly, scaly flowering stalks of this plant appear in the springtime before the leaves. There are several stalks, from 3 to 18 inches in height, arising directly from the rootstock. Each usually bears at its top a single yellow flower head having in the center numerous tubular-disk blossoms surrounded by ray flowers.

The blooms open only in sunny weather. The ripe seed head looks somewhat like that of a dandelion, golden and flat. Only after the flowers lose their freshness do the some 3- to 7-inch-wide and 5- to 8-inch-long, hoof-shaped, marine-green leaves develop, blanching the lower portion of the plant with densely matted, woolly, rather fragrant foliage, earning coltsfoot its early name of "the son before the father." Both components are medically important.

The long, perennial, crawling, fibrous rhizome is also used.

Area: Seeking brooks and other wet places, especially where the soil is claylike, coltsfoot is found from the Maritimes and Quebec to Pennsylvania, Ohio, and Minnesota and in adjoining provinces and states.

Uses: The herb, when dry, is somewhat bitter throughout and is mainly familiar as a remedy for coughs, bronchitis, asthma, and the like. The leaves are the main ingredient in the so-called British herb tobacco, smoked to relieve the symptoms of these disorders. The Indians and settlers also made a tea of the leaves for the same use, one prescription being for 4 teaspoonfuls of the dried leaves steeped half an hour in a quart of water. A cloth saturated in this hot liquid was laid over the chest or throat, wherever the trouble was centered. In more severe cases, fomentations were used, care being taken not to burn the patient. A large amount of the solution was kept hot; blankets, sheet parts, or the like were immersed in this, wrung out, perhaps sandwiched between dry cloths, and laid in place. If two sets of cloths were available, the cooled one could be immediately replaced. This was kept up from fifteen minutes to an hour, depending on the circumstances.

Up to 2 cups of the supposedly somewhat tonic tea was drunk during the day, either hot or cold, half a cupful being taken when the patient retired for the night, perhaps on a pillow stuffed with the flossy seeds of the plant. Since all parts of coltsfoot were bitter when dried, in the early days the decoctions were often sweetened, usually with honey or maple sugar.

Coltsfoot was used to bring up phlegm, for bronchitis, whooping cough, fever, ague, and for helping digestion. The dried leaves were snuffed up the nostrils for congestion or headache. Poultices made of them were applied to piles, inflammations, and swellings, the leaves being emollient and demulcent. The dried roots and the bitter, mucilaginous, yellowish green powder made from it were also smoked for coughs and applied as for scrofula, usually as poultices.

COMMON BURDOCK (*Arctium lappa*)

Family: Composite (Compositae)

Common Names: Burdock, Great Burdock, Woolly Burdock, Bur, Burrs, Bur Weed, Clot-Bur, Clotbur, Beggar's Buttons, Gobo, Wild Gobo, Happy-Major, Personata.

Characteristics: Everyone knows the burdock, which can scarcely be mistaken, particularly because its ever-clinging burrs, the seed-pods which followed the Roman legions and other warriors across the Old World, came with the first ships to America and soon spread with the trappers, the pioneers, the settlers with their wagon trains, and the gold seekers to every part of the continent.

One of the coarser cousins of the thistle, the common burdock, for example, first has young leaves that are smooth and velvetlike, if a bit furry, giving a hint of their edible qualities that are so marked that we have watched farmers cultivating the plant in the Orient. The prickly ovule carriers further spread themselves by separating when one tries to pick them off of clothing, animals, and other possessions, additionally extending their range, although they generally do not grow at elevations above some 800 feet.

The initial flowers differ in color from purplish amethyst to white. They burst from stout stalks, sometimes over an inch in diameter. The leaves, varying somewhat among the species, grow alternately on their rapidly lifting stems. They are large, vein-ridden, dark green, and a bit shaggy, a number of them a foot wide by twice that long. The flower stalks, whose rapidity of growth is astonishing, often shoot up several feet in a brief time.

For medicinal and eating uses, the roots should be gathered the first year of growth, at least by fall but perferably in early summer. What to look for is easy to determine, for the first-year burdock does not then have flowers or burs. Reaching a foot or more in length and perhaps an inch in diameter, with a grayish white covering and a creamy pith, they are ordinarily difficult to excavate. An especially

Common Burdock (*Arctium lappa*)

slim spade or even a post-hole digger is not an out-of-the-ordinary tool to use in this task. The roots should be judiciously and completely peeled before any usage.

The long, obese flower stalks should, for most favorable results, be picked while the leaves are unfurling, in advance of the time when the flower buds would be starting to expand. The extremely bitter rind should be completely peeled and cut off and the remainder cooked in two waters. The young leaves are also ordinarily cooked in two waters to remove their extreme bitterness.

Area: Prospering throughout most of the United States and southern Canada where people and their animals have ventured, except for a southern region from California eastward, the burdocks are prominent along roads, trails, paths, and throughways, walls and fences, yards and fields. They spring up in profusion about old farm buildings and yards, sawmills, logging regions, and abandoned mines, stamping mills, diggings, placer operations, and the like.

Uses: A teaspoon of the chopped roots was steeped in each cup of boiling water for a tea of many uses, having been, for one thing, considered to be an excellent urinary remedial; for another, it was considered to have been a general tonic, drunk cold, 2 cups a day, a few sips at a time. It was another of the arthritic palliatives. The tea was believed to help pleurisy, as well as to reduce the swelling of glands. It was given to women in labor. It was also used to reduce fever by increasing perspiration. In fact, the roasted and ground roots were often seen for sale for use as a so-termed healthful coffee substitute.

Interestingly, in the case of the burdocks it was the settlers who instructed the Indians in their various uses common in those early days. The red men, however, soon adapted it to their own usages; young medicine men, fasting for days at a time in their search for purity and wisdom, occasionally imbibed the bitter beverage of the plant in an effort to make what they had discovered mentally remain in their minds.

The settler and Indians alike made a wash by boiling the roots to bathe skin ailments and diseases. Root tea was even believed helpful, when taken internally, for syphilis and chronic skin ailments. The root tea was drunk by the jiggerful. Treatments to be effective were considered to be necessarily continued for at least several weeks.

The young leaves were believed to be both cooling and dehydrating and therefore were used for lingering ulcers and other sores. Juice from the leaves, taken internally perhaps with a little sweetening because of its natural bitterness, was said both to increase the flow of urine and to rid one of kidney pain.

A salve made from burdock roots was used in an effort both to decrease swelling on wounds and sores and to bring about general healing of infections. Such a salve was also used to soothe and cure burns and scalds.

Some settlers obtained seeds from the mature burrs and started them soaking in brandy for dosage by the teaspoonful for more severe skin diseases.

Another old-fashioned way to make burdock tea was to add an ounce of the root, first year as always, to 3 cups of water and to bring it to a bubble in an open pan, keeping up the simmering until but 2 cups of fluid remained. It was then strained and taken in 4-ounce, jigger-sized potions several times every twenty-four hours. Besides the usual diuretic, diaphoretic, aperient, and alternative uses, it was supposed to be generally healthful and strengthening.

In Appalachia a tea of the roots is still used for rheumatism. In the seventeen hundreds in the New World it was prescribed as a cure for syphilis and gonorrhea. A poultice made of the leaves was also used for snakebites.

COMMON MAYAPPLE (*Podophyllum*)

Family: Barberry (Berberidaceae)

Common Names: Mayapple, May Apple, Devil's Apple, Hog Apple, Hogapple, Indian Apple, May Apple Root, Wild Lemon, Ground Lemon, Citron, Raccoonberry, Raccoon Berry, Yellowberry, Yellow Berry, Wild Jalap, Wild Mandrake, American Mandrake, Mandrake, Duck's Foot, Vegetable Caromel, Vegetable Mercury, Podophyllum, Umbrella-Leaf, Umbrella Plant, Ipecacuana, Mayapple Rhizome, Duck Root, Podoph, Umbrella-Leaf Mandrake.

Characteristics: This perennial, sometimes branched, grows erectly in the springtime to a height of about 1½ to 2 feet, often forming a flat density of ground cover in pastures, moist open deciduous woods, and shaded mountain slopes, shadowing the earth below like dwarf parasols.

Two umbrellalike, palmately lobed leaves, rarely three, grow at the top of most plants. These yellowish green leaves are flattish, lobed,

99

Common Mayapple (*Podophyllum*)

and shield-shaped. A solitary leaf is an indication that the plant is to be flowerless.

Otherwise, a solitary, waxy white, cuplike blossom some 2 inches wide, with six to nine petals and twelve to eighteen stamens sags on a slender, long stem in the fork. If all goes well, this matures into a golden, edible if many-seeded, thirst-quenching, some 2-inch-long, heavily skinned fruit, eaten raw, cooked into a marmalade and jams. It is the only edible part of the plant.

The other parts of the plant are generally toxic except in small amounts, including the dark brown root which when dried can be ground into a yellowish brown powder, incidentally irritating while being made if care is not taken.

Area: The common mayapple grows, frequently in large aggregations, from the Maritimes, Quebec, Ontario, and Montana, south to Texas and Florida.

Uses: Cherokees and other Indian tribes used the root, steeped in water to make a tea, in differing small doses both as a purgative and an emetic, as well as to kill and expel worms from the digestive tract. Believed also to be somewhat narcotic, the plant was used, too, as a diuretic. It was utilized also to encourage the discharge of bile. The resin was employed as a caustic to remove benign wartlike growths, and in fact the Penobscots turned to the juice of the fruit as a wart eradicator.

Several drops of juice from the fresh fruit were sometimes let fall into the ears in the hope that they would reduce deafness.

The root—being considered alternative, antibilious, cathartic, and emetic—was also used in the treatment of arthritis. Some thought it to be a general tonic, stirring the various glands to healthy action, and it was taken in small, frequent doses for this reason. One prescription, for instance, called for a teaspoonful of the chopped dried root steeped in 2 cups of boiling water, then sipped when needed, a teaspoonful at a time. Larger amounts would have been emetic or cathartic, depending on their potency.

Interestingly, and the result of considerable later experimentation and testing, the resin extracted from the root was used successfully as a caustic to remove benign growths on the skin caused by viruses, including warts but also other epithelial tumors.

The root tea was credited with being an antidote for poisons and snakebite. It was another of the so-called spring tonics, taken by children as well as adults, but always in minute doses for children. The time adjudged by many Indians and settlers to be the best for digging the roots was when the fruit was ripening. This tea, still used sparingly, was also taken for liver disorders, rheumatism, and venereal diseases.

COMMON PAPAW (*Asimina triloba*)

Family: Custard Apple (Annonaceae)

Common Names: Tall Papaw, Pawpaw, Tall Pawpaw, Papaw, Custard Apple, Michigan Banana, Poor Man's Banana, False Banana.

Characteristics: The blossoms of the common papaw burst forth in the springtime, in the axils of the past year's leaves, just before the unfurling of the new green foliage. These flowers, some 1½ inches in diameter, are first generally green, later changing to a dark maroon or purplish brown in hue. Each has six petals in sets of three, as well as a trio of sepals. There are numerous stamens but only several ovule-carrying pistils, which mature into large, pulpy, edible fruits.

This fruit, eagerly sought on their homeward journey by the hungry members of the Lewis and Clark Expedition, should not be confused with the tropical fruit, given the same name by some but actually the papaya—an entirely different family—two species of which fatten in Florida.

That of the common papaw, known as the poor man's banana in the Ozarks in deference to its similar if stubby shape and to its color, has large brown seeds that are numerous but easily disposable. It has a delectable aroma and a very different and interesting taste.

Often becoming thickets, this refuge from the Tropics occasionally becomes a tree 35 feet or more high, with a trunk up to a dozen inches thick. Seldom, however, does it lift as high as 20 feet, and it usually has a trunk only a few inches wide.

The immature stems and the leaves are at first rusty with down that later drops away, leaving the leaves smooth and simple, with pointed tips and bases, the upper surfaces a darker verdancy than the paler lower portions.

Area: The custard apple, as it is also known in deference to the sweet, soft creaminess of its fruit, prefers shady, fertile, damp habitats, surprisingly (as it is really an escapee from the Tropics) in southern Ontario, Michigan, and New York, westward to Nebraska,

102

Common Papaw (*Asimina triloba*)

and more realistically south to often very warm Texas and Florida. Too, it frequently eludes landscaping efforts.

Uses: The large brown seeds have been used to bring on vomiting. Dried and pulverized, they have been rubbed into the scalp to eradicate head lice. The expressed juice of the fruit was said to have use in ridding the alimentary canal of worms. The fruit is also beneficially rich in vitamins and minerals.

COMPASS PLANT (*Silphium laciniatum*)

Family: Composite (Compositae)

Common Names: Wild Lettuce, Prickly Lettuce, Opium Lettuce, Wild Opium.

Characteristics: This wild medicinal gets its name, as many Boy Scouts will tell you, by the fact that wherever it grows in full sun, its leaves twist edgewise north and south at midday. Botanists think it is the origin of today's numerous varieties of domestic lettuce, although it little resembles these store vegetables except when very young; later in the summer it often grows higher than a man, with short, stiff, sharp spines bristling from the stems and the underneath parts of the leaves, themselves and their teeth keenly tipped.

The smallish dandelionlike blossoms of the compass plant are grouped together, a few to a cluster, on a number of short stems at the top of the stalk. Still resembling tiny dandelion flowers in the fall, the blooms become covered with down, each minute seed wearing its own circling crown of white fluff by which it is distributed by the breezes.

Also like the dandelion, all portions of the compass plant ooze an acrid white fluid when bruised or broken.

Area: An annual in some instances, a perennial in others, the ubiquitous compass plant thrives throughout most of the United States, as well as southern Canada.

Uses: The roots of the compass plant, all of which is edible, used to be simmered in water for use as a mild laxative, general tonic, and stimulant and as a mild remedy for arthritis and swollen glands.

The whole plant, according to the Department of Agriculture, has been used as a diuretic to increase the flow of urine, as a quietening

Compass Plant (*Silphium laciniatum*)

antispasmodic, and as a smoothing agent to the skin and mucuous membranes. As an emolient, it was thought to be beneficial to sore and chapped skin.

Early settlers believed the milky juice was useful as a nerve tonic and sedative, while the Indians brewed a tea from the leaves and gave it to new mothers to heighten their milk flow.

CRANBERRY (*Vaccinium*)

Family: Heath (Ericaceae)

Common Names: Craneberry, American Cranberry, Wild Cranberry, Large Cranberry, Small Cranberry, Bog Cranberry, Swamp Cranberry, Rock Cranberry, Lowbush Cranberry, Northern Mountain Cranberry, *Pomme de Terre,* Lengon, Lingonberry, Cowberry, Foxberry, Partridgeberry.

Characteristics: The wild cranberry, tinier and tastier than the domesticated variety, is recognized by almost everyone because of its likeness to the Thanksgiving and Christmas standby. It is regarded as the most important berry of the North. The Pilgrims learned of the fruit from their friendly Indian neighbors, and ten barrels of the long-keeping fruit were early shipped back to King Charles II in England in the slow sailing ships of the age.

The evergreen bog or swamp cranberry (*Vaccinium oxycoccus*), for example, has extremely slim stems, up to some 18 inches long, that creep through the moss and root frequently at the joints. The small, thick, leathery green leaves, whitish underneath, tend to grow alternately. The flowers, reddish or pinkish, often develop terminally in groups of one to four with a quartet of four recurving, narrow petals. The dark, red, translucent berries nod characteristically at the ends of threadlike stalks, giving the fruit generally its earlier name of craneberry.

Area: The fruit grows from Alaska to Newfoundland, south to the Carolinas and Arkansas.

Uses: Tea steeped from the evergreen leaves of the cranberry was another of the spring tonics of the Indians and settlers. This was also believed to help prevent kidney stones and bladder gravel. Thought to have diuretic properties, this tea was also considered to be of value in

Cranberry (*Vaccinium*)

treating many kidney disorders. It was said to have an astringent quality, useful in controlling diarrhea.

As if all this were not enough, there were those who considered it useful in handling diabetes. It was also thought to be a good treatment for nausea.

Cranberries themselves were claimed to be excellent in combating and eventually removing blood toxins, as well as in controlling liver ailments.

An old recipe for a beverage for invalids and convalescents was to crush a cup of cranberries and stir them into a similar amount of water. Simmer a quart of water with a tablespoon of oatmeal and a slice of lemon peel. Then add the cranberry solution and sugar, about half a cup of sherry or less, boil the whole for thirty minutes, strain, and serve chilled.

DOCK (*Rumex*)

Family: Purslane (Portulacaceae)

Common Names: Curly Dock, Curled Dock, Yellow Dock, Round-Leaved Dock, Blunt-Leaved Dock, Narrow-Leafed Dock, Narrow-Leaved Dock, Narrow Dock, Sharp-Pointed Dock, Red-Veined Dock, Red Dock, Patience Dock, Common Dock, Bitter Dock, Sour Dock, Water Dock, Great Water Dock, Swamp Dock, Arctic Dock, Mexican Dock, Wild Spinach, Wild Pie Plant.

Characteristics: Docks are plump, chunky plants with bulging masses of mostly basal leaves, generally several inches to a foot or so long. Identifiable by curly or undulating edges, these smooth dark-green leaves are occasionally heart-shaped but more often long and slimly lancelike. The flower stalks are decorated with occasional leaves that are similar but only about half the size. The many varieties of this wild medicinal plant vary somewhat among themselves.

Small greenish flowers, those of some species becoming purplish or definitely reddish with maturity, grow in circles of loosely branched clusters ascending central stems. The three modified petals of each small blossom enlarge and bear dry, triple-winged fruits that have the overall rich brown look of coffee grains, becoming all in all more interestingly conspicuous than the original flowers.

The roots are long and yellow, too firmly anchored to be pulled up. Medicinally important as they were, they had to be dug.

Dock (*Rumex*)

Area: Growing and used throughout the world, the docks in North America thrive throughout Alaska and the Canadian Arctic, south across Canada and the contiguous states well into Mexico.

Uses: Dock greens, continuing to grow despite snow and frost, are still important in places where commercial vitamins are hard to come by, both preventing and curing scurvy as they do. For these purposes the greens, which when young and tender are pleasingly lemonlike raw, are better the less they are subjected to heat. Interestingly, they are even richer in the necessary vitamin C, which the human body is not able to store, than oranges.

Dock greens are also more abundant even than carrots in vitamin A, which forms the necessary rhodopsin in the retina of the eye and, therefore, when this pigment is not up to par in the system, both add to the sparkle of one's eyes and improve night vision.

The dock roots are endowed with chrysophanic acid as well as the important alkaloid rumicin, both considered to be useful in treating liver disorders. Learning of such benefits years before the first Vikings arrived in North America, the Indians extracted these essentials by boiling the dug and scrubbed roots in water and drinking the extract several times each day.

Some of the tribes dug up the roots in the late summer or just before the ground froze in the fall, washed them throughly after trimming them, then split, dried, and stored them.

Dock root tea was made by the pioneers generally by steeping about an ounce of the dried, finely cut, yellow roots in a quart of simmering water until the latter cooled, then straining the liquid and throwing away the solids. The liquid was bottled and kept cool. Half a cup drunk shortly before breakfast each morning was supposed to be slightly laxative, tonic, blood-purifying, and appetite-stimulating. The astringent decoction was also used as a digestive remedy and externally for skin ailments. Incidentally, large amounts of the greens have a laxative effect with many.

The roots are still soaked in vinegar in Appalachia and the wash utilized to combat ringworm. There the leaves are made into a poultice for hives resulting from nervousness or from allergies. In fact, the docks have long been used for treating rashes and itchy spots on humans, and for such ailments as mange on domestic animals and saddle sores on horses, mules, donkeys, and pack dogs, one method still in use being to simmer the roots in enough vinegar to cover until the former are very soft and the majority of the fluid has been absorbed or evaporated. Then, once it has cooled, strain the pulp through a kitchen sieve. Mix one part of the remaining mass with twice its bulk of Vaseline or lard if that is handier; then stir in enough powdered sulfur to make a workable ointment. Apply this to the offending spots until they have cleared up, which on my packhorses I've seen happen within four days.

The Blackfeet and the Navajos merely pounded the dock roots into a pulp and applied them to human and animal swellings and sores, including ulcers, supposedly with satisfactory results.

A syrup was made by boiling a pound of cut bits of dock root in a quart of water until only half the amount of water remained, straining and discarding the solids, and then adding enough sugar or honey to form a sticky, thick solution. This was taken by the teaspoonful, when the throat tickled, as a cough syrup and counterirritant.

Believing in spring tonics, some of the pioneers cut the cleaned live roots of the dock into small bits, placed them in a bottle with whiskey, and let the whole stand in a cool dark place for at least two weeks, whereupon it was taken by the tablespoon with or before each meal.

Docks as a whole—eaten, drunk, or used as poultices—were believed efficacious in the treatment of rheumatism.

DOGBERRY (*Sorbus*)

Family: Rose (Rosaceae)

Common Names: Rowan Tree, American Rowan Tree, American Service Tree, American Mountain Ash, European Mountain Ash, Mountain Ash, Wild Ashe, Mountain Sumach, Quickbeam, Quick Beam, Witchwood, Wine Tree, Round Tree, Roundwood, Indian Mozemize, Missey-Moosey, Missy-Massy, Masse-Misse, Life-of-Man.

Characteristics: The dogberry grows both as a shrub and as a tree. The former range from a couple of feet to 15 feet in height. A few of the trees become as high as 50 feet, but they are commonly 20 to 30 feet high, with narrowly round tops. The compound leaves, growing stemlessly opposite one another, with a single leaf crowning the top of the branch, generally number from seven to seventeen. They are glossy, oblong to elliptic, narrowish, sharply tipped and toothed, and from about 1 to 4 inches long.

Flat densities of tiny, white, profusely stamened flowers burst forth from May through July, governed by the latitude and elevation,

Dogberry (*Sorbus*)

in snowy splendors about 3 to 6 inches across. These mature into dramatically orangish red masses of pea-sized berries, each with its distinctive rose-family dimple at the top. These dogberries can be beneficially plucked both in fall and in winter.

The bark, the other medicinal part, is smooth, thin, sometimes scaly, and light gray. It can be gathered when needed.

Area: Dogberries, preferring wet to moist habitats, grow from Newfoundland to Alaska, south to California, New Mexico, and Appalachia. They are also widely used in landscaping because of their decorativeness.

Uses: Dogwood berries, wealthy in vitamin C, have long been recognized as efficient in both curing and preventing scurvy. They were also believed useful in killing and expelling parasitic worms.

The bark was steeped in water and drunk for nausea and for biliousness. It was also believed effective as a blood-cleansing tonic in the springtime. Some Indians deemed the bark useful in medicines for heart trouble.

ELDERBERRY (*Sambucus*)

Family: Honeysuckle (Caprifoliaceae)

Common Names: American Elderberry, Canadian Elderberry, Common Elderberry, Red-Berried Elderberry, Blue-Berried Elderberry, Mountain Blue Elderberry, Black Elderberry, Red Elderberry, Scarlet Elder, Florida Elderberry, Elder, American Elder, Common Elder, Black Elder, Blackbead Elder, Sweet Elder, Dwarf Elder, Elder Flowers, Elder Blows, Boor Tree, Boutry, Boretree, Tree of Music.

Characteristics: Elderberries differ considerably in form and taste, growing from bushy shrubs a few feet high to trees close to 50 feet in height. Their usual clusters of aromatic, star-shaped white flowers vary from flat-topped bunches to globular arrays, maturing to berrylike, limb-sagging fruits that differentiate in color from blue, amber, red, to black and also changing considerably in taste.

The Indians used the long, straight, hollow stems that became woodier with age for arrows and especially selected some in the springtime, dried them with their leaves on, pushed out all the soft and poisonous pith with hot sticks, and made either spouts for gathering maple and other sap or bored holes in them to fashion flutes; this

Elderberry (*Sambucus*)

gave the medicinal its additional name of tree of music. I've bugled in elk with an elderberry whistle.

The red-berried elderberry (*Sambucus pubens*), to describe one, is a 3- to 10-foot shrub preferring rich woods on rocky slopes and in cool and moist ravines. The limbs are obese, tan, with warty pores. The opposite leaves are compound with some five to seven parts, 2 to 6 inches long, with fine, sharp teeth and smooth green tops and paler, generally fuzzy undersides, with lance-head shapes and sharply pointed tips. The small creamy blossoms grow with five petals joined and with three to five stamens, an inferior ovary with from three to five chambers and a three-lobed style at the tip, in pyramid-formed terminal clusters blooming from June to August. These mature into round, bright red, berrylike fruits, usually slightly less than ¼ inch in diameter. This particular species thrives from Alaska to Newfoundland, south to Iowa, the Great Lakes, Indiana, and Georgia.

Area: Elderberries, liking rich and moist soil, grow from Alaska to Newfoundland and throughout most of the continent from California to Florida.

Uses: Stomach upsets have followed the eating of too many of some of the red drupes, and not even all the bluish and blackish fruit is pleasant raw, although dried or cooked they are better, particularly when mixed with tastier berries. The wild fruit is among this continent's most potent in vitamin A, thiamine, calcium, and niacin, while having close to 450 calories per pound and about 9 grams of protein in the same amount. Indians and settlers used it widely.

The fruit was believed to have cooling, gentle laxative, and urine-increasing properties. Wine made from it was thought to be tonic, as well as a cooling lotion when washed over the bodies of those suffering with fever and, taken internally, to promote sweating both to reduce fever and to promote good general health. The berries, eaten regularly, were said to help arthritis, as well as gout. They were also taken to enable one to cough up phlegm.

The juice, simmered uncovered until thick, was used as cough syrup and for other cold symptoms. The Choctaws mashed the berries with salt for a headache poultice. Some boiled honey and the fruit juices together to make a medicine that, dropped into the ears, was thought to ease earache.

The rest of the medicinal was usually used with great caution and some parts of it were occasionally avoided entirely.

The white flowers were steeped into a tea that, drunk hot, was used to produce perspiring in an effort to reduce fever. It was also drunk hot, sometimes steeped for seven or eight minutes with sprigs of wild mint, *Mentha,* to relieve stomach trouble. Hot, it was also believed useful for sore throats and other cold symptoms. The cold tea had the reputation of increasing urine flow when this had been scanty. The flowers, dried and stored, were also used by some tribes when needed to control fever.

The flowers and the young fruit together, besides being utilized as a diuretic and to promote sweating for health and for fevers, were also used in ointments and balms for burns, sores, and swollen and paining joints. The properties of the flowers included those of a mild stimulant. The dried blossoms of the blue-berried *S. canadensis* were steeped for use as skin lotions and antiseptic washes. Those of the *S. cerulea* were thought to be an even more potent remedy and were also used as remedies for broken blisters, sores, rashes, pimples, acne, and hemorrhoids.

Some pioneer women mixed a strong tea made half from elderberry flowers and half with their apple vinegar for both healing and cooling purposes. The flower tea was also used to help digestion by preventing the formation of gas and the expelling of that already present. An infusion of the dried flowers was especially sought for tonsillitis, since it was thought to be stimulating to the mucous membranes. Elderberry flower water, used for sunburn, was even thought to help bleach freckles.

One ointment made from the flowers mixed all the blossoms possible with the pure white lard produced by warming black bear fat in open pans and draining off the cracklings. Once the flowers were well browned, the whole was strained through fine cloth and stored in jars for use as a skin cream, a sore healer, and, incidentally, a fly and mosquito repellent.

A fresh infusion of elderberry flowers in boiling water was, upon cooling, said to be a most excellent wash for sore eyes. In a number of areas the steeped dried flowers were used as a general help in cases of fever. It was also held to be valuable for treating consumption or any bleeding from the lungs.

The inner bark of the stems was removed, dried, and kept for use in very small amounts as a purgative. In larger doses it served as an emetic. The bark of the roots acted so drastically that it was generally regarded as too dangerous to experiment with. Some of the Indians gathered the spotted and lenticellate bark of the elderberry to mix with bear lard for an ointment with which to treat rashes, inflammations, irritations, sores, and other skin troubles. The bark also had the

116

property of acting, when steeped, both as a purgative and an emetic, depending on the dosage; in very small amounts it was but a gentle laxative.

For instance, a tablespoon sipped several times a day was depended on to act as a purgative, while for an emetic the doses were 3 tablespoons every five minutes until vomiting resulted. Again, a large number of Indians and pioneers found the bark so potent that they would use it only in an emergency. Small amounts of the tea were believed to help in cases of water retention.

Still, women drank very small amounts of elderberry bark tea for cramps during menstruation and later to ease the pain of birth and to help labor along. Sometimes when the child was born dead, the mother was given a few sips of the bark decoction in an effort to ease her pain, although it is difficult to explain how it could do this. It was also sipped to assist in phlegm expectoration from the lungs.

Externally, the bark found favor in a number of different ways. The Iroquois boiled the inner bark of the S. *canadensis* and applied it to that part of the cheek over a throbbing toothache, apparently with good results. The bark, simmered in lard, provided an ointment used to treat ulcers, boils, carbuncles, burns, and such lesser irritations as abrasions, chafing, rashes, blistering, and so forth. The bark was mashed, steeped, and so used by itself for poultices and the like to treat arthritis and similar troubles. The cooled liquid in which the bark had been boiled or steeped was used liberally as a wash in various skin afflictions. The inner bark was used too as a febrifuge and a diuretic.

The leaves, also poisonous both in mature and bud form, were carefully used by some as a potent cathartic when constipation was particularly troublesome. Tea extracted from them was also cautiously administered for dropsy, as well as for a stimulating diaphoretic.

Externally, the crushed leaves were rubbed 'on the skin as a mosquito and fly repellent. Beaten with oats or cream, they formed a lotion and ointment said to be valuable for burns, scalds, contusions, and more severe skin difficulties.

Some tribes turned to the crushed leaves as a poultice for headaches. Others used them thus with salt added. They were also so used just warmed and laid or tied on the forehead. The leaves were also pressed and crushed to give a juice valued by some as an eyewash. They were applied, too, to stop itching. They also made one of the poultices used for aching joints.

The Creeks mashed the more tender roots, agitated them with hot

117

water, and bound them on squaws troubled with sore breasts. Scrapings from the stalks were sometimes used as a substitute when the proper roots could not be located.

The wood and buds were boiled to provide what was said to be a remedy for agues as from malaria and for inflammations.

EVENING PRIMROSE (*Oenothera*)

Family: Evening Primrose (Onagraceae)

Common Names: Evening Primrose, Yellow Evening Primrose, Morning Primrose, Hooker Evening Primrose, Desert Evening Primrose, Common Sundrops, Gumbo Primrose, Sandlily, Sand Lily, Rockrose, Rock Rose, German Rampion, Large Rampion, Tree Primrose, Night Willow Herb, Coffee Plant, Fever Plant, Scabish, Scurvish, King's Cure-All.

Characteristics: The aromatic flowers ordinarily unfurl only after sunset, reproduce in the darkness by the energies of night-flying moths, usually close their four wide petals toward sunrise, shrivel for a day or so, and then fall, to be replaced by erect, hornlike, comose seed-filling capsules. A few do remain open, however, occasionally as large white flowers, reddening with age.

The common sundrops (*Oenothera fruticosa*), one of the varieties, is appropriately named as its flowers unfurl in the daylight; it is an inch or two across, with a quartet of inversely heart-shaped petals which are brilliantly yellow and a slim calyx tube with a clublike ovary. The 1- to 5-inch-long, narrow leaves differ from ovoid and oblong to lance-shaped, their rims being either smooth or wavily toothed.

Area: Seeking moist woodlands to desert habitats according to the variety of the member of the evening primrose family, these flowers occur from southern California, Utah, Nevada, New Mexico, Arizona, and Texas north to British Columbia, Michigan, and New Hampshire, south to Florida in the East.

Uses: One of the first wild plants to be exported to Europe about the time of the Pilgrims' arrival in Massachusetts, the evening primrose was often soaked for use as a poultice. It was regarded as one of the better treatments for coughs resulting from colds. It was also used to

Evening Primrose (*Oenothera*)

lessen the spasms of whooping cough. It had mild astringent properties. Also an antiscorbutic and a febrifuge, it was believed to help asthma and scrofula.

Peeled and then simmered in two changes of bubbling salted water, the stoutly branching roots were given to convalescents. A salve contrived from them was considered useful in helping cure skin inflammations and eruptions.

FEVER ROOT (*Triosteum*)

Family: Honeysuckle (Caprifoliaceae)

Common Names: Feverwort, Wild Coffee, Tinker's Weed, Horse Gentian, Genson, Wild Ipecac, Wood Ipecac.

Characteristics: Fever root, which has somewhat hairy stems, grows some 3 or 4 feet high. Its bell-formed blossoms, the petals of which are guarded by five comparatively lengthy sepals, appear in greens, yellows, and brownish purples, rising from the angles between the leaves and the stems. They mature into egglike to almost spherical berries that are orangish or reddish in hue, each oval containing three big hard seeds.

The joined green leaves of the *Triosteum perfoliatum,* tapering somewhat at their bases, meet and encircle the stems. The opposite leaves of the *T. aurantiacum* also diminish to narrow inner ends through whose middles the stalk ascends.

Area: Fever root grows from Minnesota, Wisconsin, Ontario, Quebec, New Brunswick, and Nova Scotia southward.

Uses: The scrubbed roots of *T. perfoliatum* in particular were simmered in varying strengths, governed by the tastes of the Indians or settlers preparing it and by the gravity of the disorder, for individuals on the road to recovery from weakening fever, as a beverage believed useful in cleansing the system, for arthritis, to quiet the nerves, for a generally weak feeling, and in especially strong doses as an emetic and purge.

The roots, pounded into paste as a poultice for sores, were also resorted to for snakebite.

The seeds were dried, roasted along the edges of campfires, and ground with pre-Columbian pestles and mortars of the Indians, or cracked and granulated between two smooth stones and brewed into a

Fever Root (*Triosteum*)

coffeelike beverage as a bracing drink, enjoyed especially during chill autumn evenings. The Europeans migrating to this continent brought about a level tablespoon of the grounds to a bubbling boil, set it off the fire for some five minutes to take on character, then enjoyed it as a general tonic, sometimes with honey, maple syrup, or maple sugar, perhaps with milk if they had a cow or nanny goat.

GOATSBEARD (*Tragopogon*)

Family: Composite (Compositae)

Common Names: Oyster Plant, Purple Oyster Plant, Vegetable Oyster, Salsify, Salsafy, Meadow Salsify, Yellow Salsify.

Characteristics: The name comes from the Greek word *tragos,* meaning "goat," and *pogon,* which is translated as "beard." This cognomen comes from the seed heads, at the top of each of which matures a fluffy, beardlike tuft which, the whole flower looking like a huge ripe dandelion blossom some 2 to 3 inches across, parachutes the seeds over the landscape usually in the late summer.

In fact, the most noticeable part of this wild medicinal is the single-headed bloom, principally made up of large purple or yellow ray flowers something like a daisy, beneath which pointed, long, narrow, green, grasslike leaves borne on the flower axis generally reach out in some species farther than the violet or golden petals themselves. Ordinarily closing after noon, these pretty wild flowers appear in June and July after the plant is two years old.

The biennial and sometimes perennial plants, which also like the dandelion all have a milky sap, lift, occasionally with branches, from about 1 to 4 feet and have numerous, clasping, grasslike leaves.

Thrusting vertically downward, the long roots are thin and white, which, especially before the second and flowering year, some relish for what they consider to be a parsniplike taste, while others like them for what they believe is more an oysterlike flavor, good enough in either event to encourage their commercial growth here and in Europe. Roasted and ground upon maturity, they are one more coffee substitute.

Area: Goatsbeard, said to be native to Europe, Asia, and Africa but appearing early on this continent, grows from the Atlantic to the Pacific through the contiguous United States and in southern Canada.

Goatsbeard (*Tragopogon*)

Uses: The freshly extracted, milky juice of the young goatsbeard was believed by the Indians and settlers to be useful in dissolving gallstones, the calculuses formed in the gallbladder in the biliary passages.

The white juice was also extracted, kept until it coagulated, and then chewed by both Indians and whites. Besides helping to keep the mouth moist, it was believed to be good for the digestion.

In cases of slow and painful discharge of the urine, drop by drop, an enema was prepared and used by crushing and simmering in water a couple of handfuls of the entire plant—flowers, leaves, stems, and scrubbed roots—then straining out the solids and adding a small amount of sweet oil, such as olive oil.

Extracts were sometimes used for sore eyes.

An extract procured by simmering the roots, for example, was believed helpful for indigestion, heartburn, poor appetite, and liver trouble. Well washed and scraped, then cut up raw in salads, the young roots were held to be good for the stomach, for convalescents, and for giving strength to the thin and the consumptive. When older, the roots were boiled, generally in two changes of water, for the same purposes.

The tender young leaves, eaten raw, are an antiscorbutic.

GOOSEBERRIES AND CURRANTS (*Ribes*)

Family: Saxifrage (Saxifragaceae)

Common Names: Wild Gooseberry, Eastern Wild Gooseberry, Prickly Gooseberry, Bristly Gooseberry, Smooth Wild Gooseberry, Slender Gooseberry, Whitestem Gooseberry, Round-Leaved Gooseberry, Rock Gooseberry, Sierra Gooseberry, European Gooseberry, Swamp Gooseberry, Garden Gooseberry, Northern Gooseberry, Missouri Gooseberry, Wild Currant, Black Currant, Wild Black Currant, Western Black Currant, American Red Currant, Red Garden Currant, Swamp Red Currant, Trailing Black Currant, Northern Black Currant, California Black Currant, Blue Currant, Golden Currant, Fetid Currant, Skunk Currant, Wax Currant, Sticky Currant, Buffalo Currant, Squaw Currant, Bear Currant, Missouri Currant, Hudson Bay Currant, Clove Bush, Dog Bramble, Quincy Berry, Feverberry, Groser.

Characteristics: Ordinarily the thorned and bristly fruit of the *Ribes* genus are gooseberries, while the smoother species are currants.

124

Top: Gooseberries (*Ribes*); *Bottom:* Currants (*Ribes*)

There are exceptions, however, and the black currant of the North (*R. lacustre*), the red currant (*R. prostratum*) of the North, and the *R. glandulosum* or skunk currant of the same general locale are bristly. All furnish good fruit, especially when cooked.

The *Ribes*, a name from the ancient Arabic, is not now so well known as it was in the early days, as it has been discovered that the blister rust fungus, destroying the five-needled pines, spreads to the pines from the *Ribes*. So by eradicating the currants and gooseberries in and near our conifer forests, the spread of the destructive rust can be controlled.

The yellow, red, and black berries of the golden currant (*R. aureum*), to cover one species, were among those enjoyed by the Lewis and Clark Expedition as a survival food. The typical green leaves of this currant, nearly smooth, up to about 1¼ inches wide, with three to five lobes, are characteristically maplelike. The perennial shrub lifts up to a smooth 8 or 10 feet in height. The long, bright, golden flowers, with a tubular calyx and five short lobes, grow in racemes in the axils of the leaves, giving forth a pleasantly spicy odor. A quintet of stamens alternate with the petals.

The single pistil produces a pulpy, ¼-inch berry, sometimes golden like the blossoms but equally delicious when red or black, fresh, cooked, or dried by the Indians for pemmican. Blooming in April and May, it is found naturally in moist soil from California to British Columbia, throughout the Rockies east to New Mexico and Saskatchewan, growing up to some 8,000 feet above sea level.

Area: Gooseberries and currants grow from the Gulf of Mexico to Alaska and from the east to the west coasts.

Uses: The Hopis resorted to the fruit of the *R. cereum* for stomachache. Concerning the wax currant, wild gooseberry, squaw currant, and bear currant—*R. inebrians* and *R. cereum*—this same tribe also found that devouring a large quantity of the red berries at one time could make an individual ill, and that those eaten raw in quantity were emetic.

Other early experiences indicated that the berries of the genus as a whole promoted the flow of urine and helped to dissipate a fever.

A general medicine for feminine difficulties was concocted by making a tea from the leaves of the American red currant (*R. triste*). For women incurring uterine difficulties after a number of births, a root tea from the prickly gooseberry (*R. cynosbati*) was sometimes recommended.

Some pioneer women's answer to a cold was to add a little red currant jelly to a glass of whiskey punch and to give this to the patient just before sleep.

The juice of the black currant stirred into honey was regarded by some as an almost infallible remedy for throat irritation.

Poultices from currant roots were used for everything from bruises to boils.

Indians in the Rocky Mountains ate what they called a porridge of cooked gooseberries for fever and for seizures of malaria marked by paroxysms of chills, fever, and sweating recurring at regular intervals. Pregnant women often had a yen for gooseberries, especially because of their cooling qualities to the stomach and their ability to quench thirst. They were said to be conducive to good appetite and a remedy for catarrh.

The young leaves, steeped, were tried to help break up kidney stones and pass gravel. Used as a mouthwash, the tea had a reputation for helping cure cankers.

GRAPE (*Vitis*)

Family: Vine (Vitaceae)

Common Names: Wild Grape, Indian Grape, Small Grape, Winter Grape, Sweet Winter Grape, Frost Grape, Summer Grape, Fox Grape, Northern Fox Grape, Southern Fox Grape, Turkey Grape, Possum Grape, Cat Grape, Mustang Grape, Skunk Grape, Pigeon Grape, Chicken Grape, Downy Grape, Blue Grape, Bush Grape, Rock Grape, Dune Grape, Canyon Grape, Mountain Grape, Riverbank Grape, Post-Oak Grape, Pinewood Grape, Bullace Grape, California Grape, New England Grape, Arizona Grape, Silverleaf Grape, Plum Grape, Bunch Grape, Sugar Grape, Muscadine, Scuppernong.

Characteristics: Half, at least, of this globe's innumerable grapes are native to North America, the many species of the trailing, climbing, tendril-clasping, wide-leaved, quickly picked fruit being an Indian and pioneer standby and, therefore, one of the mainstays of the hungry Lewis and Clark Expedition. The leaves are mainly heart-shaped and often have no tendril or fruit cluster opposite every third one.

For instance, the fox grape (*Vitis labrusca*), the ancestor of the now famous Concord grape, is a loftily climbing vine that thrives in

Grape (*Vitis*)

rich woods, by streams, and in thickets. It has shallowly and sometimes deeply cleft, three-lobed leaves with roughly toothed rims. Somewhat leathery, these are some 4 to 9 inches long, smoothly green atop, and rather rustily fuzzy beneath. The three- to six-seeded, sweetish, and somewhat musky fruits are usually on the purplish side.

The trailing or climbing muscadine, differing from all other grapes in growing with smooth bark marked with paler pores, unbranched tendrils, and no woody divisions separating the pith at the leaf joints, has roundish or widely egg-shaped 2- to 5-inch-wide leaves with toothed rims, usually glossy above and below, but sometimes somewhat yellowish and downy along the veins beneath. The small clusters of generally blackish purple, tough-skinned, up to an inch wide, muskily sweet fruits having gleaming instead of frosty or grainy surfaces. The vines climb high in woods, swamps, and thickets.

Area: Wild grapes grow through southern Canada and the United States, many domestic species including those cultivated by some of the Indians having gone wild. They have fortunately been immune to the grape phylloxera, the louse accidentally brought to France, where it nearly destroyed all that country's priceless arbors.

Uses: Despite the fact that a 100-gram edible portion of North American grapes is more than four-fifths water, it contains 158 milligrams of potassium, 12 of phosphorus, 4 of iron, 100 international units of vitamin A, 4 of vitamin C, and measurable amounts of vitamin B complexes, plus trace minerals and other nutrients.

These mineral and alkaline-rich fruits aid the body in clearing itself of amassed toxins, at the same time benefiting the kidneys by neutralizing uric acid in the urine. Its rich tartaric acid is said further to assist the urinary system in ridding itself of stones, gravel, and calculous concentrations in the kidneys and bladder in general.

The freshly pressed juice has been used as a blood invigorator. In large amounts it has been used to control diarrhea.

The leaves were chewed to relieve thirst, useful in regions where water was scarce. Soaked in water, they were pressed into service as poultices for everything from fresh wounds to snakebite.

Following childbirth, a tea steeped from the twigs of the frost grape (*Vitus vulpina*) was given to the new mother to relax her and to help bring back her strength.

The juice from freshly crushed, preferably ripe grapes proved to be valuable in helping cleanse the eyes of irritating matter such as the dust from cattle drives and the chaff from threshing.

GREAT WILLOW-HERB (*Chamaenerion*) (*Epilobium*)

Family: Evening Primrose (Onagraceae)

Common Names: Spiked Willow-Herb, Grand Willow-Herb, French Willow-Herb, Bay Willow-Herb, Bay Willow, Flowering Willow, Persian Willow, Willowweed, *L'Herbe Fret,* Fireweed, Firetop, Burntweed, Pilewort, Wild Asparagus, *Asperge,* Indian Wickup, Herb Wickopy, Blooming Sally, Sally-Bloom, Deerhorn.

Characteristics: I've ridden up on deer who—while a great forest fire was still smoldering immediately behind them, where it had been started to clear grazing land beside the Peace River and spread out of control in the early northern springtime—were nibbling on fresh green shoots of the great willow-herb, already sprouting to cover this blackened wasteland with what would soon become a solid wild mass of purple flowers.

This wild medicinal so quickly follows burned-over land, logging operations, new wilderness roads, ditches, pipelines, electric-power swathes, oil-drilling operations, and settler-cleared areas that it turns man- or nature-disturbed regions into vast spreads of rapidly growing and profusely expanding masses of green, rose, reddish, purple, bright pink, lilac, magenta, and infrequently white blossom spikes.

The rapidly blooming, single-stemmed perennials start their strongly decorative flowering from the base and ascend fairly slowly, so that the underneath portions of the numerous spikes may be heavy with long seed-packed pods, while the center is still beautiful with flowers and while the tip is yet budding.

The masses of pods are filled with tightly and trimly layered seeds that toward autumn break open with their bulges of gossamer-parachuted seeds that, wind-borne, soon whiten landscape, roads, trails, and bodies of water.

The great willow-herb, or fireweed, as it is often so appropriately called, grows as high as a man if the location is damp and sunny enough, but usually it is some 4 to 5 feet tall. Its willowlike leaves themselves enhance the otherwise often jackpotlike locales where the plants thrive.

Area: Millions of acres of man- and nature-disordered regions lighten to turquoise from June through September from the foggy Aleutian Islands to Greenland, south to Quebec, South Dakota, Colorado, and Oregon.

Great Willow-Herb (*Chamaenerion*) (*Epilobium*)

Uses: Having abundant vitamin C, the great willow-herb was used as an antiscorbutic by the Indians and settlers who picked the fresh green sprouts when they first came up in the springtime and simmered them sparingly like asparagus. Even with the older stalks, the Indians used to split them open and eat the sweet, glutinous, invigorating, vitamin-rich pith.

Swellings were washed by many Indians and pioneers with an extract made by boiling the well-washed roots in a small amount of water, and this was continued many times until the elevation, if it were nothing too serious and lingering, disappeared.

A strong decoction made by boiling the roots and stalks was one of the wilderness emetics in the New World.

Being astringent, 2 level tablespoons of the root and herb were covered with a cup of boiling water and allowed to steep for some twenty-five minutes. Sipped during the day when it was cold, up to 2 cupfuls during a twenty-four-hour period, it was used to alleviate diarrhea.

HAW (*Crataegus*)

Family: Rose (Rosaceae)

Common Names: Black Haw, Scarlet Haw, Red Haw, Hawthorn, Cockspur Hawthorn, Downy Hawthorn, River Hawthorn, Western Black Hawthorn, English Hawthorn, Hawthorne, Thorn, Bicknell's Thorn, Thornbush, Thorn Apple, Thorn Pear, Thorn Plum, White Thorn, Cockspur Thorn, Hagthorn, May, May Blossom, Mayflower, May Haw, Bread and Cheese.

Characteristics: The 1- to 5-inch, straight or only slightly curved, single thorns of the haw are not found on any of the outer native shrubs or trees on this continent (although many regard the haw as originally an English import); this makes the genus easy to differentiate. The same cannot be said of the many species, numbered by some in the hundreds.

All in all, the haws are a large, complex group of shrubs and trees, with generally thorny twigs and branches, although a few species are spineless. The leaves are single and what is known as simple, growing alternately in varying shapes and different degrees of lobing and serration. The conspicuous flowers have five creamy and sometimes pinkish blossoms and loom up importantly in this coun-

Haw (*Crataegus*)

try's history, as they gave the Pilgrims' ship *Mayflower* its name. Growing in ordinarily fragrant clusters in midsummer, they usually thrive in flattish, terminal groups.

The small applelike fruit, characteristically tipped with the remnants of the outer floral leaves, are really pomes, a fleshy reproductive entity with five seeds enclosed in a capsule and an outer more or less thick, fleshy layer which differs markedly in taste on each shrub or tree, especially when it is raw. Mostly reddish, they are also sometimes yellow and rarely bluish, purplish, or black, often with a high sugar and low protein and fat-content pulp, generally less than ½ inch in diameter.

One of the more common species is the cockspur hawthorn, with its lengthy thorns and its glossy, somewhat egglike leaves, broadly rounded at the top and tapering to the base. Another is the downy hawthorn, with generally thorny branches and soft, ordinarily egglike but lobed leaves with heart-shaped or spiral bases.

Area: Haws abound, often in landscaping efforts, from the Atlantic to the Pacific Oceans across the original forty-eight states and southern Canada.

Uses: The haw in the early days of America had the widespread reputation of being valuable as a diuretic in helping those with water-retention problems, such as some alcoholics, and particularly those suffering with dropsy, which is an abnormal accumulation of serous fluid in the tissues and cells of the body.

Its active parts, crataegin and amygdlin, the latter also being found in the elsewhere considered wild cherry, were separated from the other substances and used both as a heart stimulant and as a help in bringing down and controlling high blood pressure. They were therefore considered to contribute considerably in helping decrease the distress incurred in heart and urinary ailments.

The less informed regarded the haw as a heart tonic, especially valuable in helping ease the agony and difficulties of angina pectoris and as a steadier of the heartbeat, as well as assisting those with other heart disorders.

One dose was made by drying and powdering the fruit of the haw and taking up to about a dozen grains morning, noon, and night. Another was to blend an ounce of this powder with a pint of brandy and take this in the same number of drops. If dizziness resulted, the dosage was reduced. A stimulating tea was brewed from the leaves. The bark of the pear hawthorn was boiled for the same reason. If one had some semblance of pain in the vicinity of the heart, the tea was made of the twigs. Tea steeped from haw leaves was resorted to both for nervousness and as a stimulant.

Besides being employed for emotional pressure and general nervousness, as well as for nervous indigestion, the haw was also used to deal with arthritis and for the aches and pains of overexercise. The powder of the dried pits was believed useful in treating kidney stones and gravel.

The flowers, leaves, and pomes were all believed to be helpful in stopping all types of diarrhea. The Ojibwas, members of the Algonquin nation living about Lake Superior, thought the bark and pomes useful in what they generally referred to as squaws' medicine. The bark of the black haw (*C. nigra*) was often used in stopping uterine hemorrhaging. The young twigs were boiled to bind and stop fluxes. This haw as a whole was resorted to as an astringent, nerve sedative, general stimulant, and diuretic. Other Indians thought the fruit, especially that of *C. rotundifolia*, to be good for stomach disorders.

Finely powdered haws were applied to lingering sores to cause them to dry up and scab. Some Indians and pioneers chewed the leaves to apply to temporary swellings and contusions. All in all, every part of the various haws growing throughout the continent had different definite uses; for one thing the so-called distilled water from them was used to draw out splinters and thorns.

HORSETAIL (*Equisetum arvense*)

Family: Horsetail (Equisetaceae)

Common Names: Field Horsetail, Common Horsetail, Horsetail Grass, Scouring Rush, Dutch Rush, Pewterwort, Bottlebrush, Shavebrush, Shave Grass, Joint-Grass, Joint Weed, Pipes, Bull Pipes, Devil's Guts.

Characteristics: Another wild medicinal, notably simple to identify, is the horsetail. Nearly every camper, hiker, or fisherman has made his way through stands of this small green plant which prospers along corduroyed tote roads, about shaded brooks, at the mouths of mountain streams, and in other cool, moist locations. Ever notice, when you've been relaxing on a log, how some of these give the impression of miniature pine forests? Others are reminiscent of whimsically dwarfed bamboos. The reason? The horsetail grows in two different forms.

The infertile horsetail has a single thin stem which resembles the

135

Horsetail (*Equisetum arvense*)

trunk of a tiny pine all the more because of green shoots that branch out from it in a series of levels. The fertile horsetail thrusts upward in one bare stalk. This ascends in joints which many people pull apart idly, section by popping section.

Both varieties are also known as the scouring rush. The gritty, silica-coated surfaces of the older plants make them convenient articles to grab by the handful for scrubbing pans after an outdoor meal. As for eating, the outer tissues can be removed from the young shoots of both varieties and the somewhat sweetish interiors eaten raw. Older, they are poisonous, and the aconites in them sometimes kills grazing horses in particular.

Many botanists believed that flowering plants commenced with this genus.

Area: Horsetail is found throughout Canada and the northern United States down into California.

Uses: The barren stems, stripped of their silica-impregnated covering, are said to have diuretic and astringent qualities. Indians and the early settlers used a decoction of them for dropsy. This was also believed to encourage menstruation.

For preparation as a diuretic, one recommended method was to steep 2 tablespoonfuls of the chopped, jointed stem, covered, in a pint of bubbling water for half an hour. This was allowed to cool, was strained, and 1 or 2 cups were sipped daily. Used externally in poultices, the solution was applied to stop bleeding.

Sipped, this was also thought to be of benefit in disintegrating and removing stones and gravel from the urinary system.

The Paiutes burned the ground leaves and used the ashes for cankers and sore gums. The Shoshones did the same thing with the dried and powdered roots.

INDIAN FIG (*Opuntia ficus indica*)

Family: Cactus (Cactaceae)

Common Names: Prickly Pear, Eastern Prickly Pear, Western Prickly Pear, Prickly Pear Cactus, Plains Cactus, Opuntia, Devil's Tongue, Tuna, Beavertail, Nopal, Slipper Thorn.

Characteristics: Indian figs are the cacti with the flat-jointed stems. Those members of the same *Cactaceae* family with round-jointed

Indian Fig (*Opuntia ficus indica*)

stems are called chollas and are fibrous and dry. On the other hand, the Indian fig family, protecting their bitterish moisture by having spines instead of leaves and by being layered with a thick covering of wax, have long been a source of emergency drinking water for the desert Indians and for those who followed them. This juice is so mucilaginous that it is still sometimes used in making mortar.

The pale, oval seeds are about 5 millimeters in diameter and have a depressed center and margin. The dramatically lush red and golden flowers that grow on the padlike joints of the Indian fig during the late spring and early fall evolve into the fruit that gives the genus its name. Ranging in size from that of small plums to oranges, the mature colors extend from golden green and dark purple to the red of the big delicious prickly pears, as they are also called, of the *Opuntia megacantha* of the Southwest.

The family is much more easily recognized than harvested, which, because of its sharp spines, is best accomplished with substantial leather gloves and a knife.

Area: Distribution of these cacti has been extended throughout North America because of their popularity as garden and house plants, from which domesticity many have escaped to the wilds. Native only in the Americas, these cacti thrive best in Mexico, where you see the cattle eating them. Within the United States and Canada they grow from California to British Columbia in the West, extending well eastward into the interior. In the East one finds them from New England to Florida.

Uses: The Indians, and the plainsmen, mountain men, prospectors, trappers, and settlers following them often in dusty wagon trains, long peeled the stems of the Indian figs, dampened bandages and compresses with their rather acrid, sticky juice, and bound these on abrasions and other wounds to promote healing.

Poultices were also prepared from the mashed pulp and applied to suppurating sores on man and domestic animal alike, being especially useful among horses, mules, and burros for the treatment of saddle sores. Too, the peeled stems were bound over wounds like bandages. The young joints were also secured before the spines had time to grow, roasted or boiled, and used as compresses for arthritis. The carefully despined and peeled lobes were, and in some cases still are, regarded as efficacious for the alleviation of arthritic swelling, redness, heat, and pain. These so-prepared, warmed pads were even applied to the breasts of new mothers to increase the flow of milk.

The split joints, care being taken with the spines, were roasted and applied to help heal ulcers. Roasted over campfire coals, they were bound over the swelling of mumps. The stems were also boiled in water to provide a wash to relieve sore eyes, headaches, rheumatism, and even insomnia. Even regarding the Indian fig as useful against gout, the Indians found relief, and in New Mexico, for instance, claim they still do with the split baked joints.

The fuzz of the young Indian fig plant was rubbed into warts with the idea of both removing them and guaranteeing their not recurring.

The arduously peeled Indian figs themselves were used as a fever-reducing agent in cases of pleurisy, mental disorders, and chills. They were believed to abate and cool arthritic pain. The fruit, from which candy is commercially made today, was used to treat everything from asthma and diarrhea to gonorrhea. It was believed to increase the flow of urine—a useful phenomenon in the hot regions.

A tincture made from the flowers and stems was prescribed to ease spleen disorders and diarrhea. A tea brewed from the flowers alone was imbibed to increase the flow of urine.

Western frontiersmen simmered the well-washed roots in milk and drank this to relieve dysentery. Slaves infected with severe diarrhea, in which mucus and blood were passed, often drank only half a cup of milk simmered with 8 cups of water, to which a little Indian fig root was added, both to stop the diarrhea and to restore mucus to the intestinal tract.

The Navajos made enclosed shelters and arranged steam baths by pouring infusions of Indian fig, sage, juniper, and piñon over heated stones to treat rheumatism, eye trouble, insomnia, and headache.

INDIAN GINGER (*Asarum*)

Family: Birthwort (Aristolochiaceae)

Common Names: Wild Ginger, Sierra Wild Ginger, Canada Wild Ginger, Snakeroot, Canada Snakeroot, Vermont Snakeroot, Heart Snakeroot, Southern Snakeroot, Coltsfoot Snakeroot, Black Snakeroot, Black Snakeweed, Heartroot, Coltsfoot, Colicroot, Catroot, False Colt's Foot, Hot Potato, Sturgeon Potato, Asarabacca, Broad-Leaved Sarabacca.

Characteristics: Indian ginger is a low-growing plant, with a stem that creeps below the ground, and therefore it is usually thought of as

Indian Ginger (*Asarum*)

a stemless perennial. This subterranean stem emits an aromatic odor when bruised or broken, hence some of the names.

A pair of extremely veiny leaves, their heart shapes lifting only some 6 inches above the ground, rise from the tip of the rhizome. A small and solitary flower, often hidden beneath forest litter—thick, bell-shaped, brownish outside, and purplish within—grows softly and pointedly three-lobed but without petals at the base of the leaves. There are a dozen stamens and an ovary with half that many chambers and a six-lobed stigma.

Area: Indian ginger grows often in rich woodlands across southern Canada and the northern United States south into the moist coniferous forests of California in the West, the Carolinas and Georgia in the East, and Missouri and Texas in the central regions.

Uses: Indian ginger, also known as snakewood, was used in potent decoctions by some of the Indians to induce abundant sweating and may well have been the drug the famous author, A. Hyatt Verrill, was referring to when he wrote, "Many a white man owes his life to the medicinal knowledge of the Indians, and I can personally testify to the efficiency of Indians as physicians, for I was safely brought through an attack of yellow fever by Indians and Indian medicines."

The part of the plant used to bring on copious perspiring to break fevers was the dried rhizome and roots, strong enough to cause dermatitis in some individuals just by the handling of them, which were used as a carminative, among other things. Doses differed, but one was a teaspoonful of these, dried and powdered, to 2 cups of boiling water, generally taken by the jiggerful as needed. This dosage was, of course, increased in potency for fever-reducing purposes.

The underground stem was considered to have value as an expectorant, antiseptic, and tonic. In parts of Appalachia today a tea is still made from the root to relieve stomach gas. Canada wild ginger, as it was also called, was turned to in colonial America in place of Jamaica ginger.

It was much used throughout the country as a febrifugal agent, to mitigate or cure fever, as a diaphoresis and carminative for flu, grippe, and cold symptoms, and for colic. It was believed to help eject viscid matter from the kidney system. The roots and rhizome were ordinarily used in a decoction, but a few Indians steeped the leaves to reduce fever.

As a spring tonic turned to by many old wives and grandmothers, it was valued, especially as it was reassuringly bitter, and particu-

142

larly as it had a stimulating effect. The roots were bound to cuts and wounds to stanch bleeding and promote healing, and there were those who believed they had worth when one was bitten by a poisonous viper, as may be surmised from many of the names the medicinal picked up. The tea was also resorted to for nervousness and for heart difficulties including overrapidity of the beat. The Ojibwas used it as a poultice while setting, splinting, and bandaging broken limbs.

Some of the early Americans believed that it aided the digestion of ill members of their groups. It was also supposed to sharpen the appetite of anyone with a jaded feeling.

Some tribes advocated the use of the root and spicy underground stem for troubles with the respiratory system, especially the lungs, and for sore or aching ears.

An infusion of the root and subterranean stem was relied on by some Indians and their adherents as one of the earlier oral contraceptives, hopefully believed to bring about temporary sterility.

The roots were dug by some in the early springtime, dried, powdered between two smooth rocks or by other primitive means, and used as a snuff to ease the aching of head and eyes.

INDIAN JACK-IN-THE-PULPIT (*Arisaema triphyllum*)

Family: Arum (Araceae)

Common Names: Jack-in-the-Pulpit, Northern Jack-in-the-Pulpit, Small Jack-in-the-Pulpit, Swamp Jack-in-the-Pulpit, Woodland Jack-in-the-Pulpit, Green Dragon, Brown Dragon, Dragon Root, Dragonroot, Dragon Plant, Dragon Turnip, March Turnip, Meadow Turnip, Indian Turnip, Wild Turnip, Swamp Turnip, Pepper Turnip, Wild Pepper, Starch Plant, Starchwort, Memory Root, American Arum, Thrice-Leaved Arum, Devil's Ear, Priest's Pintle, Wake-Robin, Bog Onion, Cuckoo Plant, Lords and Ladies.

Characteristics: First of all, the acidity and the biting pungency of this plant, especially the root, which is the part generally used in medicine, despite many assertions to the contrary cannot be removed by any amount of boiling.

Prolonged drying, as people have found the world over, must be resorted to. The quickest way to do this is by roasting. The simplest and most satisfactory method is to slice the roots into very thin bits, then to place these in a dry place for upward of three months, at the

Indian Jack-in-the-Pulpit (*Arisaema triphyllum*)

end of which time they will be white, delicate, nutritiously starchy, and as crisply pleasant as a potato chip. Or, they can be satisfactorily ground into a flour or powder for medical use.

Even handling the fresh rootstocks can cause inflammation of the skin in individuals more sensitive to them. Eating a tiny sliver of the raw root might be likened to swallowing a teaspoonful of red pepper, and its violently corrosive effect can linger for hours.

The perennial has two stalks of three leaves each, between which grows a third stalk topped with a green tubular *pulpit,* which has a hood turned down over it that protects an inside greenish or dark purple tube or *preacher.* The spathe, itself green or purple and usually palely or whitely striped, resembles an old-time canopied pulpit from which the minister *Jack* preaches. This latter is a clublike, projecting upper part of the spadix which bears dense clusters of pistillate flowers and later brilliant crimson, berrylike fruit toward its base, better revealed when the hood withers after the blooming between late March and June. Male and female flowers, and therefore the berries, are often on separate plants.

The round roots or corms, irritating and toxic, with needlelike calcium oxalate crystals, are the parts most often used by human beings.

Area: The Indian jack-in-the-pulpit seeks rich, moist woodlands from New Brunswick and Nova Scotia to Florida and Mississippi, west to Minnesota and Louisiana.

Uses: The only Indian use of the raw corm that I have reliably heard of was as a salve, sparingly mixed with lard, for ringworm and as a counterirritant for snakebite.

If it was dried long enough to remove the corrosiveness, that was another story. Then, boiled in milk, it was used to treat tuberculosis, sore throats, and coughs. The dried ground corm has its advocates in the alleviation of arthritis, asthma, bronchitis, and trouble with an overabundance of phlegm in the lungs, bronchial tubes, and throat. It was used to promote sweating.

The dried and powdered root was placed on the forehead and temples to ease headache. It was considered useful as a diuretic, to ease stomachache and gas and chronic bronchitis. Poultices made from it were used on irritated eyes. It was tried as another of the multitudinous treatments for cold symptoms. The powder was employed as an insecticide.

There were reports of Indians discreetly using the not entirely neutralized roots for some of these purposes, but this had to be done with a great deal of care and at times when skin-blistering was actually sought or a counterirritant really desired. Even then, drying and never boiling was the method used to remove successfully the greater part of the acridity.

INDIAN LETTUCE (*Montia perfoliate*)

Family: Purslane (Portulacaceae)

Common Names: Spanish Lettuce, Miner's Lettuce, Naiad Spring Beauty, Winter Purslane.

Characteristics: A distinguishing feature of the invaluable Indian lettuce is that some two thirds of the way up each of its several stems there grows a cuplike disk of a leaf through whose center the particular stalk continues. Each is then topped by tiny whitish to pinkish blossoms.

Every one of these pretty flowers swings and sways in the fresh breezes on its own comparatively longish stem, generally with five petals and a duo of sepals, the modified leaves each comprising a calyx. These blooms mature from the lower portions of the stalk upward so that there are often flowers below and buds above. All eventually grow shiny black seeds.

Indian lettuce commonly starts with a whirl of slim, narrow, basal leaves through which several stalks push their way upward some 4 to 12 inches.

Area: The native Indian lettuce flourishes throughout the greater area of western North America from Mexico, California, and Arizona northward to British Columbia and southern Alaska, where the aborigines have also long relished it, eastward to Utah and the gold-rich Black Hills of South Dakota.

Uses: Indian lettuce first sprang into national prominence when the forty-niners stampeded to California by every means of transportation available after the discovery of gold at Sutter's Mill. Generally greenhorns, ill equipped, plagued because of their very numbers and the fact that almost overnight nearly everyone became a prospector, they had little means, time, and money for fresh food. Loose teeth, spongy gums, and inner bleeding into the skin and the membranes rich in mucous glands soon manifested themselves in what are now the dry and dusty remains of historic camps and ghost towns.

Indian Lettuce (*Montia perfoliate*)

The Indians and the Spanish—hence the names Indian lettuce and Spanish lettuce—saved hundreds of the rip-roaring forty-niners, who dispensed justice with six-guns and hangmen's ropes but couldn't conquer scurvy on their own, by showing them the antiscorbutic. This, eaten raw when tender and preferably briefly simmered in a minimum amount of water when tougher, saved the lives of many of our ancestors, whether or not they otherwise struck it rich.

INDIAN RICE (*Zizania*)

Family: Grass (Gramineae)

Common Names: Wild Rice, Water Rice, Water Oats.

Characteristics: Indian rice grows in a pair of native varieties, sometimes stretching up about 10 feet from muddy and silty habitats in and around swamps, marshes, pools, ponds, lakes, brooks, streams, and rivers, where it has long been sought by Indians, settlers, and hunters of migrating ducks and geese. With its obese stem up to about ½ inch thick at the base and its large, coarse, seed-bearing, plumelike tops, it can hardly be mistaken for anything else.

It is actually a luxuriantly growing grass, thriving in shallow water which has enough movement to keep it from becoming inactive and stale. The flower clusters are seed-receptive on top and pollen-rich below. Fertilized, the seeds become long and dark within hairily tipped husks. Once dried and husked, the blackish seeds must be amply bathed in cold fresh water before they are eaten or they will be too sweetly smoky in taste.

In fact, if they are to be planted, they must be stored in water at 32°F for maximum germination. They lose their ability to germinate if they are exposed to the air for more than a few days.

The name of the Menomini Indians means "Indian Rice" and in their country, bisected by the circle of 50° north latitude, the moon in September is known as the Rice-Is-Ready-to-Harvest Moon.

Area: Indian rice thrives in great stands from Maine and Quebec to the Great Lakes, Wisconsin, and Minnesota, southward along the coast to Florida. Its range has been considerably increased by the plantings of duck and geese hunters.

Uses: An Indian treatment for cholera was intense cathartics and perspiring, brought on by one of the aspirin-containing wild medici-

148

Indian Rice (*Zizania*)

nals such as willow or poplar cambium or checkerberry, or by heavy steam baths, then abundant meals of porridges of Indian rice.

This wild rice, as it was also called, provided the diet of Indians and colonists who had incurred stomach trouble. It was considered, and still is by many, to be an ideal intake for those with the symptoms of high blood pressure and heart difficulties. Too, thin gruel made from it was and is favored for the ill and convalescent.

JERUSALEM ARTICHOKE (*Helianthus tuberosus*)

Family: Composite (Compositae)

Common Names: Sunflower Artichoke, Sunflower Root, Wild Sunflower, Canada Potato, *Pomme de Terre.*

Characteristics: This native perennial, its tubers being the important part, has stalks, slim and branched, that grow up to some 10 feet tall, with leaves which, unlike those of some of the other sunflowers, are greenish beneath. Formed like roughly toothed lance heads, either ovate or oblong, they are sharply pointed and coarse and hairy above. Low down, they grow opposite one another but frequently tend to alternate as the stems rise and branch.

The often many blossoms, golden but lighter in color and smaller than most of their cousin sunflowers, lack the colorful, seed-filled centers of the latter and are much smaller and less conspicuous. What this wild medicinal fails to be endowed with above ground is more than made up for by slender, fleshy, potatolike rootstocks that bulge from a densely creeping root skein. Ideally dug in the fall, these are marked by the tall old stalks above and are many times easier to harvest for growing on the rims of bogs and marshes.

Area: At one time cultivated by some of the eastern tribes and later by the colonists, these have widely escaped and now grow in damp but not wet locales from Ontario to Georgia, west to Manitoba and Arkansas, and in widely separated parts of the United States and Canada.

Uses: The leaves were long used hopefully for the control of malaria. A tincture of the blossoms was many times prescribed for the treatment of bronchitis. In fact, this was considered particularly useful in handling a chronic dilation of the bronchi or bronchioles—each the minute, thin-walled branch of a bronchus, either of the two primary divisions of the trachea that lead, respectively, to the left and right lungs.

Jerusalem Artichoke (*Helianthus tuberosus*)

The fleshy, watery, and sweetish tubers, simmered in bubbling water with their skins on until a fork can easily be inserted and withdrawn, then cooled and skinned, was nutritious and so easily digested that it was recommended for invalids and convalescents.

A few of the tubers were usually reserved and dried, to be pounded when necessary and then chewed to relieve a sore throat.

JUNIPER (*Juniperus*)

Family: Pine (Pinaceae)

Common Names: Ground Juniper, Common Juniper, Red Juniper, Dwarf Juniper, Scrub Juniper, Prostrate Juniper, Trailing Juniper, Mexican Juniper, Mountain Juniper, Shore Juniper, Chinese Juniper, Bush Juniper, Irish Juniper, Greek Juniper, Swedish Juniper, Shrub Juniper Bush, Juniper Bush, Hackmatick, Savin, Horse Savin, Scent Cedar, Red Cedar, Eastern Redcedar, Gorst.

Characteristics: One has only to smell or sip gin to distinguish the scent and taste of juniper. Although it also grows as a tree, one generally thinks of the juniper as a low, scraggly, creeping, prostrate evergreen with miniature pinelike needles instead of leaves and fragrant blue berries which provide a nourishing and pleasant nibble. I've sat in many a mat of it on a mountaintop and glassed the country for game. But as the eastern redcedar (*Juniperus virginiana*) it grows over 100 feet high, with both needlelike leaves when young and scalelike leaves about ½ inch in length, twice as long, when mature.

The common juniper (*J. communis*) is a low evergreen shrub up to a dozen to 30 feet high, growing low and spreading upright. The bark of the trunk is reddish brown and shreddy. The pine-family needles are straight, sharply tipped, ridged, and nearly at right angles to the branchlets. The dark purple fruit is round and about ¼ inch wide, fleshy, and berrylike.

In the characteristic creeping juniper (*J. horizontalis*), which grows at altitudes up to nearly a mile high from Alaska to Newfoundland, south to New York and Nebraska, the two to six scales of the tiny cones unite to form fleshy, aromatic ovals which we regard as berries. The needlelike leaves of the ground-sprawling plant, often used in landscaping, are about ½ inch long and agreeably prickly.

The junipers do not yield seeds until they are about ten years old. The Rocky Mountain juniper (*J. scopulorum*) flowers in the spring,

©AJA

Juniper (*Juniperus*)

and its seed dispersal is long and persistent, the commercial seed-bearing age being from 10 to 300 years. It produces on the average some 1,790 seeds per ounce. The treatment recommended by the U.S. Department of Agriculture for germination is layering them in moisture-holding material such as earth or peat for two to four months at 68 to 80°F, then for a similar period at a cool 33 to 41°F. Seeing that such a tremendous amount of seeds has some three centuries during which some of them may accomplish this, it is little wonder that juniper is so widely spread and prolific.

Area: As might be expected, junipers prosper from Alaska to Labrador and Newfoundland, throughout Canada and the United States, wherever conditions are right, even on dry sterile hillsides.

Uses: All parts of the juniper were used in Indian medicine and passed along to the pioneers and settlers, many of them with much imagination. For instance, once a campfire had burned down to mere embers, these were scattered, fresh damp juniper branches piled onto them, and a patient suffering with arthritis made to recline on them, at the same time drinking a hot tea of juniper berries to help along his perspiring.

Too, heated damp bundles of boughs were bound to joints three or four times a day, steaming berry tea being imbibed consecutively. Solutions of boiled juniper twigs and berries were also bound to rheumatic parts in compresses. Similar sweat baths were used for fevers. Too, fresh hot juniper tea was drunk in cases of fever such as that brought on by flu to cause temperature-lowering sweating.

In connection with heating parts of the shrub and tree, the needles and also the scalelike leaves were crushed, dampened, heated over the fire, bound to the jaw over an aching tooth with a cloth or strip of leather, and kept warm there with a hot stone. Somewhat similarly, the minutely grated twigs were heated and bound around a sore throat, renewed when they cooled. Leafy ends of branches were also bound hot around sprained and swollen parts, such as ankles, as they were on aching rheumatic joints.

A decoction made by boiling the tips of juniper twigs, to which the leaves and resin was sometimes added, was drunk cold for syphilis and gonorrhea.

An oil extracted from the wood of such junipers as the common juniper (*J. communis*) was used to cause menstruation to recommence, but that from the eastern redcedar (*J. virginiana*), when employed for abortion, sometimes proved fatal. Teas of twigs and berries were also tried more safely for the same purpose. However, during their final few weeks of pregnancy, numerous squaws from many tribes started drinking a half cupful of boiled twig tea daily. After birth, nursing mothers took it to hold off renewed menses.

For hemorrhaging, hot juniper tea was resorted to as an astringent. Before battles too, young twigs and berries were eaten each day to hasten coagulation of bleeding after any wounds. The daily drinking of cold berry tea each day for a week or longer was faithfully followed for the same purpose after it had been steeped overnight, then strained.

A similar procedure was followed, incidentally, by those with lumbago.

As is still occurring today, the Indians and those from the Old World were also already trying to find a cold remedy, and the various parts of the juniper were included in the attempts. Some of these so-termed cures were so unpalatable, for instance, that the New Mexican women where we once lived by the Sangre de Cristo Mountains disguised them with the aromatic juniper, also tried by itself in various forms as a cold and flu remedy. One corrective attempted was inhalation of the smoke from smoldering juniper limbs. One refinement was breathing the fumes from juniper berries, heated under covers over a receptacle of hot embers.

Medicinal fumigation of quarters and individuals after illnesses and especially after childbirth was carried out by burning, or preferably allowing to smolder and smoke, dampened green juniper branches over hot embers, fuming recepticles of fresh berries in particular sometimes being carefully carried about and controlled for such purposes.

The heated berries were applied to wounds and sores. Decoctions of every part of the shrub or tree were resorted to for antiseptic and healing washes. Poultices made from the crushed berries and leaves were resorted to for scalds, burns, and sores. A combination of warmed resin and terminal berries is still used by some of the tribes to bring boils to a head and to keep them drawing and clean.

Scanty urination and kidney troubles were common complaints in hot, dusty regions where there was little water, and the fruit was used to treat them, being considered especially useful as a diuretic. It was later distilled in some edible oil for what were considered to be even more effective results.

Tea boiled, steeped, and otherwise brewed from the fruit was used for everything from a tonic, to ease gas and other digestive troubles, to kill and expel worms from the alimentary tract, for hardening of the arteries, for snakebite, for hiccup attacks, for fevers, for stemming hemorrhaging, and for stimulants. One refinement was a half cup of berries, steeped in the evening, strained, and then kept cold overnight, and drunk every morning for a week by those with impaired digestion and by those needing a tonic.

The dangerous oil of the eastern redcedar (*J. virginiana*) was in early times used for chronic trouble with the genito-urinary system.

The Indian use of the juniper for uterine obstructions was commended nearly two centuries ago by an Old World physician.

Juniper needles, and scalelike leaves, were dried, crushed and pounded, and dusted on slowly healing sores, as well as on far less serious strains and bruises. The similarly powdered twigs were used to cover the rashes and eruptions of such diseases as measles and smallpox. The heated twigs, or potent decoctions of them, were also applied to such trouble spots and to ulcers and other serious sores. The crushed ripe berries were also smoothed on as a salve for these and many other difficulties.

Juniper was another of the antiscorbutics, a pleasant way of taking it being by covering about a dozen young berryless sprigs with a quart of cold water, bringing this to a boil, covering and simmering ten minutes, then removing from the heat and steeping for an additional ten minutes. For a higher vitamin C content, cover a handful of young sprigs with boiling water and set it aside to steep overnight before drinking.

KELP (*Nereocystis*)

Family: Brown Algae (Phaeophyceae)

Common Names: Edible Kelp, Ribbon Kelp, Bull Kelp, Giant Kelp, Bladder Wrack, Sea Wrack, Black Tang.

Characteristics: Every species is good to eat, although they differ considerably in composition. For instance, there is the extremely noticeable giant kelp of the Pacific from California to Alaska, with its lengthy hollow stalks and large gas-filled, floating bladders—among which whale and sea lion and otter cavort—sometimes growing as high as 80 feet from its roots at the bottom, in huge offshore patches amid long, thin, gleaming blades, all valuable to human beings. Much usable fresh kelp is washed ashore during heavy seas.

156

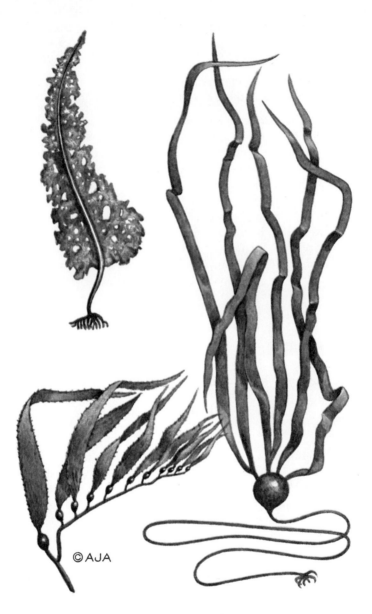

Kelp (*Nereocystis*)

Then there is the less spectacular kelp, which has a short, chambered stalk with a primary, longish, green or brownish leaflike thallus, with a distinguishing heavy middle rib extending from the stalk, and innumerable roundish openings among the winglike sides which give the whole a colanderlike appearance.

Area: These plentiful marine algae flourish throughout the oceans of the world, including those of our forty-ninth and fiftieth states.

Uses: Kelp, heartily recommended by dieticians and sold powdered in the health-food stores, is abundant in potash salts, with some 27 percent to 35 percent potassium chloride dry weight. An edible 100-gram unit with 21.7 percent water, boasts 5,273 milligrams of potassium, 3,007 of sodium, 1,093 of calcium, 240 of potassium, plus many trace elements. But you can get the same invaluable nutrients by eating the kelp when it's gathered, its flavor becoming even more pleasant when it is kept and dried. The Indians turned to it so that they would not get "big necks," goiter, like their Old World neighbors, who sometimes suffered from a lack of the essential iodine.

Some of the Indians, especially those near the seacoasts, used kelp fronds to relieve and help cure burns and scalds.

Kelp was used to combat overweight. The medicinal was also valued as a blood purifier and as an alternative—a medicine gradually changing a condition and bringing back health.

KNOTWEED (*Polygonum*)

Family: Buckwheat (Polygonaceae)

Common Names: Common Knotweed, True Knotweed, Spotted Knotweed, Beach Knotweed, Japanese Knotweed, Giant Knotweed, Yard Knotweed, Shasta Knotweed, Leafy Dwarf Knotweed, Spurry Knotweed, Spotted Knotweed, California Knotweed, Silver-Sheathed Knotweed, Sawatch Knotweed, Pennsylvania Smartweed, Heartweed, Smartweed, Doorweed, Snakeweed, Viviparous Bistort, Bistort, American Bistort, Western Bistort, Alpine Bistort, Goose Grass, Serpentgrass, Knot Grass, Knotgrass, Dragonwort, American Bamboo Shoots, Patience Dock, Nine Joints, Lady's Thumb, Bigwood Lady's Thumb, Swamp Persicaria, Pennsylvania Persicaria, Bindweed, Beggarweed, Wild Buckwheat, Bird's Knot, Birdstongue, Heartease, Water Pepper.

Knotweed (*Polygonum*)

Characteristics: There are some thirty to fifty species of knotweed on this continent, depending on which school the botanist surveying the subspecies attended. All these members of the buckwheat family are delicious eating, incidentally, none being poisonous.

Common species include the *Polygonum pensylvanicum* and *P. lapathifolium,* both 4 feet tall or higher, with mostly lancelike leaves. The first has erect pink spikes, the latter drooping and somewhat greenish spikes. The gland-tipped hairs on the stems of the blossom cluster of the former serve to differentiate it from similar knotweeds or smartweeds, as they are also known.

P. punctatum and *P. persicaria* are ordinarily shorter medicinals with lanceolate leaves and fringed or lacerated stipular sheaths, the first with greenish white blossoms and the second with generally pink blooms.

The slender perennial *P. bistortoides,* whose delicate and striking flower spikes give no hint of the obese and starchy rootstocks beneath, blossoms without petals, generally with a quintet of short white or greenish sepals, the stamens attached to the calyx, and oblong erect leaves.

Perhaps most widely known in much of this country is the Japanese knotweed (*P. cuspidatum*), whose hollow stalks, when lifeless, loom up against the landscape like bamboo thickets, clattering in the breezes and serving to identify the asparagus-shaped young shoots when they thrust up robustly in the spring. Innumerable greenish white blossoms later erupt in multibranched clusters between the stalks and the leaves which, being pointed, serve to distinguish this medicinal from the others in the widespread family whose common names vary in differing localities.

Area: Knotweed grows in nearly every part of the United States, as well as in most of Canada.

Uses: Knot grass, bindweed, and beggarweed (*P. aviculare*) were boiled and blended with the bitter and astringent bark of the oak (*Quercus*) as a replacement for quinine when the latter was unavailable.

For diarrhea with children as well as with adults, some tribes and their pioneer neighbors soaked the stems and leaves of the bigwood lady's thumb (*P. coccineum*) in cold water and gave it to them internally. This medicinal was also used in a root-tea mixture to heal an injured womb after the birth of a child. A root tea from this plant was used as a mouthwash, especially when cankers and other sores were present.

P. persicaria—also called lady's thumb, heartease, and spotted knotweed—has been utilized as a whole to increase urine flow when this was scanty. For this, a teaspoonful was steeped in a cup of bubbling water and sipped when cold during the day, 1 or 2 cupfuls every twenty-four hours. The juice was believed useful in easing and helping to cure abrasions, cuts, wounds of all sorts, and even bruises.

Stones and gravel in the urinary system were believed to be dissolved when a tea of knotgrass (*P. aviculare*) was imbibed regularly. For some reason, holding this plant in the hand at least until it became warm—and for even longer periods with some more severe difficulties—was supposed to arrest an attack of nosebleed. This particular species was also regarded as a diuretic and astringent.

The bitterish tea that was brewed from the Pennsylvania smartweed or Pennsylvania persicariam (*P. pensylvanicum*) was given to individuals hemorrhaging from the mouth.

The root of the patience dock, snakeweed, or dragonwort, as *P. bistorta* was variously known, was often turned to when a diuretic, alternative, or astringent seemed called for. This type produced an S-shaped rhizome that bends back upon itself which was used in small bits to make a tonic drink. It is reddish brown, thick, channeled or flattened, with root scars beneath, and contains tannin, starch, and calcium oxalate. Since it is one-fifth tannin, it is very bitter and astringent.

The entire *P. punctatum* was steeped in warm water and used as a wash and on damp compresses for sore, rough, reddened, or inflamed skin. It found service as a gargle for coughs arising from colds or irritations and was one of the medicinals turned to for alleviating cold symptoms. A cup a day of a decoctation made by steeping a teaspoonful of the cut-up herb was prescribed as a diuretic and as a stimulating tonic.

The generic cognomen *Polygonum* means "many joints," indicating to many that the plant was useful in arthritis—that is, for swollen and aching joints.

LABRADOR TEA (*Ledum groenlandicum*)

Family: Heath (Ericaceae)

Common Names: Narrow-Leaved Labrador Tea, Hudson's Bay Tea, Muskeg Tea, Bog Tea, Moth Herb, Marsh Tea, Continental Tea.

Labrador Tea (*Ledum groenlandicum*)

Characteristics: Labrador tea is a 1- to 4-foot-high, resinous, evergreen shrub, which prefers bogs, swamps, muskegs, tundras, damp open woods, and moist meadows. The woolliness that covers the underneath parts of the inwardly rolling leaves, grayish the first year and more of a rusty reddish brown in older foliage, quickly identifies these wild medicinals. The 1- to 4-inch-long leaves are alternate, thick, blunt, leathery, narrow, simple, darkly green above, with smooth, curling rims. The plant is pleasantly aromatic when bruised or crushed.

The small, regular, whitish to yellow flowers, each with its own slender stalk, have five to seven stamens and a five-sectioned ovary and grow in roundish, showy clusters, at the tops of the leaved stems.

One of the names of this plant, Hudson's Bay Tea, takes note of how it is still used as a beverage by Company employees in the Canadian north, once largely owned by the Hudson's Bay Company, which still maintains its far-flung trading posts with white buildings with red roofs in remote regions, although in later years it has become more a big-city retailer.

Area: Labrador tea grows across the Arctic and subarctic from Alaska to Greenland, southward to British Columbia and Washington, Alberta, Michigan, Wisconsin, Ohio, and New Jersey.

Uses: Brewed like store tea, Labrador tea is pleasingly antiscorbutic and stimulating. It was also used by the Indians and settlers as a tonic supposed to purify the blood. A few leaves, chewed raw, act on many as a quick stimulant. Large quantities are said to be cathartic. Drunk in more moderate amounts, however, it was supposed to halt chest troubles and ward off chills. It was also employed to treat wounds.

Ledum palustre, according to a fairly recent *U.S. Dispensatory,* contains the glucoside ericolin, tannin, and valeric acid, among other things.

It was another of the warm, stimulating beverages turned to during the American Revolution that still provide an agreeable drink.

LIVERBERRY (*Streptopus*)

Family: Lily (Liliaceae)

Common Names: Liver Berry, Scoot Berry, White Mandarin, Cucumber Root, Twisted Root, Clasping Twisting Root.

Liverberry (*Streptopus*)

Characteristics: The thing to regard when identifying a liverberry is the singular bend or twist in each solitary flower or berry stem near its midsection. These thin stems lift individually from where the tapering and pointed, smooth, generally ovate leaves, with a flourlike bloom on their undersides, alternately clasp the 2- to 5-foot-high stalks. In fact, the *Strepto* part of the Grecian genus name means "twisted."

When viewed from the front, the tiny, oval, pulpy fruits seem to be suspended from near the middle of the 1- to 2-inch-broad, green leaves. Their colors range from yellowish white to orange and red. They bloom from early spring to July, with light green to pink bell-like flowers.

Area: The liverberry grows where the ground is damp from Alaska to California and in moist shaded woods, boggy regions, and along stream banks from Iowa, Ontario, and southern New England southward, where conditions are sufficiently cool. They occur on mountains well over a mile high, as well as in vales.

Uses: The young shoots and leaves, especially when they are tender enough to relish raw, are strongly antiscorbutic. The several berry-recognizing names tell the rest. Indians enjoyed a very few for their cool, somewhat cucumberlike flavor. But in numbers they have a most definite carthartic effect.

MAPLE (*Acer*)

Family: Maple (Aceraceae)

Common Names: Red Maple, White Maple, Chalk Maple, Silver Maple, Black Maple, Carolina Red Maple, Scarlet Maple, Scarlet-Flowering Maple, Virginia Ash-Leaved Maple, Ashleaf Maple, Striped Maple, Stripe-Leaved Maple, Drummond Red Maple, Sugar Maple, American Sugar Maple, Black Sugar Maple, White-Barked Sugar Maple, Rock Maple, Hard Maple, Soft Maple, Common Maple, Goosefoot Maple, Ivy-Leaved Maple, Bigleaf Maple, Vine Maple, Hedge Maple, River Maple, Water Maple, Mountain Maple, Rocky Mountain Maple, Mountain Maple Bush, Florida Maple, Montpelier Maple, Siberian Maple, Italian Maple, Norway Maple, Japanese Maple, Tartarian Maple, Spiked Maple, Sycamore Maple, Shoe-Peg Maple, Moose Maple, Moosewood, Box Elder.

Maple (*Acer*)

Characteristics: Being the emblem of Canada, the maple leaf is recognized by nearly everyone. Coloring with oxidation as it does magnificently at the end of summer, it is a principal cause for the unforgettable fall beauty of New Hampshire, Vermont, Maine, and the Bay State of Massachusetts.

The seeds also are distinctive, composed of a tan duo of wings in whose center bulge a plump pair of edible seeds.

The sugar maple, to pick the most famous member of the family, is a large tree 60 to more than 100 feet high which thrives in fertile, moist, to well-drained and frequently rocky soils. Three- to 6-inch-wide leaves, generally with a quintet of pointed and frugally wavy-toothed lobes which are divided by broadly U-formed sinuses, are deep green above, paler and many times somewhat whitened below, and smooth or almost so, making the tree seem more beautiful.

The blossoms, forming from April to June, are yellowish green, clustered on lengthy and sagging hairy stems. The paired fruits, centered between wings about an inch long to form a brownish U, ripen from June until September.

Certain of the maples develop mature seeds in no more than two months after flowering, whereas the bigtree (*Sequoia gigantea*), to note a contrast, requires about 125 years. The familiar winged seeds of the sugar maple (*Acer saccharum*), for example, disperse from October to December. They average 380 seeds per ounce.

Area: The maple family, which includes numerous refugees from elegant landscaping, grows as a whole throughout southern Canada and the contiguous states except for the Great Plains and the lower Rockies. The sugar maple, valuable for its hardwood and the major source of maple syrup and sugar, prospers from Newfoundland to North Carolina, northern Georgia, and northern Louisiana, west to southern Ontario and Minnesota.

Uses: A wash decocted from the soaked pith of a twig of the mountain maple (*Acer spicatum*) was often cupped in a hand and used to bathe an eye to remove such foreign matter as dust. A calming, moderating, and tranquilizing douche for the uterus was also brewed from this particular tree. The bark from the mountain maple was used, too, for the treatment of general eye infections, of worms in the alimentary canal, as poultices for abrasions, and, incidentally, to tone the appetite.

In fact, the Indians often turned to the various maples in general for getting rid of intestinal worms, for treatment of eye trouble from minor irritations to infections, and for increasing the appetite.

167

An extract obtained by boiling both leaves and bark was said to strengthen liver activity, as well as to open obstructions there and in the spleen, at the same time relieving pain from such disorders.

The gathering of maple syrup, having been common on this continent since pre-Columbian centuries, produced a liquid and sugar far more important medically in B vitamins, phosphorus, calcium, and enzymes than today's commercial products, from which they are now largely refined. Scarce and expensive as these maple delicacies are today, it is a commentary on the times that colonists apologized for serving maple sugar in lieu of the then-costly, difficult-to-obtain, inferior, manufactured brown sugar.

MARSH MARIGOLD (*Caltha*)

Family: Buttercup (Ranunculaceae)

Common Names: Cowslip, American Cowslip, *Ahklingquank,* Meadowbright, Meadow Bouts, Mare-Blobs, Palsywort, Water Dragon.

Characteristics: The American cowslip, as it is also known, should not be mistaken for a different wild edible and medicinal of the same name in England—a situation further confused by the fact that a similar *Caltha palustris* thrives and is used internally there.

The species, a member of the buttercup family, when raw is poisonous with the volatile hellebore—a powder or extract formerly used medically, fatal if improperly utilized, which in the old days was employed as a heart and respiratory depressant and as an insecticide—fortunately driven off with delicious results when cooked.

Because of the fact that the marsh marigold must always be cooked before being eaten, it is a good idea to collect the plants by themselves. Furthermore, precautions should be taken not to include mistakenly any poisonous water hemlock or white hellebore which seek a similar area. The fatal water hemlock, unfortunately, looks like and smells like a parsnip with a dahlialike root, growing tall on thin hollow stems with terminal clusters of small white flowers. The fatal white hellebore is a leafy plant somewhat resembling the skunk cabbage, with loose cabbagelike leaves.

Our marsh marigold (*C. palustris*), grows smoothly, with an obese, forking, hollow stalk some 1 to 2 feet high, bearing on stout, long stems heart-shaped or kidney-formed roundish, basal

Marsh Marigold (*Caltha*)

leaves up to some 7 inches in diameter, glossily dark green above and paler below, their rims smooth, undulating, or roundly toothed. The smaller, higher leaves grow almost from the stalks themselves.

The five to nine petallike sepals of the 1- to 1½-inch bright golden blossoms fall early, leaving a tiny concentration of seed containers to lengthen and expand. Incidentally, the 1- to 2½-millimeter, elliptic to pear-shaped, brown seeds can be sown a quarter of an inch deep along a wet margin in the woods, or in a pot that must be kept constantly wet, until they are ready for transplanting. They naturally grow in wet meadows, open woods, and swamps, one of which habitats must be simulated in a home garden if their domestic growth is to be successful.

Area: The bright-yellow marsh marigolds, presaging spring, prosper from the wet and cloudy Aleutians in an easterly direction along the damp Gulf of Alaska, northeasterly across the Arctic coast to Labrador and Greenland, then as far south as the Carolinas.

Uses: The marsh marigold when raw is poisonous, harsh, and pungent, but a drop of the corrosive juice dropped on a wart once a day is said sometimes to make the horny, virus-caused protuberance vanish.

The surest and least vitamin-wasting method of making the medicinal safe for taking internally was to drop the young leaves, flowers, and stems into bubbling water, let it come to a boil again, and drain away the fluid; then pour in more simmering water and let this once more come to a boil before draining. Finally steam or simmer until tender. The water then remaining was used for dropsy, as a diuretic, and for other kidney troubles. The leaves were also eaten by some for these same purposes.

Claimed to be effective for treating trouble with the chest and lungs, it was also utilized as an expectorant, for coughs, and as a component of cough syrups.

A tea of the third water of the boiled flowers was said to give favorable results in treating fits, as was the concentrated scent of the marsh marigolds themselves.

MINT (*Mentha*)

Family: Mint (Labiatae)

Common Names: Peppermint, Brandy Mint, Apple Mint, Orange Mint, Corsican Mint, Lamb Mint, Lammint, Spearmint, Brown Mint,

Mint (*Mentha*)

Curly Mint, Common Mint, Garden Mint, Canada Mint, Mackerel Mint, Lady's Mint, Scotch Mint, Scotch Spearmint, Lemon Mint, Squaw Mint, Water Mint, Horsemint, Moon Mint, American Mint, Wild Mint, Fieldmint, Pennyroyal, American Pennyroyal, Western Pennyroyal, Mountain Pennyroyal, Giant Hyssop, Sage of Bethlehem, Wild Bergamot, Beebalm, Yerba Buena, Horehound, Oswego Tea.

Characteristics: The numerous wild mints have been well known to us from ancient days to the present as medicines, scents, flavorings, and foods. Although there are numerous varieties, all have square stems, opposite leaves, and a pleasing familiar aroma. This fragrance may not permeate the surroundings if just a few mints flourish together, but you only have to rub or crush a leaf in your hand to recognize it.

Area: The wild mints, a number of them escapees from gardens, are broadly distributed from the southern half of Canada throughout the contiguous United States down into Mexico. They prefer damp soils.

Uses: For giving a sickroom a clean, agreeable odor, introduce the steam of mint leaves boiled in water. Otherwise, to conserve the highly volatile aromatic aroma of the oil-filled cells of these plants, as well as to save most of the abundant and medicinally valuable vitamins A and C, plunge a large amount of the freshly gathered green leaves into bubbling water, cover tightly, and let them steep overnight before straining and using. The highest available counts of these two invaluable vitamins are, of course, secured by eating the newly picked, tender young leaves raw. For out-of-season use, young mint leaves are best gathered on a dry morning, dried at room temperature, and then kept in a cool dark place in closely covered jars.

Mint tea, made the same way and in the same proportions as a regular tea, has long been considered a pleasant palliative for both colic and indigestion, partly because it tends to relieve the digestive system of gas.

Peppermint (*M. piperita*), held by many of the Indians and colonists to be the most effective of the mints, was believed to increase bile secretion. This mint, with its distinctive odor, grows about a yard high, has dark green and toothed leaves which are somewhat rough beneath, unlike the smooth spearmint leaves, and produces spikelike groups of purplish blossoms at the tops of the stalks and in the angles between the leaves and the stems.

The leaves were and are chewed to sweeten the breath. The newly plucked leaves were also bound over painful areas for relief. Pepper-

172

mint tea, a teaspoon of the leaves and flowering tips to a cup of bubbling water, was drunk cold for headache, heartburn, digestive gas, colic, indigestion, and as a sedative. The crushed, freshly gathered leaves, said to have mild anesthetic properties, were sometimes rubbed into the skin to relieve headaches and local pain. Peppermint has also been among those ingredients recommended as a seasickness preventative.

The milder spearmint, also recognized as a distinctive flavoring agent and, like peppermint, brought to the New World by the colonists, grows unbranched in thick clumps from heights of about 1 foot to 1½ feet, with bright, smooth, oblong or lance-head-shaped, unevenly toothed leaves and whitish to deep violet flowers. A handful of the fresh leaves to a cup of boiling water, steeped for no longer than five minutes and then strained, makes a pleasant tea that some of our older family members still regard as a prompt remedy for nausea, indigestion, chills as well as even colds and influenza, and both as a sedative and as an inducement to sleep.

Our forefathers also prepared for the long, cold winters by gathering in dry weather the fresh, young, green leaves of their preferred mints, drying them at room temperatures until they were brittle enough to crumble, and storing them in cool dry places in tightly closed jars to preserve the volatile aroma, then measuring, timing, and using them exactly like Oriental tea. Because there were no English taxes on them, mint teas were popular during the American Revolution, while they were also resorted to during the Civil War, when importation of orange pekoes, Formosa oolongs, and the like were curtailed. Mint teas were enjoyed in the various ways that regular tea was imbibed, one favorite being with a bit of lemon and sugar.

The other mints, none of them harmful but having a variety of odors and flavors, were also widely used by the Indians and settlers. For instance, the horsemint (*Monarda Punctata*) which has other names such as wild bergamot, beebalm, and lemon mint—with unbranched square stalks growing up to about 3 feet tall, a general hairiness, and bright rather than dullish opposite green leaves, with distinctive pink to purple round flowers heads from about 1 to 3 inches in diameter—was regarded as the most potent of the mints, giving relatively the greatest amount of pungent and aromatic oil.

This extract, when applied to the skin as a liniment, produced redness and had to be used with care to prevent blistering. It was regarded professionally in the old days as useful externally in typhoid fever, arthritis, and even deafness. It was served by the Dakotas and the Winnebegos both internally and externally as a treatment for

173

Asian cholera and was later used by white doctors. Other tribes bruised the fresh green leaves and let them soak in cold water, which was later drunk to ease backache. This was believed to be stimulating. The Creeks, members of a confederacy of Indians mainly of Muskogean stock who formerly occupied most of Georgia and Alabama as well as parts of Florida, steeped and soaked the entire plant to extract an aromatic solution for bringing on sweating.

It was boiled with the familiar red willow for use, both internally and externally, for swollen legs and for dropsy in general. Some Indians sought the tops of the plants to alleviate chills and fever. It was also used in combination with other wild plants as a drink to reduce delirium and as a snuff for headaches.

The U.S. medical profession from the early to the latter part of the nineteenth century prescribed the leaves and tops of the horsemint to check vomiting, to induce perspiring, to alleviate arthritis, and to relieve gassy cholic. It was also taken internally for the expulsion of general gas from the alimentary canal and for the increase of sweating for such purposes as breaking up a fever. Externally it was used in liniments as a stimulant, to produce superficial inflammation with the aim of reducing inflammations in deeper adjacent parts of the body, and to produce blistering.

Another derivative still used, thymol, is available from this wild medicinal. This aromatic antiseptic, used as a fungicide and as a preservative and today largely made synthetically, was officially listed in *The Pharmacopoeia of the United States* from 1820 to 1882 and in the *National Formulary* since 1950. Besides being utilized as an antiseptic, it was long found effective against various fungi and especially against hookworm.

With as much vitamin C as the same weight of oranges and about the same amount of vitamin A as carrots, the freshly gathered mints have long been valuable in preventing and curing scurvy and in aiding night blindness and dull-looking eyes, as well as imparting a glossiness to the hair.

MOUNTAIN TEA (*Ceanothus*)

Family: Buckthorn (Rhamnaceae)

Common Names: Tea Tree, Jersey Tea, New Jersey Tea, New Jersey Tea Tree, Wild Snowball, Red Root, Redroot.

Mountain Tea (*Ceanothus*)

Characteristics: Mountain tea is a straggling, downy, deeply rooted shrub that grows 2 to 3 feet high. It is widely distributed in generally dry soil in upland hardwood forests, on prairies, in arid open woods and glades, and along roadsides and rocky, gravelly banks.

It has ovate or oblong to lanceolate leaves, finely toothed, simple, alternate, pale green, and somewhat hairy on their undersides, although dark green above. Appearing from May to September, small, white flowers on long stalks grow in terminal clusters and in the angles between the leaves and stems. These mature into dry, splitting capsules, each with three seeds.

The so-called New Jersey tea (C. *americanus*) is distinguished by ovate or oblong leaves, generally more than an inch wide, and somewhat elongated flower clusters. The so-named redroot (C. *ovatus*) has narrower leaves and more flat-topped, umbellike flowers in closely grouped bunches.

Mountain tea got its name from the brewing of the leaves, both green and dried, in the thirteen colonies in the same manner as commercial tea and Indianlike, before and during the American Revolution, when imported teas were at first unpopular because of the English tax and later during the hostilities when they became scarce. Especially after they had been dried, the leaves made a happily hot, pleasantly palatable, and somewhat nutritious tea resembling the Oriental blends.

Area: Mountain tea grows from New Brunswick, Nova Scotia, and Prince Edward's Island across Canada to Ontario, south to the Gulf of Mexico and Florida, and west to Texas and Kansas.

Uses: Besides being drunk for pure pleasure, the astringent beverage was used as an expectorant, mouthwash, and gargle for irritated throats. An extract made by simmering the leaves and seeds was also used to treat ulcerated throats.

A commercially manufactured and dispensed tincture of mountain tea has been widely used medically to increase the coagulation of the blood, particularly to prevent hemorrhaging after surgery.

A decoction of the red roots, credited by different sources both as a sedative and as a stimulant, was used to loosen sticky mucus secreted in abnormally large amounts in the respiratory passages. The Indians turned to it for a wash for syphilis.

The shrub, a teaspoon of the root bark being steeped in a cup of boiling water until cool and then drunk 1 or 2 cupfuls a day, was used by the Indians to treat dysentery and gonorrhea. Externally, it was utilized as a wash for syphilitic sores and for eye diseases in

children. The dried roots were also ground between two smooth stor
to a powder for dusting the former sores.

The deep taproots, capable of fixing nitrogen in the soil, were also
used as an astringent, as an antispasmodic, as a treatment for respiratory difficulties, for reducing high blood pressure, and for enlarged
spleens.

MULBERRY (*Morus*)

Family: Mulberry (Moraceae)

Common Names: Red Mulberry, Black Mulberry, White Mulberry,
Texas Mulberry, Virginia Mulberry Tree, Virginia Mulberry, Bul-
berry, Murier Sauvage, Red Morus.

Characteristics: The native red mulberry (*Morus rubra*), regarded
as the most useful of the varieties that grow on this continent, occasionally becomes a large tree, thrusting upward to some 75 feet, but is
more usually 20 to 30 feet in height. The leaves are simple, alternate,
shiny, and broadly egg-shaped to irregularly lobed. They are distinguished by fine, short, closely spaced, more or less blunt teeth along
their edges and by being often hairy on their tops, which are darker
than their undersides. When broken off, the leaf stems have a
sweetish, milky sap which is also found in the twigs. The thin bark of
the trunks, which are tough and rot-resistant, tends to flake and is a
grayish to reddish brown.

Before Revolutionary days the English brought over white mulberries (*M. alba*), the food of the silkworm, in a failing attempt to start
a silk industry in the New World. These are similar trees but with
hairless leaves and a brownish yellow bark.

The small, greenish white flowers of the red mulberry blossom in
springtime in dense, pendant spikes suspended by short stems that
hang between the individual leaves and the branches. Male and
female blossoms often grow on the same tree. The juicy, pleasantly
sweet berries, about an inch long, are made up of densely clustered,
one-seeded drupes, like those of the blackberry, and darken to a deep
purple when ripe.

On the other hand, the similarly shaped fruits of the white mulberry, which often take on a more pinkish hue, do not have the same
pungent flavor but are rather insipidly sweet.

177

Mulberry (*Morus*)

Area: Its fruit relied upon by the Indians and settlers, the ⌐ mulberry grows from New England west to southern Ontar ┐ nesota, and the Dakotas, south to Florida and Texas. The whit ┐ berry, introduced east of the Appalachians, now grows as far we⌐ Minnesota and Texas. The Texas mulberry (*M. microphylla*), a shr ┐ or small tree usually scarcely more than 10 feet high, grows in the ┐ state, south into Mexico, and west through New Mexico and Arizona. The range of the mulberries has been extended by their having become popular as a garden and lawn tree.

Uses: The berries of the mulberries were crushed and squeezed to make a cooling drink believed beneficial in bringing down a high fever. The juice was also regarded as a sedative and mild narcotic. Too, the fruit eaten in quantity was used as a moderate laxative. The inner bark, that part scraped from the wood after this had been exposed by the removal of the outer bark, was boiled with water into a syrup or steeped as a tea which, depending on its strength, acted as a purgative or laxative for children.

The Indians who lived near the Rappahannock believed that rubbing the skin with the sap of the native red mulberry rid them of ringworm. Some Indians and settlers made an extract by simmering the outer bark with water, which potion they drank to destroy and expel parasitic worms.

MULLEIN (*Verbascum thapsus*)

Family: Figwort (Scrophulariaceae)

Common Names: Common Mullein, Great Mullein, Mullein Dock, Flannel Mullein, Mullen, Feltwort Flannel Leaf, Flannelleaf, Flannel Plant, Old Man's Flannel, Adam's Flannel, Blanket Flannel, Blanket Leaf, Feltwort, Velvet Plant, Velvet Dock, Torch-Wort, Cow's Lungwort, Bullock's Lungwort, Crown's Lungwort, Hare's Beard, Lady's Foxglove, Peter's Staff, Juniper's Staff, Jacob's Staff, Shepherd's Club, Aaron's Rod, Hedge Taper, Candlewick, Ice Leaf, Indian Tobacco, Wild Tobacco, Big Tobacco.

Characteristics: Mullein is a tall, weedy, unbranched biennial, hairy and soft, that grows up to about 8 feet high. It lifts strikingly from a basal rosette about 2 feet wide with winged stems and a soft, downy or woolly foliage. The leaves are single, alternate, and widely oblong or lancelike, 2 inches to a foot long, with smooth unlobed rims.

Mullein (*Verbascum thapsus*)

The high, clublike seed spike does not form until the second year, when, from late June until September, yellow flowers become dense along it, each with a five-part calyx, five-lobed corolla, and the same number of stamens, eventually forming a fruit that is a pod or seed-filled capsule. Incidentally, even after 70 years the seeds of the *Verbascum blattaria* are still able to germinate.

Mulleins seek old meadows and pastures that have been over-grazed, rocky or gravelly banks, wastelands, roadsides, and embankments. They also grow in Europe where the ancient Greeks and Romans dipped the dried stems into wax to make wicked candles.

Area: Mullein grows throughout southern Canada and the United States.

Uses: The reason for some of its names is that it was smoked in pipes and cigarettes to help throat congestion. Also, the Navajos blended it with ordinary tobacco and smoked it in the hope of straightening out mild mental disorders. The Mohicans were among the tribes smoking the dried leaves to relieve asthma. Some Indians made a smudge over the dwindling coals of their campfires and inhaled the smoke for catarrh and other pulmonary troubles. The fumes were also used in efforts to revive an unconscious patient.

The leaves and flowers were classed as astringent, cough-relieving, as a sedative to the respiratory system, as a fungus in-hibitor, and as a pain reliever. They were supposed to contain a mucilaginous substance whose protective coating prevented added ir-ritation to the digestive system and, externally, softened and soothed the skin.

Mullein was used to ease coughs and the ejection of unusually heavy phlegm. For this, one prescription was for an ounce of the dried leaves to be simmered in either water or perhaps milk for some ten minutes, strained to remove the hairs and other solids, and sipped warm, with honey or possibly maple sugar added for smoothness and flavor. The same infusion was utilized for diarrhea.

The dried flowers were soaked in some edible oil for several weeks, then used to treat earaches, hemorrhoids, sunburn, rashes, inflamma-tions, and even bruises and contusions. The flowers were also thought to be diuretic and were credited with curing coughs and lung and chest trouble, both they and the leaves being listed as official medicines in the *National Formulary* for twenty years up to 1936.

Mullein oil was considered to be effective against disease germs in the old days as what we would now consider to be an antibiotic.

Mullein roots were boiled to relieve convulsions, and the decoction was also reputed to be antispasmodic and an aid for nervous indigestion. Tea from the roots was regarded as an aid to liver trouble. Inflammations of the digestive and urinary systems were said to be relieved by steeping about an ounce of the dried leaves in 2 cups of boiling water, straining, and then drinking it cold.

Indians suffering from gout often turned to a decoction of mullein. Poultices made from it were put on sprains. A tea brewed from the heart of the young plant was believed to relieve spasmodic intestinal pain.

An Indian device to relieve foot pain was to soften a large leaf on a hot stone, fold it, and bind it to the sole of the foot.

MUSTARD (*Brassica*)

Family: Mustard (Cruciferae)

Common Names: Yellow Mustard, Red Mustard, Black Mustard, Common Black Mustard, Brown Mustard, White Mustard, Indian Mustard, Chinese Mustard, Field Mustard, Charlock, Kerlock, Kidlock, Senvy, Scurvy-Senvy, Rape, Bees Rape, Summer Rape, Wild Navette.

Characteristics: The whole large mustard family can be recognized by the four petals of the blossoms, arranged in the form of a cross. Narrowing at its base, each petal is broadly flat at the top. There are also always four leaflike green sepals growing close against the lower portions of the petals, also in the distinctive crosslike shape that gives the genus its name, derived from crucifix, *Cruciferae*. Half a dozen tiny, lean stamens carry the pollen.

In the middle of each flower, hidden until the petals and stamens fall away, is a singular, green, seed-bearing concavity. It then expands into an elongated, thin pod which is jammed with tiny, deeply colored, pungent seeds, dozens of these peppery fruits lifting alone from the stalks. The erect four-sided pods with their oily, hotly but agreeably biting contents mature during the warm summer months.

Entire fields and mountainsides become golden in the springtime when the annual black mustard, the most important member of the clan, grows into tall, tasty greens which, while they are still young and tender, are found in the markets.

182

Mustard (*Brassica*)

Interestingly, the U.S. Department of Agriculture scientists have found that the seeds of the black mustard can still bloom when they come in contact with moisture after being in the ground for up to half a century.

Area: Wild mustards prosper across southern Canada and the United States, where they flourish especially along the Pacific.

Uses: The Mohicans bound the bruised leaves of the black mustard in place to relieve both toothaches and headaches. Other tribes found that grinding the dark hot seeds of the same species into powder, then sniffing this into the nostrils, helped dry up head colds.

Mustard seeds were also ground by our early ancestors in this New World and made into a paste by mixing them with something such as bear lard, hog fat, mutton tallow, beef lard, or a similar domestic shortening. This was applied and bound where its heat could do the most good for such ailments as lumbago, rheumatism, and bad strains.

The ground seeds were also mixed with an equal volume of flour, made into an adhesive by stirring in warm water, and applied with bandages, compresses, and tapes. Such plasters, still used sometimes for chest colds, can be so powerful that care must be taken to prevent blistering. Some home prescribers said that the addition of the whites of eggs would prevent this. Portions of the body were also heated by the rubbing on of crushed mustard leaves.

The additions of the crushed seeds to hot baths were commonly used for those who were chilled or who were treating colds. Hot foot-baths were concocted the same way. These still are prepared by some in an effort to draw congestion from the head and lungs.

Steeping a tablespoon of the seeds in a quart of bubbling-hot water was used as an emetic. The same effect was also sought by steeping a teaspoon of the crushed seeds of the mustard in a large cup of water, stirring this during the process. Once this had cooled enough to take comfortably, it was quaffed in a single drink. If this did not at first prove effective, it was resorted to a second and even a third time, ten minutes apart.

The essence of the seeds was mixed with honey as a cough medicine, believed to be particularly useful if the cough had been persistent and of long duration. The crushed seeds, added to honey or to wax, were also used cosmetically for roughness of the skin, for scabbiness, and even to eradicate spots or bruises.

When mustard was in flower, the entire plant was simmered in a small amount of water, used as a wash for itch and for freckles. It was also believed to be especially effective in cases of poisoning, depression because of narcotics, drunkenness, and for relieving an overfull stomach without oppressing the rest of the body.

An infusion made by steeping mustard seed was believed to bring on the menses. It was also believed helpful for women in childbirth and later to prevent hardening of the breasts. Used as a wash, it was credited with reducing the swelling of the testicles.

Today's Department of Agriculture experts affirm that mustard greens are an aid to general health, 100 grams of them simmered and drained boasting 183 milligrams of calcium, 32 of potassium, a slightly lesser 30 of phosphorus, 3 of iron, as well as a hearty 7,000 international units of vitamin A, 97 milligrams of vitamin C, plus worthy amounts of riboflavin, niacin, and thiamine.

OAK (*Quercus*)

Family: Beech (Fagaceae)

Common Names: Georgia Oak, Oregon White Oak, Western White Oak, California Black Oak, Spanish Oak, Red Spanish Oak, Oglethorpe Oak, Durand Oak, Chinquapin Oak, Gambel Oak, Black Oak, Scarlet Oak, Red Oak, Southern Red Oak, Northern Red Oak, Yellow Oak, Blackjack Oak, Blackjack, Bluejack Oak, Swamp Oak, Swamp White Oak, Swamp Chestnut Oak, Northern Pin Oak, Willow Oak, Valley Oak, Water Oak, Live Oak, Scrub Oak, Low Oak, Post Oak, Bur Oak, Basket Oak, Mossycup Oak, Tanner's Oak, Iron Oak, Rock Oak, Corkoak, Chestnut Oak, Cherrybark Oak, Laurel Oak, Shingle Oak, Bear Oak, Cow Oak, Turkey Oak.

Characteristics: Everyone knows the fruit of the oak, the acorn, likely both the Indians' and our wildlife's principal food. Acorns are divided into two main groups, the sweet and the bitter. The bitterness of the latter is due to tannic acid, the acid in our tea and injurious to the human digestive system only in large amounts; but once the substance is leeched out as in water, these acorns, too, are nutritious.

Oaks, furnishing about half the hardwood lumber milled in this country and being a favorite shade and landscaping tree, are also familiar to all.

Oak (*Quercus*)

The single, deeply lobed leaves that grow from short stems alternately on the limbs generally oxidize beautifully in the fall and clatter down to cluster on the ground, although a few shrivel and rattle on the trees throughout most of the winter. There are also smaller-leaved evergreen oaks like the live oak.

Maturing in a single season, the acorns of the white oaks, which have a characteristic scaly gray bark, are sweet and the insides of their saucerlike shells smooth.

The nuts of the red oaks, their shallow cuplike shells' inner surfaces being hairy, take two growing seasons to become ripe, and they are ordinarily bitter. The leaves are bristled, and the bark is darkly furrowed.

Area: Close to fifty species of oaks thrive throughout the original forty-eight states except in the northern prairies, as well as through southern Canada.

Uses: The Indians had their own antibiotics, one of them being the mold that collected on the bitter acorns during the sweetening process, which was carefully collected, stored in a cool and damp spot, and eventually utilized on sores, wounds, infections, and the like.

It is the bark of the oaks that has been most widely used medicinally. Being so rich in tannin, oak bark is exceedingly astringent and was therefore, after being soaked or simmered in water, valuable as one of the aborigines' antiseptics and astringents. The decoction was given for piles.

Indians in New England drank it for bleeding and for internal hemorrhaging in general. The Ojibwas, for one, boiled the inner bark of trees and the root bark for diarrhea. Other tribes steeped the inner bark and imbibed it sparingly, as too much would disrupt the digestive system, for loosening phlegm in the lungs and deep respiratory passages and allowing it to be coughed up. Other tribes used the infusion in enemas for piles.

One formula called for a pound of pounded oak bark, boiled with a gallon of water until but 2 quarts remained. This was then strained. Among its other uses was that of bathing a feverish patient to bring down his temperature. It was used as a wash, too, for ulcers, gonorrhea, and general inflammations. It was given internally to anyone spitting blood, and was used as a vaginal douche.

The white oak (*Quercus alba*) was considered to be particularly valuable as an astringent, tonic, and hemostatic, as well as a medicine for a long list of ailments that included dysentery, cholera, hemoptysis, leukorrhea, phthisis, intermittents, and gonorrhea. Poultices made from it were even used for gangrene. Powdered, the dried inner bark became the basis for gargles and tooth powder.

Oak bark, soaked in alcoholic beverages, was considered useful as a liniment for arthritis and the like.

Powdered acorns, mixed with water, were an old remedy for diarrhea.

The inner bark of the red oak (*Q. rubra*), first chewed and then soaked in water, provided a wash that was said to be good for sore eyes, even those of long duration. The bark of this tree was also thought to help heart trouble.

The bark of the black oak (*Q. nigra*) was also steeped and crushed, as between two smooth stones or with a mortar and pestle, and boiled to make another bath for sore eyes.

The inner bark of the bur oak (*Q. macrocarpa*) was used to make a gargle for sore throats, especially for tonsillitis, and as a general astringent. Interestingly, the bark of this tree was stripped off for use as primitive bandages to hold broken bones in place, particularly those of the legs, feet, and arms.

The inner bark of the oaks was scraped or cut off, after the heavy outer bark had been stripped away, and steeped in more water than usual to make a mild medicine for children with intestinal troubles.

The inner bark of both the white oak and the bur oak were among those boiled to make douches for vaginal inflammations and infections. Decoctions of white oak bark were also used by Indians and colonials alike to quell dripping sinuses and chronic mucous discharges.

The galls found growing on the oaks were strong with tannic acid and a smaller amount of gallic acid and were used by the red men and the immigrants in attempts to heal skin diseases, including inflamed sores and ulcers of long standing, and to check bleeding.

One reason some Indians particularly relished acorns for food was that they brought on thirst; their belief was that drinking a lot of water was healthful.

OREGON GRAPE (*Berberis aquifolium*)

Family: Barberry (Berberidaceae)

Common Names: Mountain Grape, Dragon Grape, Mountain Holly, Mahonia, Pepperridge, Barberry, American Barberry, European

Oregon Grape (*Berberis aquifolium*)

Barberry, California Barberry, Common Barberry, Jaundice Barberry, Blue Barberry, Creeping Barberry, Berberry, Sourberry, Wood Sour, Sowberry, Piprage, Algerita, Guild Tree, Japonica, Yellow Root, Pepperidge Bush.

Characteristics: Pioneers clattering westward along the Oregon Trail found these shrubs and berries to be an important source of medicine and food, hence the popular name. Commonly, yellow flowers, each about ¼ inch in diameter, grow in fragrant masses of long, drooping clusters in the springtime. The leaves are rich and gleaming expanses during the summer, showing gray when turned by the wind, and then oxidizing to glowing crimsons and brownish yellows in the fall. The inner wood itself, often made into small pendant crosses, is colored a beautiful gold. The fruit differs from scarlets, oranges, and royal purples to the lovely blues of the so-named Oregon grapes and the California barberries.

The leaves, about 1 to 1½ inches in length, extend from usually rounded or sagging grayish branches. Growing with rounded tops and narrowing bases, they are toothed and bristly. A trio of pointed spines replace them on some of the younger branches of these bushlike herbs, which grow from some 6 to 12 feet tall.

Area: The various species of the Oregon grape family, some of them introduced into gardens, grow in pastures, thickets, and alongside fences, walls, and roadways from Alaska to California eastward to the Atlantic Ocean. They are scattered through the rough country of the Rocky Mountains.

Uses: The fruit, rich in vitamin C, is useful in preventing and curing scurvy, used both fresh and as a sort of lemonade. The latter was also enjoyed as a cooling drink to reduce fever and to settle stomachs, as well as to stimulate appetites. Moreover, it was also believed effective as a mouthwash and gargle.

The root and stem were also harvested, mostly in the autumn, for use in Indian and frontier medicine. The bark of the root was adjudged the most powerful, and a teaspoon of it, dried and then pulverized between two smooth stones, served as a cathartic. The roots were also scoured, cut into small sections, and boiled. The infusion, authoritatively bitter, was believed to be effective in treating chronic indigestion. It was also used as a laxative and emetic and, in smaller amounts, as a tonic. The roots, soaked in beer warmed just below the boiling point, was also believed to be of service, in small, frequently repeated doses, in relieving both hemorrhaging and jaundice. It is astringent.

The bark of the roots has been found in laboratories to be some three times stronger in alkaloids than the bark of the stems. Both lose strength rapidly with age.

PIGWEED (*Chenopodium album*)

Family: Goosefoot (Chenopodiaceae)

Common Names: Smooth Pigweed, Wild Spinach, Goosefoot, White Goosefoot.

Characteristics: Pigweed, a native of Europe and Asia brought by the explorers to North America where it was early adopted by the Indians, is a freely branching annual which renews itself by its abundant seeds, over 70,000 having been counted on a single plant.

Not only does it have bluish green and grayish green leaves, but its blossoms are initially green. Small and inconspicuous, these cluster in spikes at or near the tops of the some 1- to 6-foot-high plants, as well as where the leaves with their mealy white undersides grow from the branches. Often maturing to a redness, they produce hundreds of small, black, many times dull seeds which at second glance prove not to be flat but convex. The stalks of the older plants also often take on reddish streaks.

Area: This spinach relation thrives throughout the United States and Canada, from Labrador to Alaska southward.

Uses: Pigweed is a rich source of calcium for youngsters and for everyone else needing this bone-making element, especially those who do not drink a lot of milk, inasmuch as it is the richest source of this silver-white bivalent metallic member of the alkaline-earth group known among the leafy green vegetables. It is also unusually rich in vitamin A which, if the absence of this is the cause, takes away dullness in the eyes and contributes to keener night vision. The lavish amount of vitamin C in its fresh green leaves both prevents and cures scurvy.

Indians and backwoods folks used and still use poultices of simmered pigweed leaves for the aches and pains of arthritis and for all sorts of swellings. They also wash such afflicted parts with a decoction

191

Pigweed (*Chenopodium album*)

made from the steeped leaves. Not only does the calcium in pigweed help the teeth nutritionally, but the fluid extracted from the boiled leaves, the warmer the better, may be held in the mouth to allay the discomfort of toothache.

PINE (*Pinus*)

Family: Pine (Pinaceae)

Common Names: Eastern White Pine, Western White Pine, White Pine, Black Pine, Red Pine, Eastern Yellow Pine, Yellow Pine, Gray Pine, Alaska Pine, Norway Pine, Oregon Pine, North Carolina Pine, Monterey Pine, Scotch Pine, Austrian Pine, Jersey Pine, Virginia Pine, Cambria Pine, Walter Pine, Parry Pine, Oldfield Pine, Table Mountain Pine, Digger Pine, Rosemary Pine, Jack Pine, Loblolly Pine, Sand Pine, Bank Pine, Marsh Pine, Swamp Pine, Pond Pine, Mountain Pine, Stone Pine, Pocosin Pine, One-Leaved Pine, Four-Leaved Pine, One-Leaved Nut Pine, Shortleaf Pine, Longleaf Pine, Scrub Pine, Northern Scrub Pine, Giant Pine, Slash Pine, Poverty Pine, Prickly-Cone Pine, Hard Pine, Nut Pine, Blister Pine, Pitch Pine, Sugar Pine, Bur Pine, Lodgepole Pine, Tamarack, Larch Piñon, Ponderosa, Hackmatack.

Characteristics: The North American genus of pines includes the trees and shrubs collectively known as the evergreen conifers, embracing the two or three dozen pines themselves, depending on which school of thought the botanist doing the counting follows—the arbor vitae (literally the Tree of Life, so named because it saved a group of early explorers from dying of scurvy), the great hemlocks (the poison hemlock; any of the small poisonous herbs of the carrot family having finely cut leaves and tiny white blossoms differ vastly and visibly and are no relation), the prolific spruces, the tamaracks, the larches, the bald cypresses, the sequoias, the life-giving junipers (which one winter saved Jacques Cartier and his crew in the frozen St. Lawrence River, which they had discovered), the true and the false firs, and the numerous cedars.

If you make an error between a pine and the Christmas-tree fir or the more similar spruce, they will be the same medicinally. All have a life-sustaining edible inner bark and the all-important vitamin C, without which one painfully dies, since the human system cannot accumulate it. All too often we hear of the occupants of small downed

Pine (*Pinus*)

planes starving to death or succumbing to scurvy when lost amid the innumerable pines that clad this continent. Medically, it is all so useless. The cambium, that coating that lies between the outer bark and the wood, can be scraped or sliced off and eaten for sufficient nourishment, raw or cooked, in any way that's handy. An even more pleasant tea, steeped by soaking a handful of needles in any convenient container of water, will provide the antiscorbutic. Or the greenest, newest needles, themselves tender enough to eat in the spring, can be chewed. The Christmaslike aroma makes the whole procedure memorable.

The pines flower in the spring, coating everything with thick yellow pollen. Once this overabundance fertilizes the female stigmas of the pistillate blossoms, the common cones commence forming. Very edible when young, these require a couple and sometimes three years to mature and let fly their own winged seeds, the commonest food of the chattering squirrel.

Most of the vast pine family is evergreen, but native conifers like the deciduous tamaracks, larches, and the bald cypresses drop their needles in the autumn.

Area: Pines green much of the United States and Canada up to timberline except in the tundras, the deserts, and the central plains.

Uses: In addition to the two lifesaving characteristics too important not to cover earlier, the pines have numerous medicinal uses. For instance, the Indians simmered the bark of the younger pines to draw the heat and inflammation out of burns and scalds and to guard against infection.

The bark of the white pine particularly, easily recognizable because its bluish green foliage—needlelike, flexible, soft, and generally curved 4 to 8 inches long—grows in bundles of three, was so treated by a number of the tribes. The fact that its sticky and fragrant resin becomes a white crust early gave the white pine and the eastern and western white pines their names.

The dried cambium of this particular species, having the property of ejecting mucus from the lungs and throat by coughing or hawking and expectorating, was adopted from the Indians by several manufacturers for this purpose. The steeped cambium of the young white pines especially was also resorted to internally for pains in the chest.

Some tribes ground and hammered the inner bark to a paste which they applied to ulcers and carbuncles, as well as to wounds and everyday sores, regarding it as one of their prime medicinals. Indians who pitched their wigwams around Lake Superior crushed the trios of needles and spread them over the foreheads of supine patients, or tied them there with deerskin bands, to ease headaches. For pain and discomfort in the back, they breathed in the hot fumes emitted from the same needles warmed over the fringes of their campfires, often on hot rocks. The pitch oozing from these and other pines was spread on sores and inflammations as salves.

Another use for the three-leaved bundles was simmering them for a drink regarded efficacious for treating sore throats arising from colds and even for consumption. The aborigines in what is now Connecticut steeped the bark and took the solution internally in the belief that it eased cold symptoms. The bark was also crushed into a poultice for piles and ulcers, as well as boiled to make a potion for bringing boils to a head. Some Indians just soaked the bark of this eastern white pine and, as soon as it was soft, used it on sores of all sorts.

The cambium of saplings, though, they boiled for drinking to quell dysentery. A drink made of the steeped buds was held to be laxative. The Indians and settlers made poultices by simmering the scrubbed roots of these evergreens.

The amber-colored resin seeping and solidifying from the pines was plastered over parts where there was muscular soreness, as after games or hard work and from arthritis. This resin, easily picked and scraped from the trees where it exuded prolifically from cuts and lacerations, is brittle at first but soon chews into a soft and pleasantly flavored pink gum which had many uses: sweetening the breath, increasing or quickening menstrual flow, treating kidney disorders and tuberculosis, smearing on the body to ease localized swellings, curing itching and even ulcers, and internally for treating sore throats.

The colonists dissolved it in brandies and other alcoholic beverages to wash inflammations, itchy spots, scalds, and burns.

This resin, found on all the pines, was heated and smeared on the chest for pneumonia, for helping rheumatism and muscular soreness, for bringing boils to a climax, for taking the soreness and inflammation out of wounds and cuts, and even for treating annoying mosquito and other insect bites.

One tribe burned and damped pine wood to charcoal, encompassed this in a wet cloth or strip of deerskin, and tried the whole around the throat for laryngitis.

Pine oil and tar was widely used as a disinfectant, insecticide, antiseptic, parasiticidal agent, expectorant, and deodorant; a number of these uses it still enjoys in modern times.

The tips of the dense, scalelike foliage of the arborvitae, so important in vitamins, were used for gout, fever, and lingering coughs. Half an ounce of the young leaves, steeped or soaked overnight in a cup of water, then sipped a tablespoon at a time, was relied on by some to produce menstruation, as well as to increase the flow of urine. Externally, it was used in an effort to eradicate wars and to cure athlete's food and ringworm.

Then there is the piñon. Indians in New Mexico simmered its needles in water, added sugar to the decoction, and took it internally as a remedy for syphilis. Whether or not this had any beneficial effect, there are definitive reports from Department of Agriculture scientists that just a 100-gram portion of the pleasant little nuts boasts 635 calories, 60.5 grams of fat, 20.5 of carbohydrates, 13 of protein, in addition to a great 604 milligrams of phosphorus, 5.2 of iron, 4.5 of niacin, 1.28 of thiamine, and 0.23 of riboflavin, all in a medically important, pleasantly piquant package.

POKE (*Phytolacca*)

Family: Pokeweed (Phytolaccaceae)

Common Names: Pokeweed, Pokeberry, Virginia Poke, Poke Root, Pocan, Pocan Bush, Scoke, Skoke, Caokum, Coakum, Cucum, Cokan, Inkberry, Red-Ink Plant, Redwood, Red Wood, Garget, Pigeonberry, Chongras, Jalap, American Nightshade.

Characteristics: The ripe, deeply purple, reddish purple, or orangish purple berries, growing in racemes some 4 to 7 inches in length (each fruit being a bit more than ¼ inch in diameter) has a red juice that was one of the first natural inks of the New World, so enduring that it is still to be seen in museums. They also produce multitudes of bright, long, black seeds. Birds become intoxicated when eating these berries—another distinctive sign.

Beside the withered remains of the former season's plants spring the fat young sprouts that, up to some 7 inches in height, are the only part of the plant that, unless used very carefully, is not poisonous. The shoots proved so popular to the first mariners and explorers in the New World that they took the sprouts back to Europe, where they were equally regarded as delicious.

The mature, then poisonous stalks take on a purplish hue in place of the lush, appealing greenness of the young plants. The annuals

197

©AJA

Poke (*Phytolacca*)

mature into roundish stalks that soar upward for some 3 to 9 feet. They have multitudinous, tiny, greenish white flowers which grow on long, fat separate stems in lengthy clusters. The leaves, known botanically as ovate-lanceolate, grow in the form of rather stout lance heads with individual stems at their bases and sharp points at their tips. Scattered except for a little cluster at the top, and sometimes other small clusters on the stalks, they are some 10 inches in length. The leaves, smooth both top and bottom, have slightly undulating rims.

All in all, the perennials are plump and strong-smelling, not at all difficult to recognize.

Area: The poke, native to tropical America and a hearty perennial especially in the South, now is common in the eastern part of the country except along the Canadian border, west to Minnesota and the Lone Star State of Texas, southward through Mexico.

Uses: First, it should be reemphasized that except for the stout young shoots which grow to some 6 to 7 inches high, and the leaves growing from these sprouts, poke can be very harmful if not used with extreme caution. As for the shoots, they are so popular that they are regularly grown domestically, in such places as cellars, and they are sold in some grocery stores. Cut off just where they emerge from the ground, they are cooked like asparagus, rich in vitamin C.

The large, poisonous roots used to be collected in the fall by the pharmaceutical industry, as affirmed by the U.S. Department of Agriculture, and utilized in small portions as an emetic, for which it was favored because of its slow and harmless behavior, and for treating arthritis. The poisonous berries contain a strong laxative. The Indians and colonists, using those roots, mainly cut them into small pieces and steeped a level tablespoonful with 2 cups of boiling water, then dosed themselves sparingly by the tablespoon. The roots, like the berries, also have a narcotic action.

The poke's major medicinal component is said to parallel the action of cortisone in stimulating the complete glandular network, which would account for its help with rheumatism, for one thing. But, again, caution was always the governing principle.

Poke was believed to be extremely useful as an alternative, perhaps the most effective in this respect of all wild medicinals; that is, a drug used empirically to alter favorably the course of an ailment. For this purpose, a tea prepared by steeping a tablespoon of the cut root or ripe berries with 2 cups of boiling water was taken by the tablespoonful.

The dried root is still used in Appalachia, according to the Department of Agriculture, for the treatment of hemorrhoids. The dried berries are used in some regions as poultices to bring boils and other sores to a head.

A number of tinctures and ointments have also been made of this powerful medicinal and used to reduce glandular swelling and to help chronic arthritis and stiffness of the joints. It was also regarded by some as being efficacious externally in such skin diseases as scrofula, eczema, and even syphilis. A decoction made from the roots was washed over the skin to do away with itching. Apparently it could be applied externally as often as necessary without undue risk, and it was believed to be very helpful in reducing such annoyances.

A number of tribes used the cut roots on the soles and palms of Indians suffering with fever, and the pioneers followed suit. The fresh leaves were made into poultices for scabs of long standing. They were also dried for application to swellings, ulcers, carbuncles, and wounds of one sort or another.

PUSLEY (*Portulaca oleracea*)

Family: Purslane (Portulacaceae)

Common Names: Purslane, Low Pigweed, Purslance.

Characteristics: The earth-embracing pusley, whose shoots seldom stretch more than an inch or two toward heaven, is a sprawling annual whose stems and tendrils creep over many a yard where, spurned by most as a lowly weed, it does not usually gain the attention it should, since it is unusually rich in medically important minerals and vitamins. Native and widely used in Persia and India long before the birth of Christ, it spread early to Europe and was one of the plants widely adopted by the Indians after its immigration to the New World with the first settlers. It spread quickly and widely because of its profusion of tiny seeds, well more than 50,000 having been counted on a single plant.

The corpulent, narrow, paddlelike, ½- to 2-inch-long leaves, growing almost opposite, prosper in rosettes lifting from fleshy, forking stems. Each disk of leaves, which have a lovely reddish to regal purplish green tinge to them, centers a tiny golden medallion of a flower which reveals itself only in warm, bright sunlight. These stemless delicacies have some five to seven yellow petals and about eleven

Pusley (*Portulaca oleracea*)

elegant stamens that mature into small round pods whose tops lift off like crowns when the tiny seeds are ready to be revealed.

Area: Preferring as it does sandy fertile soil, pusley reigns from the balmier provinces of Canada throughout the continent to each of our southern states.

Uses: Pusley has become even more widely appreciated in this country since Henry David Thoreau extolled it in 1854 in the classic *Walden:* "I learned that a man may use as simple a diet as the animals, and yet retain health and strength. I have made a satisfactory dinner off a dish of purslane which I gathered and boiled. Yet men have come to such a pass that they starve, not for want of necessaries but for want of luxuries."

As a medicine, pusley is important because of the fact that, according to U.S. Department of Agriculture tests, a 100-gram portion has been found—despite the fact that it is more than 92 percent water raw and more than 94 percent water following boiling—to boast 2,500 international units of vitamin A raw and 2,100 cooked, 0.1 milligram of riboflavin raw and 0.06 simmered and drained, 25 milligrams of vitamin C raw, and a robust 3.5 milligrams of iron. Although the Indians did not know of vitamins and minerals, any more than did the colonists, they recognized the health-giving qualities of pusley, and where we once lived in Taos several of the women in the towering pueblo there canned quantities each year to give to their growing families.

The seeds, which U.S. government scientists have found will stay alive in the ground for more than forty years until moisture comes along to start their growth, were made into a tea by the Indians, who also used the tender stems and tips for the same purpose, to bring about relaxation and sleep.

Pusley tea had many uses among the American aborigines who, of course, passed along their particular findings to the Europeans who, knowing some of the virtues of the wild medicinal from the Old World, had been using it particularly for lightning and gunpowder burns.

The Indians found the decoctions useful in cases of gout, for reducing agitation and nervousness just as we use sedatives today, for gonorrhea, as a diuretic, for headaches, particularly those arising from exposure to the sun and weather, and for stomach, intestinal, and liver ailments.

The decoctions, not made so potent as usual, were considered mild enough to be safe in killing intestinal worms in children. Brewed stronger, it was considered effective for adults with the same problem.

The juice, gained by crushing and straining the plant, was stirred into wild honey for a cough medicine. It was also used externally as is for bathing inflammed generative organs. Mixed with oil, sometimes that rendered from grizzly fat, it was rubbed into stiff necks. It also seemed to help piles, used both internally and externally, the latter particularly when the ailment caused soreness of the skin.

Mixing it with wild honey or with maple sugar was claimed to help shortness of breath and immoderate thirstiness except when this arose from diabetes.

Bathing the body with cool, crushed pusley was resorted to in cases of fever and, less critically, for inflammation.

The multitudinous small black seeds, which the Indians and hungry pioneers crushed, sieved, and used for flour, were steeped for tea which some of the tribes looked to for help with painful urination, as a bath for eye irritations, and for stomach trouble. Boiled in wine, it was given in small doses to children to kill and pass worms.

Juice from the crushed and strained plant, used externally, was esteemed many centuries ago for ulcers and other sores in the generative parts, for inflammations in general, for soaking compresses which were laid where the head ached, for easing other aches and pains, for gout and fever, for trouble with the genitourinary organs and functions, and as a generally accepted antiseptic.

RED LAVER (*Porphyra*)

Family: Red Algae (Rhodophyceae)

Common Names: Laver, Seaweed, Sea Lettuce.

Characteristics: Red laver is the lean, leaflike frond sighted during low tides on both the Pacific and Atlantic seacoasts of North America, expanding from reefs, ledges, rocks, pilings, dock supports, and the like. Afloat in the sea, the young wild medicinals have a red luxuriant radiance, like the rarest red jadeite. This dulls when it loses its moistness. The solitary blades, growing in groups, tumble and sway gracefully beneath the surface in sheltered inlets and elsewhere when the high tide is still and the surface tranquil, unruffled by wave or wind.

Adhered solely by a small disk, the fragile fronds are many times ripped away in large quantities by heavy seas and hurled ashore. When fresh they are then still harvested.

Maturing, the thallophytes, which when youthful have but one

Red Laver (*Porphyra*)

layer of cells, take on thickness when pairs of sexual organs begin to increase along their rims, the jellylike substance that surrounds the reproductive entities then ripening and swelling. The widening and generally deeply slashed blades then assume a hazy greenish, grayish, and purplish brown tinge.

Spores are freed by the hundreds of thousands upon maturation and swirled by the restless tides until those which are destined to find a satisfactory adhering surface, and when other conditions are suitable, come to rest and begin germinating without delay. Thus a brand-new crop of laver shows up at the start of the next season, with the ecstatic gloss and resilience of adolescence.

Area: Sea lettuce, as it is also called, thrives along both ocean coasts of North America.

In Japan I've seen harvesters making it easy on themselves by submerging groups of bamboo, tied together for easy handling, then retrieving them when the laver crop is ready—one reason why an industry of importing red laver to America from the Orient has grown up, when exactly the same thing can be gathered here freely.

Uses: Red laver is important in the prevention and treatment of goiter, an enlargement of the thyroid gland visible as a swelling of the front of the neck. Edible raw, it is tastier chopped, ground, and sun-dried to a blackness. By reason of its zestful salt content, it is successfully and regularly stored in closed containers by the Alaskan aborigines for healthful eating throughout the year, either raw like popcorn or cooked as in fish stews.

Rich in selenium, the nonmetallic element, red laver has also been considered efficacious in the control and curing of dandruff.

ROCK TRIPE (*Umbilicaria*)

Family: Rock Tripe (Umbilicariaceae)

Common Names: Tripe, Blistered Rock Tripe, *Tripe de Roche*, Lichen.

Characteristics: Rock tripe is not actually a plant but a green alga that joins with a fungus, the former making an organic substance from the air and from the moisture in it, the latter procuring inorganic material from the rocks and ground, forming a slowly growing entity that makes the bristlecone pine seem a youngster by comparison. It

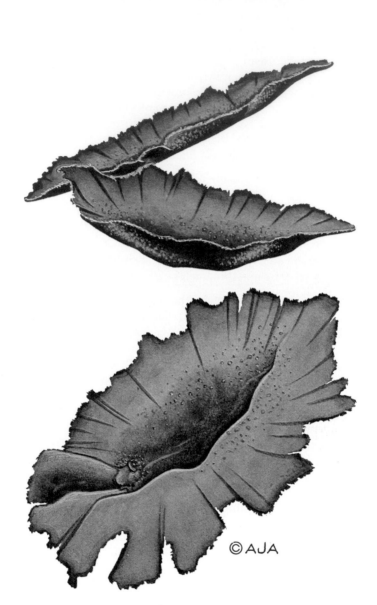

Rock Tripe (*Umbilicaria*)

has no root or stem, looking more like a dark, leathery, pocked, non-succulent, upwardly curling lettuce leaf whose middle has somehow attached itself to a rock or ledge.

Colors vary from green, brown, grey, to black, and it clings so closely to its host that frequently it has to be scraped free. Perhaps best described as crustaceous, membranous, and spreading, rock tripe can scarcely be mistaken for anything else.

Area: Rock tripe grows about the top of North America and down through the Dominion of Canada, several species extending to the southern states particularly in the East.

Uses: In the early and hungry decades of Arctic exploration, before the days of concentrated rations and before Vilhjalmur Stefansson turned the problem of living off the country in the Far Northern spaces to a science, such Arctic explorers as Sir John Franklin, Sir John Richardson, and their following and often starving fellow adventurers sometimes lived on rock tripe for months with scarcely any change in diet, since it was extraordinarily rich in starches, vitamins, and minerals.

Ideally first soaked for several hours usually in cold water to rid it of its purgative and bitter properties, it could then be simmered until tender to give a gumbolike richness to soups or, if some other ingredients were available, to stews.

Scraped from rocks and powdered, it was used farther south to treat cankers, tender gums, and other mouth sores, even with children. Also, rock tripe was soaked overnight, and then the otherwise usually discarded cold water was sipped in small amounts to combat diarrhea.

Rock tripe was used, too, as what is now called an antibiotic to restrict infectious staphylococcus bacteria.

The North American Indians, many of whom suffered through what was for them harsher winters than the newcomers from the Old World were accustomed to, were more aware of the so-called blood-purifying spring tonics than the initially arriving Europeans. The settlers followed them in turning to rock tripe as one of their bitters.

A common formula in the old days ran something like pouring an earthenware pot full of boiling water over a quantity of laboriously gathered rock tripe fragments, letting this soak and cool overnight, and then placing the receptacle onto the back of the stove, or settling or suspending it over the fringes of a campfire, where the heat was such that only an occasional bubble plopped to the surface, and keeping it there the better part of a day. Then the practice was to strain it, add a cup preferably of gin per quart of the resulting spring tonic, and set it aside in a cool dark place. A common dose was 2 tablespoonfuls upon arising and then again upon retiring for each adult member of the family, studiously less for children according to their ages.

ROSEWORT (*Sedum*)

Family: Stonecrop (Crassulaceae)

Common Names: Roseroot, Western Roseroot, Stonecrop, Scurvy Grass.

Characteristics: Rosewort is unmistakable when you bruise, scrape, or cut one of the large fleshy roots because of the strong and pleasant roselike perfume it then emits, despite the fact that it is not a member of that family.

The flat, equally spaced, about ½-inch-long leaves, are obese in comparison to those on surrounding plants and are a beautiful light green to pinkish white. They throng over the several stalks which arise from 4 to somewhat more than a dozen inches high on this squat bush, the descriptive appellation *Sedum* coming from the Latin *sedere,* meaning "to sit." Either oblong or oval, some have smooth, others toothed rims.

Dense flat heads of reddish violet to dark brownish and golden flowers crown the tops of the branches. Each of the multitudinous tiny blossoms has a quartet of narrow, pollen-floured petals, blooming from May to August, depending on the latitude and elevation. They produce capsulelike crimson to purplish seed-filled pods, each of the latter with four or five spikes.

Area: Roseworts are found in many rocky, moist seacoast spots and in more than 2-mile-high elevations in the interior from northern California east to Nevada, New Mexico, and Colorado north to British Columbia, the Yukon Territory, and Alaska, then across the Arctic regions and the tundra to Labrador and damp Newfoundland, south in the East to the mountains of North Carolina.

Uses: Roseworts, being one of the first wild medicinals to green in the spring, were eagerly sought by sea captains with scurvy-ridden crews troubled with spongy gums, loosening teeth, and a bleeding into the mucous membrances and skin caused by a lack of ascorbic acid. Readily and swiftly curing these conditions, it also was called scurvy grass.

Rosewort (*Sedum*)

The tender, young, acidulous leaves and stems early in the season were eagerly devoured raw at first, while later many were cooked, preferably as briefly as possible. The rough, large, tasty roots were also relished.

SAGE (*Salvia*)

Family: Mint (Labiatae)

Common Names: Wild Sage, Meadow Sage, True Sage, Garden Sage, Golden Sage, Scarlet Sage, Chia, Texas Sage.

Characteristics: Sage is a fuzzy perennial with soft, downy hairs. One characteristic is that, when a bunch is wadded together, it clings to itself, remaining a compact mass. The erect stems are grayish with down and have, on pubescent stalks toward their bases, up to about 18-inch-long leaves. These grow with a series of opposite lanceolate to narrow elliptic leaflets, with rounded teeth and wool beneath, narrowing at their bases to long petioles. Several wheels of tiny blue or whitish, and sometimes reddish, flowers grow in whorls of four to eight, depending on the particular species. The plants have an easily recognized strong, unique, aromatic odor.

The chia (*Salvia columbriae*), a distinctive annual springing up in the Southwest at the start of the late fall rains and an Indian standby, is a rough sage with deeply incised, coarse, usually hairy, dark-green leaves that grow mostly close to the ground. Three or so whirls of small blue flowers circle, mintlike, in separated densities above prickly, dark-red, leafy bracts. These mature into seed-filled pods that remain like skeletons when the rest of the plant has withered, not giving the winds enough purchase to blow them free and leaving them for the Indians to harvest.

The seeds of the Texas sage (*S. coccinea*) are oblong, angular, or bowed, and about 2 to 3 millimeters in size. Those of the annual scarlet sage (*S. splendens*) run about 7,700 per ounce and take two or three weeks to emerge at 65 to 75°F.

Area: Sage grows throughout southern Canada and the United States, the very important chia (*S. columbriae*) in Arizona, Utah, Nevada, and California.

Sage (*Salvia*)

Uses: The medicinal part of this plant in general is the leaves, harvested during the flowering period in June and July. In the case of chia, the vital part is the seeds, which are gathered from the then nearly dead annual in July.

Steeped like tea and in the same proportions, sage tea was slightly tonic and quieting to a disordered stomach. Its peculiar but pleasant odor was retained in the beverage by the warmish, somewhat bitter aroma of the thus extracted volatile oil. With a long-remembered agreeable taste, it was said to benefit a ticklish and somewhat irritated throat, to quiet and help expel bothersome and often painful gas that was sometimes present, and to assist the liver, kidneys, and gallbladder, helping to break up and expel stones and gravel from these latter two organs.

Still regarded in a few regions as effective in treating sore throat—severe inflammation of this part and surrounding areas often accompanied by fever, cankers, sore gums, mouth ulcers, and swollen tonsils—it is to this day thought by many to be an effective gargle and mouthwash.

A marked diaphoretic action was said to assist in the flushing of catarrhal secretions from the mucous membranes of the bronchial and alimentary passages, aiding and sometimes preventing pectoral and gastric troubles.

As long as two centuries ago, the juice from the bruised fresh leaves was credited with helping remove warts. They were also pressed into service to treat sores, cuts, and wounds, the Indians being among those making a salve of the crushed fresh leaves and edible lard for these purposes. The Catawbas, on the other hand, made their salve for the same use from the roots of the wild sage (*S. lyrata*).

A somewhat stronger tea than usual was both used as a gentle laxative and to reduce the flow of milk from breast-feeding mothers at weaning times. This was also used to strengthen loose teeth. It was said to help make the menstrual periods regular.

Gargling with sage leaves crushed in vinegar was believed to help heal, as well as ease the pain, of ulcerated gums. Others mixed these with nutmeg to help toothaches. Too, ground seeds were mixed with water to make a wash that was believed to keep the mouth and throat moist at such times as during dusty cattle drives.

The oil too was said to help in preserving meat—an important matter before days of refrigeration.

A particularly refreshing drink for hot weather was made by mixing chia seeds with cool water, each seed becoming separately suspended in its own white, mucilaginous cloudiness. The minute white, gray, and brown seeds are so nutritious that a teaspoonful was regarded as enough to sustain an Indian for a day on a forced journey.

SALTBUSH (*Atriplex*)

Family: Goosefoot (Chenopodiaceae)

Common Names: Ball Saltbush, Crown Saltbush, Silver Saltbush, Australian Saltbush, San Joaquin Saltbush, Truncate Saltbush, Arrow Saltbush, Saltweed, Orach, Red Orach, Spear Orach, Garden Orach, Sea Scale, Silver Scale, Crown Scale, Shad Scale, Sea Purslane, Desert Holly, Quail Brush.

Characteristics: A number of the saltbush species are lone stems that, touched only by the higher tides, sprawl along the upper sands and pebbles of beaches. Others more resemble amaranth and pigweed, covered elsewhere in this volume, although the taste is more temptingly salty, while both their blossoms and the sites where they grow naturally differ.

The small, creamy green flowers, separated one from another, raise on slim, often bending spikes that lift from the upper angles between the stalks and stemmed leaves, appearing about July. The tiny, starchy, olive-hued seeds mature not long afterward.

The distinguishing quality of the leaves is a broad, triangular, arrowhead shape, about ½ to 3 inches long, sharply pointed, with the barbs at either basic corner turned outward. The margins are smooth. The leaves are usually a light green , ordinarily granulated and even paler beneath.

Area: Saltbushes thrive profusely along beaches, damp flats, and in salt marshes from Labrador to Virginia, and from British Columbia to California, while often appearing on wet alkaline spots in the interior.

Uses: An eighth of a pound of the freshly gathered ripe seeds, crushed and then covered and steeped for six weeks in 1½ cups of brandy, provide a light and rather pleasing tincture that was used as an emetic during the Pilgrim days in Plymouth. The dose was a tablespoon, taken in a cup of water porridge. Its effect was milder than that of ipecac and was said not to bind the bowels afterward. The patient was advised to go to bed afterward, where a gentle sweat could carry off additional waste matter. Inasmuch as vomiting comes harder

Saltbush (*Atriplex*)

with some individuals than others, a second dose of the same strength was advised if the first one did not produce the desired result.

Besides the usual stomach disorders and the other reasons for which an emetic was prescribed, the saltbush tincture was recommended for troublesome headaches and for the first attacks of arthritis. It found a place in not a few pioneers' medicine chests.

The vitamin C content of the tender tips and juicy young leaves of the fresh saltbush is effective as an antiscorbutic.

SASKATOON (*Amelanchier*)

Family: Rose (Rosaceae)

Common Names: Saskatoonberry, Sour Cherry, Sugar Plum, Sugar Pear, Sweet Pear, Grape Pear, Indian Pear, *Poires,* Currant Tree, Shad, Shadberry, Shadbush, Shad-Bush, Shadblow, Serviceberry, Service-Berry, Downy Serviceberry, Western Serviceberry, Sarviceberry, Juneberry.

Characteristics: The saskatoon's conspicuous white flowers, with their quintets of strap-shaped petals, appear in the spring, among the initial blossoms to decorate North America's shrubs and trees each year. The wild medicinal gets its names of shad, shadberry, shadbush, shadblow, and the like because its blooming occurs along the northeastern coast at the same time as the spawning of the shad, who then climb the freshwater rivers and streams of this continent to breed and reproduce.

Having about twenty stamens, appearing in short duration in long, slender assemblies, the white flowers are often so thick and showy that their parent trees and shrubs many times seem rimed with frost and snow, silhouetting them against abrupt slopes and swarthy undergrowth. They mature into a large, blueberrylike fruit that is reddish to blackish purple, with the rose family's distinctive five-pronged pucker at its summit. They are actually an applelike pome rather than a berry. Ten large seeds give an almondlike flavor—when they are dried or cooked—to the otherwise rather insipid berries.

The bushes, otherwise inconspicuous with smooth gray bark and elongated, sharp-pointed buds, grow simple, alternate, ovate to obovate leaves with finely serrated margins, densely pubescent when opening.

Saskatoon (*Amelanchier*)

The saskatoon differs from other members of the genus in the fact that its fruit and ovary are separated into chambers, each of which holds a single seed. The filiform prolongation of the plant ovary bearing a stigma at its top, however, generally numbers five. The petals are much more narrow than those in the other *amelanchiers*. Rather than being arranged in a cluster, the fruit ascends the small branches one by one. Deciduous leaves, usually in the form of longish ovals, have marginal teeth pointing sharply forward toward the apexes.

Area: Despite its initial density, slow in returning to regions blackened by fires, the saskatoon grows throughout Alaska across the north, then southward beyond the United States into Mexico. In spite of the fact that thickets of shrubs give life to otherwise bare, dry, rocky hillsides, painting them a dusky red in the fall when the berries are at their plumpest, the markedly flexible small trees and large bushes prosper best in damp if sunny and open situations.

Uses: Widely used by the Indians to give fruit to their seldom equaled concentrated trail food, pemmican—by weight half dried lean meat and half rendered fat—saskatoons except when fresh did not provide the vital vitamin C which had to be secured from other sources, but it was considered to have other valuable uses elsewhere.

A wash made by simmering the inner bark of this medicinal was used for eyes sore and blurred from sun as from climbing and hiking, from glare as from canoeing, from dust as from traveling in dry weather, and from snow blindness, which is not blindness at all but rather inflammation caused from too long exposure to the continued shine and glint of ice and snow on insufficiently protected eyes. (Interestingly, snow blindness can be incurred on an overcast day and through the canvas of a tent.)

Before they matured, the crushed pomes were used to bind the bowels after the bowels had been weakened by excessive and abnormal discharges. They lost this restringent quality with ripeness.

SASSAFRAS (*Sassafras*)

Family: Laurel (Lauraceae)

Common Names: Saxifrix, Saxifras, White Sassafras, Red Sassafras, Common Sassafras, Silk Sassafras, Tea Tree, Mitten Tree, Gumbo, Cinnamonwood, Smelling Stick, Saloop.

Sassafras (*Sassafras*)

Characteristics: Christopher Columbus is said to have been helped in his successful efforts to quell mutinous seamen, who feared to sail any farther westward, by the sudden sweet smell of the sassafras tree, which indicated the nearness of land. Sassafras even exceeded tobacco during the early days as a North American export to Europe. In fact, special ships were carrying cargoes of sassafras from this continent back to the Old World before any other New World product made an impression on medicine there.

The distinctive and agreeably aromatic odor and flavor of this small- to medium-sized tree, varying in height from about 10 to nearly 50 feet, is as pleasant as it is characteristic. Even the roughly furrowed grayish to reddish brown bark has this fragrance both in taste and smell. The leaves, which unfurl before the golden greenish blossoms appear in latter April and early May, are of three shapes even on the same tree—a thumbed mitten, a three-fingered glove, and a smooth egg shape. The spiciness of darkly blue, one-seeded berries, up to about ½ inch in diameter but mostly of pea size, attract birds to the female trees in the autumn when they mature on their reddish stalks.

Area: The majority of our sassafras trees grow from Iowa, Indiana, Illinois, Michigan, southern Ontario, Ohio, Pennsylvania, New York, and Massachusetts, south to Texas and Florida, thriving mainly along roads and fences, in thickets on the edges of woods, and within pastures and cleared lands which have been deserted.

Uses: Wine made from sassafras berries was frequently imbibed for colds. During the flowering period from March to April, the blossoms were simmered to make a tea to lessen fevers. An old-fashioned idea, still adhered to in many parts of the country, is that the blood should be thinned and purified in the spring, and among the roots used to prepare brews for this were and are those of the sassafras.

Also, a tea made of the root bark is still utilized in Appalachia for such general and varied purposes as to increase the flow of urine, to treat kidney troubles, to ease the discomfiture of a gassy and upset stomach, to produce an increase in perspiration, to help dysentery, and to relieve respiratory troubles. About two centuries ago the tea was believed to slow the milk flow in nursing mothers when this seemed expedient. The tea has also been used as a stimulant and for the treatment of bronchitis.

The bark has been made into a poultice for sore eyes. Pioneers thought that chewing it would help break the tobacco habit, a problem even then.

Jesuit priest Paul Le Jeune who lived among the Iroquois in the middle of the seventeenth century said that sassafras leaves, pounded together and laid on wounds of all kinds, would heal most of them in short order.

Other early Europeans spoke of beating the bark of the root and using it to cleanse ulcers; also of applying it to swellings or contusions to ease the pain and to heal the parts. It was generally used along the eastern seaboard as an ointment for bruises. The leaves were chewed and laid on wounds to stop bleeding. Teas made from the sassafras were thought beneficial in the treatment of venereal diseases. Even years ago, the roots were distilled to make an oil for flavoring beverages such as ginger ale, sarsaparilla, cream soda, and root beer, as well as toothpaste and the like. It was used in such concoctions as Kickapoo Oil, featured at old-time medicine shows. The bark was favored as an insect repellent. Tea made from it was thought to be effective in helping the passage of gravel and kidney stones.

The fragrant and mucilaginous southern soups which have varied little since Indian times still are considered by many to be very healthful and beneficial.

The Rappahannocks made a tea from sassafras roots to bring out the rash to reduce fever in measles—a disease which in modern times has been determined to be much more dangerous than was previously thought.

The Catawbas showed the white man how to treat lameness by abrading the spot where the lameness lay, bathing it both during and after the bleeding with warm water, then drying some sassafras roots in the coals of a campfire, scraping off the thus-loosened bark, pounding it well between two smooth stones, spreading it over the afflicted part, and bandaging it there for several days, after which the patient was often adjudged cured.

One way to making sassafras tea was to put two roots, each a couple of inches long, in 3 pints of water, first scrubbing the roots vigorously with a stiff brush, rinsing them, and then scraping away the bark, which was included with the roots in a pot. Bring this to a boil, then reduce the heat, simmer for fifteen minutes, and finally remove from the heat, cover, steep for ten minutes, strain, and serve. Another dosage, especially used as a spring tonic, was made by cutting or grinding a teaspoon of the bark, steeping this in a cup of boiling water for ten minutes, then drinking cold, a few sips at a time, throughout the day. Still another formula called for dropping several roots into a quart of bubbling water, setting this off the heat, and steeping five minutes.

Or, you can use the entire root, first scrubbing and cutting it into pieces that will easily fit into a pot holding a gallon of water. A pound of roots will thus make 4 quarts of tea and can be used several times before they lose their strength. Merely simmer until the tea has a yellowish red hue, a rich smell, and a pleasing taste. Then you can treat it like Oriental tea, drinking it as is, or thinning with milk or cream and, if you wish, sweetening it.

Some scientists have been warning lately that the sipping of sassafras as a spring tonic is, like the alleged cumulative dangers of cranberries and Red Dye No. 2, dangerous to the health. But it has been added that the Red Dye No. 2 which proved dangerous to laboratory mice would have to be consumed at a rate of 1,200 pounds per day to pose a threat to human beings. Perhaps this proves that using sassafras tea to put spring into your spring is one of the few age-old customs that bureaucrats shouldn't mess with.

Sassafras was also used to make a mouthwash, held to be as beneficial as many of the commercial products now on the market.

SAXIFRAGE (*Saxifraga*)

Family: Saxifrage (Saxifragaceae)

Common Names: Red-Stemmed Saxifrage, Purple Saxafrage, Spotted Saxifrage, Brook Saxifrage, Swamp Saxifrage, Early Saxifrage, Tufted Saxifrage, Lettuce Saxifrage, Mountain Lettuce, Deertongue.

Characteristics: Somewhat over sixty species of saxifrage inhabit North America. In general, the medicinals usually have five whitish petals, five sepals, ten male-gamete-producing stamens, and an ovary around which the receptaclelike tip of the stem frequently extends in the form of a cup. This ovary is made up of two chambers and is generally divided into a duo of somewhat rounded projections with a filiform prolongation, a stigma at its apex, extending from each. The fruit that matures from these under ideal conditions is a tiny, double-sprouted podlike seed vessel.

Our commonest and most widespread species of saxifrage is the so-called early saxifrage (*Saxifraga virginiensis*), which grows mainly on stony slopes and on damp to dry rock ledges where its appearance in crevices gives the genus its erroneous Latin equivilent of "rock-splitter." The fact that it can exist with a minimum of water lets it grow in such a confined fissure.

Saxifrage (*Saxifraga*)

The early saxifrage has a gluey-haired flower stem only 4 to 6 inches tall when it starts flowering in early April or a few weeks before. Continuing to bloom, as it does, many times into June, this stalk often branches and extends up to a foot in height. At its base lifts a rosette of somewhat fleshy, oval, or ovoid-shaped leaves from 1 to 3 inches long which, while green, often take on a violet hue beneath. Their rims can be undulated, roughly serrated, or briefly and bluntly notched. Similar leaves often subtend the natural subdivisions of the flower stem.

The blossoms, which give off a vanillalike aroma when dried, grow in neat little throngs at the tips of the medicinals. Only about ¼ inch in diameter, they have five oblong and narrow white petals, whose ends have a tendency to curl backward. Ten masculine stamens with brilliant golden uprights of pollen give color to the delicate flowers, beneath each of which is a minute, five-pronged emerald cup or calyx.

Area: The saxifrage copiously brightens the Appalachians in the East and, in fact, most of the continent, except for the west-central dustinessess, from Alaska—where species such as the red-stemmed saxifrage (*S. lyallii*), the spotted saxifrage (*S. austeromontana*), the purple saxifrage (*S. oppositifolia*), and the tufted saxifrage (*S. caespitosa*) blossom late in the season within mountain ravines where the snow often remains until the hot all-day sunlight—to California, Arizona, and New Mexico; in the East from Newfoundland to northern New England.

Uses: The saxifrage is another green sought for its antiscorbutic properties. Although they had never studied in Latin classes how Roman doctors turned to it for diseases of the kidneys and bladder, the Indians early discovered these uses. The saxifrage was also considered to be an excellent diuretic.

SCURVY GRASS (*Cochlearia*)

Family: Mustard (Cruciferae)

Common Names: Spoonwort.

Characteristics: Scurvy grass is unmistakable because of its rugged, horseradishlike odor and for its similar, although far less sharp, flavor. If one still has any doubts, he need look only for the crosslike effect of the four white petals, arranged in opposite pairs, giving the medicinal its mustard-family name of *Cruciferae.*

Scurvy Grass (*Cochlearia*)

The dainty-appearing, tiny, white blooms grow on branches stalks, several inches high, which lift from the older rosettes of leaves of the biennial. Half a dozen pollen-laden stamens surround the solitary ovule-bearing pistil. From most of the latter will mature flattened, oval pods that become crammed with minute seeds.

The fact that the leaves of the spoonwort, as it is also called, take on the superficial form of spoons gave it the Latin name *Cochlearia* from *cochlear,* which translates as "spoon." The leaves are what is known as simple, meaning that they lack teeth, lobes, or other divisions. Juicy and fleshy, varying somewhat with the species, they have a pleasant sharpness that made them particularly relished by scurvy-ridden seamen.

Area: This antiscorbutic abounds in mountainous, stony, loose granular soil resulting from the disintegration of rocks, as along the damp, foggy seashores of the Aleutians, the complete Alaskan coast, and that of the Yukon and Northwest Territories to Labrador and Newfoundland.

Uses: In the seventeen hundreds, well before the days of lime juice's becoming a regular if ineffective issue of the British navy, Captain James Cook and other mariners and explorers of his day knew scurvy grass as the only herb to be relied upon for the cure and prevention of scurvy among crews sailing around the world. At that, they did not comprehend that it had to be fresh to be effective, and the bales of it, found wild and stowed hopefully in the stuffy holds, soon became impotent with age.

Scurvy grass's long list of curable maladies were mainly scurvy symptoms, although the juice was also supposed to be effective as a mouthwash to make less obnoxious those with foul breaths, to purify the blood, and to rid the skin of spots, marks, and scars where it was applied externally.

SEA MOSS (*Chondrus*)

Family: Red Algae (Rhodophyceae)

Common Names: Irish Moss, Carrageen Moss, Lichen, Curly Moss, Jelly Moss, Pearl Moss.

Characteristics: Naturally reddish before being washed ashore and sun-bleached, sea moss also takes on greenish, blackish, purplish, and

Sea Moss (*Chondrus*)

brownish hues. In situ, it is mainly found anchored by tiny disks to rocks, shelves, ridges, and reefs that are under the sea except sometimes during low tides. Although quantities of the algae wavering in ocean pools do look somewhat like masses of sea moss, the individual plants do not have that aspect. Instead, they grow in readily cleaving bulks of flattish, cartilagelike, branching stems, and thalloid shoots, generally some 6 inches long but sometimes twice that length.

Having been harvested along Irish, Swedish, and other Atlantic coasts in Europe for long before post-Columbian centuries, sea moss was early and widely sought by our forefathers in the New World during neap and low tides. It is also found in usable quantitities where it has been cast up on the shores by heavy seas and here often bleached by the sun to a creamy white—a process also carried on by private and commercial harvesters, despite the fact that the naturally dark sea moss boasts more vitamins. Our predecessors, sometimes making special trips to the seashore to gather it, often kept sea moss for years before finally taking advantage of its mineral-replete goodness.

Area: Sea moss is well known on this continent along the Atlantic Coast from South Carolina to Labrador.

Uses: Department of Agriculture scientists have proved that a 100-gram edible quantity of sea moss, besides being highly nourishing, contains a huge 2,892 milligrams of sodium, a nearly equal 2,844 of potassium, 885 of calcium, 157 of phosphorus, and 8.9 of iron, in addition to magnesium, chlorine, sulfur, copper, iodine, and important trace minerals.

Too tough to eat directly from the sea, it becomes nearly bonelike when dried. Yet, once it is washed free of salt in fresh water, a small amount of simmering makes it valuably and pleasantly usable. As well as being nourishing, it is so soothing to the digestive system that the pioneers used it to quell diarrhea. Dosage was a teaspoon of dried Irish moss, as it is also called, to a cup of boiling water, drunk cold a few sips at a time, 1 or 2 cupfuls a day.

Considered refreshing to anyone with the fever of a cold, flu, or allied difficulty, sea moss lemonade is still concocted by soaking a cup of the seaweed, all of which, incidentally, are edible, in sufficient water to cover until the former is soft, then draining, putting the malleable moss with a quart of bubbling water in the top of a double boiler, and simmering about thirty minutes or until the solid has dissolved. Then strain, add the fresh juice of two lemons, which will be rich in vitamin C, sweeten to taste, ice, and serve as desired.

Blancmange, a favored nourishment for convalescents, if you want it to look its best, is started by washing the sand and salt from blanched sea moss, extracting any dark segments, and adding half a cup of the moss to 2 cups of milk, scalded in a double boiler. Mix in a third of a cup of sugar and, by taste, any necessary salt. Add a fourth of a cup of cold milk. Cook fifteen minutes over bubbling water, stirring constantly until the pudding thickens; then only occasionally. Allow to cool, add a teaspoon of vanilla extract, chill to firm, and serve. This will make about four portions, depending on your patient's appetite.

A jelly made from the well-washed bleached and dried moss by simmering however much you want until dissolved, then cooling, was relied upon by many of our ancestors to ease coughing from colds and flu, as well as to help bronchial, digestive, and kidney disorders.

SILKWEED (*Asclepias*)

Family: Milkweed (Asclepiadaceae)

Common Names: Cotton Tree, Cottonweed, Wild Cotton, Butterfly Weed, Pleurisyroot, Tuber Root, Silky Swallow-Wort, Common Silkweed, Milkweed, Butterfly Milkweed, Common Milkweed, Pink Milkweed, Orange Milkweed, Coast Milkweed, Narrow-Leafed Milkweed, Showy Milkweed, Clasping Milkweed, Orange Wort, Orange Apocynum, Rabbit's Milk, Canada Root, Swallow Root, Wind Root, Rubber Root, Wine Tree, Pleurisy Root, Tuberous-Rooted Swallow-Wort, Chigger Flower, Indian Nosy.

Characteristics: Some twenty-five species of silkweed grow throughout the United States, but it is the common *Asclepias syriaca*—also called silkweed, common silkweed, milkweed, common milkweed, and wild cotton—that is widely recognized by edible wild plant devotees. The silklike fluff which causes the tiny seeds to be wafted away by the fall winds was experimented with by U.S. Department of Agriculture scientists during World War II to see if it could take the place of kapok, then widely used by the navy and air force in flotation devices. The milky sap of the plant—a latex that will yield rubber, gutta-percha, balata, and chicle—was experimented with by government authorities at about the same time as a possible rubber substitute.

In the eastern part of the continent the native perennial extends

228

Silkweed (*Asclepias*)

its single, straight, stout stalks some 2 to 5 feet high in gardens, pastures, meadows, fields, swamps, as well as beside walls, fences, and roadways, where it maintains itself by the millions of parachuting seeds swooped up by the autumn breezes. All these come from rounded clusters of pleasingly fragrant blossoms whose stems, many rising from the central stalk in the same angles produced by the short-stemmed, opposite leaves. Varying in color from near white to greenish violet, these numerous tiny flowers, though appearing delicately harmless with their quintets of pollen-holding stamens and outer sepals, are composed of deadly petals, each of which has an erect cowl and an inwardly curving hook to trap honey-seeking insects.

The fragrant flowers develop into wartily long, green pods, which become about 3 to 5 inches in length and upon maturing crack along one side to expose a complexly interrelated mixture of flat, silkily turfted seeds.

Thriving in similar sites in the West, where it is also known as silkweed and milkweed, the also perennial *A. speciosa,* with the same general habits, thrusts somewhat higher than its eastern relation, with somewhat coarser and thicker opposite leaves with similarly distinctive central spines from which curve numerous stalwart ribs, all in all forming pointed lance-head-like leaves, in this case growing up to about a foot long in contrast to the shorter leaves of the eastern species, which are more like 4 to 9 inches in length.

Area: Thriving from the Atlantic to the Pacific, silkweeds grow from southern Canada to southern California and the Gulf of Mexico. The familiar eastern variety, *A. syriaca,* is seen from New Brunswick and Nova Scotia to Saskatchewan, down to Kansas and North and South Carolina. The common western *A. speciosa* is found in some of the drier sections of British Columbia east of the coastal range to Minnesota and down throughout California to the Gulf of Mexico.

Uses: The Indians and pioneers had to take care in using the silkweeds for medicine, as some plants with similar characteristics are poisonous.

The orange milkweed (*A. tuberosa*), also called butterfly weed and pleurisy root—a very leafy, somewhat hairy perennial growing 2 to 3 feet high, with alternate, narrow, short-stemmed leaves 2 to 6 inches long, and umbrella-shaped clusters of orange-yellow blossoms—has been used as an expectorant, perspiration inducer, and emetic, as well as for the treatment of arthritis. The Indians of Appalachia brewed a tea from the leaves to induce vomiting; they also used it to relieve fever. The root was dug, scrubbed, and chewed raw in sparing amounts for pleurisy. It was relied upon here, too, for the treatment of wens, moles, and warts.

The root was taken in small amounts for digestive gas. This same species was regarded in carefully small doses as a mild astringent and as an inducement for the increased flow of urine. An extract obtained by boiling the dried and powdered root was praised as a remedy for hysteria, colic, and hemorrhaging.

Summarizing the claims made for this plant by most of the writers on American materia medica in the early eighteen hundreds, Dr. Charles Millspaugh wrote: "The Pleaurisy Root has received more attention than any other species of this genus, having been regarded almost since the discovery of this country, as a subtonic, diaphoretic, alternative, expectorant, diuretic, laxative, escharotic, carminative, anti-spasmodic, anti-pleuritic, somachic, astringent, anti-rheumatic, anti-syphilitic. . . . It has been recommended in low typhoid states, pneumonia, catarrh, bronchitis, pleurisy, dyspepsia, indigestion, dysentery, helminthiasis, and obstinate eczemas."

The raw root was eaten for pulmonary and bronchial ailments. It was also chewed and then applied to wounds, the dried roots being powdered and used for the same treatments. It was sought for use on persisting sores. It was also taken internally as a poison antidote.

The Shoshones compressed silkweed sap in the hand until it was firm, then chewed it like spruce gum to keep their mouths and lips moist.

The roots of the swamp milkweed (A. incarnata) were simmered to make a tea which was taken internally in small quantities both as a general purge and to destroy or expel parasitic worms. It was also believed to act quickly as a diuretic and as a stomach stimulant when drunk, either hot or cold, in a tea made by steeping half an ounce of the powdered root in 2 cups of boiling water.

The milky white sap of the familiar eastern variety of silkweed, A. syriaca, was rubbed on warts to eradicate them. The Rappahannocks rubbed it on the skin to cure ringworm. Equal parts of the root of this silkweed and of the pulverized roots and leaves of the marshmallow (Althaea officinalis) were steeped by the teaspoonful in a cup of boiling water. Drinking 3 cups of this tea daily, and one relaxingly hot just before retiring, was said to dissolve gallstones in a few days. This tea was also regarded as being good for dropsy, as it was said to increase the flow of urine. It was likewise considered effective in the treatment of asthma, troubles with the digestive system, for making a patient hot with fever break into cooling perspiration, and for the pains of menstruation.

Once the silken tuft had been burned off the ripe seeds, the latter were ground between two smooth stones by some tribes and used as a salve for sores. However, the major Indian use of the seeds was boiling and steeping them in a small amount of water, then resorting to this for the drawing out of rattlesnake poison.

SLIPPERY ELM (*Ulmus fulva*)

Family: Elm (Ulmaceae)

Common Names: Elm, Indian Elm, Moose Elm, Rock Elm, Soft Elm, Sweet Elm, Red Elm, Tawny Elm, Gray Elm, American Tree.

Characteristics: The important slippery elm is a medium-sized tree, ordinarily about 60 to 70 feet high, and well known for centuries to many a youngster who has chewed its alluring mucilaginous and aromatic bark. The twigs, too, have the same qualities. The medicinal variety does best in rich soil, especially if the soil is impregnated with limestone, along stream banks, river terraces, flood plains, and bottomlands. However, it is also to be found on occasion in dry and poor sites. The slippery and pleasantly fragrant inner bark, once smelled and sampled, is unforgettable.

The rough and abruptly toothed leaves, intensely and darkly dull green on top, as well as somewhat abrasive—soft, fluffy, and lighter colored below—grow from brief, fuzzy, obese stems. Unfurling from downy, stubby, dully pointed, ovoid buds that in winter are an especially deep brown, the oblong to ovate, simple and alternate leaves, doubly serrated on the margins, are generally an uneven 4 to 7 or 8 inches in length and from 2 to 3 inches wide. The buds at the branch ends ordinarily have orange tips.

Interestingly, the slippery elm leaves, with their straight parallel veins from the midribs, are scratchy when rubbed either back or forth, while those of their cousin elms are scratchy only in one direction. In autumn they take on a rich golden hue with oxidation, not frost. The branches stretch out into wide, airy, relatively smooth and even crowns; hence this is one of America's most popular shade and decorative trees.

Small, greenish flowers in short-stacked assemblages enhance the slippery elm from February to April. They mature into winged seeds,

Slippery Elm (*Ulmus fulva*)

dispersed from April to June by the winds, that are samaroid—that is, they resemble the small, dry, winged, seedlike fruits of the maples (considered elsewhere in this book). There are an average of 2,500 slippery elm seeds per ounce, the range being from 2,180 to an astonishing 3,370. The commercial age bearing of this elm's seeds is from 15 to 200 years, those in the open usually bringing these forth earlier and more abundantly than those in stands.

Area: Slippery elms, still regarded as extremely valuable medicinals in Appalachia, are distributed from the Canada-United States St. Lawrence River to the Dakotas, south to the Lone Star State of Texas, east along the Gulf of Mexico to Florida.

Uses: In Appalachia people still soak the inner bark of this tree in warm water to produce a mucilage that is used as a protective, as a soothing agent for an abraded mucous membrane, as an alleviative substance, too, for injured skin, and for healing wounds. There and elsewhere a tea made by steeping a teaspoon of the powdered inner bark to a cup of boiling water, still, as it did back in pre-Columbian times, provides a laxative. Softening the skin, this still is also believed to help prevent chapping.

The Indians mashed the bark and used the pulp both for gunshot wounds and to ease the painful removal of the lead. Poultices made from such bark has been lightly pressed over burns to assist in keeping them antiseptic and to hasten their healing. The Indians, as they showed the settlers, also used it to help infections concerned with the lungs and their allied channels and organs. It was another of the wild medicines relied on for diarrhea.

Tea brewed from the roots was trusted to assist pregnant women at the time of their giving birth. In fact, the slipperiness of the bark, or of the sap and juice, was depended on by midwives to ease the births themselves. Indeed, it was considered useful when anything had to be expelled from the body, even phlegm, when this viscid mucus became secreted in abnormal quantities in the respiratory passages.

Soaking from 1 to 2 ounces of the inner bark in 2 cups of water kept below the boiling point for at least an hour, preferably longer, then straining it, gave an extract that had many uses—for enemas, diluted for vaginal douches, and in small sips for digestive troubles. When it came to enemas for constipation, some wholesome oil and warm milk were often also combined with the decoction.

The powdered inner bark was often the major ingredient in suppositories. For the sick and convalescent the powdered and apparently

234

easily digestible product was frequently flavored with honey or maple syrup and eaten as a strengthening gruel, a practice still often followed in some backwoods communities with the present-day common addition of cinnamon or nutmeg.

SOLDIERS HERB (*Plantago*)

Family: Plantain (Plantaginaceae)

Common Names: Ribwort, Ripple Grass, Ribgrass, Ribworth, Buckhorn, Indian Wheat, Cuckoo's Bread, Way-Bread, Cart-Track Plant, Fleaseed, Plantago, Indian Plantago, Goosetongue, Bird Seed, White Man's Foot, Englishman's Foot, Snakeweed, Devil's Shoestring, Plantain, Narrowleaf Plantain, Broadleaf Plantain, Plain Plantain, Common Plantain, Bracted Plantain, Pale Plantain, English Plantain, Great Plantain, Greater Plantain, Rippleseed Plantain, Seashore Plantain, Seaside Plantain, Psyllium, Psyllium Seed, Blond Psyllium, Black Psyllium, Indian Psyllium, French Psyllium, Spanish Psyllium.

Characteristics: The settlers in the New World knew this plant as soldiers herb, this persistent common weed whose sturdily ribbed, spadelike, green leaves with their troughlike stems thrust up from the roots about the solitary or several short, straight, leafless spikes even through sidewalk cracks in the largest cities of the United States and Canada—a phenomenon made possible by the fact that the tiny seeds remain alive in the ground for over forty years, according to tests started by Professor W. J. Beal of Michigan State in the autumn of 1879. It is a perennial, thriving from sea level up to 9,000 feet. Everyone will instantly recognize it from its picture.

The spikes of this early and popularly used wild medicinal flower have minute bronze to greenish blossoms, usually so unnoticeable that they are seldom seen, from which long clusters of equally unnotable seeds manifest themselves. Small differences exist among the some nineteen varieties in the Eastern Hemisphere.

Area: The soldiers herb grows from one ocean to the other throughout Canada and all fifty states, one reason why the Indians and so many early emigrants to the New World found varied medicinal uses for it.

Uses: The seeds were, and still are in many parts of the continent, valuable as a bulk laxative. Incidentally, soaking these seeds in water

235

Soldiers Herb (*Plantago*)

causes them to exude a clear sticky gum which has been used by the manufacturers of lotions and hair-wave applications. The seeds were also regarded as effective in treating jaundice and dropsy, a tea being made by steeping one teaspoon of them to each cup of boiling water.

The Shoshones were among the tribes binding a hot, wet dressing of leaves on wounds. The colonists used such a dressing for cuts, scratches, and abrasions. The wet leaves are still used in parts of Appalachia as a poultice for wounds and snakebite. Here the crushed fresh leaves still find favor when rubbed onto wounds and skin eruptions. They are also utilized for easing rectal itch. Crushed leaves of the soldiers herb were also bound to the body to reduce fever. Some Indians used such poultices to treat arthritis.

The mashed leaves used to be applied to wounds to reduce bleeding. Such a paste was also regarded as useful for carbuncles, ulcers, and lesser sores. The crushed fresh leaves or pastes made from the simmered leaves were bandaged to cuts, broken blisters, and other wounds both to prevent and cure infection. Such a paste was also used to relieve pain in instances of bone dislocations. Primitive bandages were improvised by wrapping an abraded or wounded finger with a bruised leaf and tying this with grass or some other natural fiber.

The mashed green leaves were also regarded throughout much of the continent as effective in treating snakebites and for bites from poisonous insects and the black widow spider. Indians and settlers used such a preparation to draw out felons and even festering splinters. The leaves were also steeped for a tea which was taken for general intestinal disorders. The folk medicine of Hawaii still includes the gathering of the leaves of all the varieties of *Plantago* growing in the Islands.

Poultices made of the entire plant were applied for sprains. The Indians, who also suffered from gout, relied on extracts made from the soldiers herb. So did the whites. A tea was made for this and other purposes by placing a heaping teaspoonful of the chopped herb into a cup, covering it with boiling water, and allowing it to steep for half an hour. If the powdered plant was used, a level teaspoonful was added instead and the time reduced to fifteen minutes. Both were imbibed by the cupful four or five times a day until relief was obtained.

The tea was used internally, the mashed leaves externally, for scrofulous disorders. Both were also so used, although with doubtful effects, for syphilis. The tea was believed to help clear the nasal passages of mucus and even to relieve menstruation when the flow seemed overabundant. It was used to kill and expel worms in the intestinal system. Tea made with distilled water or rainwater was claimed to be efficacious in treating inflamed eyes.

Piles and hemorrhoids? A strong tea was prepared by steeping an ounce of the chopped plant in 2 cups of bubbling water for half an hour. For the former, cotton or gauze saturated with this was applied to the piles, in severe cases being held in position by bandaging in the most convenient way possible. For the latter, a teaspoonful of the tea was injected with a syringe several times a day, particularly after each evacuation, more frequently in particularly severe cases. In feminine difficulties, it was used as a douche.

The scrubbed and dried roots, made into a powder by the Indian rock mortar and pestle or by rubbing them between two smooth stones, were used in past centuries for toothaches. Preferably this was stuffed into the troublesome cavities.

In snake country, pieces of the root were carried for possible emergency use in case of rattlesnake and similar poisonous bites.

Even the fruit was used to make a tea used to lower fever. This was also taken as a mild laxative.

SQUAW BUSH (*Viburnum*)

Family: Honeysuckle (Caprifoliaceae)

Common Names: Cramp Bark, Genuine Cramp Bark, Cranberry, Cranberry Bush, Cranberry Tree, European Cranberry Bush, High Cranberry, Highbush Cranberry, High Cranberry Bush, Mooseberry, Squashberry, Guelder Rose, Snowball Tree, Pimbina.

Characteristics: Once you've smelled this sweetish-sour viburnum, you'll ever after recognize the presence of this medicine and food, particularly valuable as it remains usable the year around. The distinctive reddish orange berries, growing at the ends of the limbs, expand from usually white spring flowers into flat clusters, shriveling but clinging throughout the nearly barren woodlands the winter through. Like many another established gourmet treat, enjoying eating the berries is an acquired taste. But let a few of the frozen, juicy fruits melt in your parched mouth like flavored ice on a subzero day, and you'll likely become a convert for life.

The generally maple-shaped leaves, becoming beautifully spectacular like those of that tree in the fall, have coarsely irregular teeth and about three to five major veins culminating near the base.

Squaw Bush (*Viburnum*)

Area: Squaw bushes thrive from Newfoundland and Labrador across the continent to Alaska, then down through Canada and the contiguous northern states.

Uses: These are many. But although it was for the bark that the squaw bush was named and has been medicinally notable, the berries are invaluable as a scurvy cure and preventative because of the fact that by weight about one part in a thousand is pure vitamin C.

The most favorable time adjudged to collect this bark was when it was most easily available on the straggly bushes that could be reached by human beings in the sap-flowing spring. Then a healthy handful of the stems was sliced off, the coverings slit lengthwise, the dark bark peeled away as best one could, dried thoroughly as in a warm half-open oven, and stored tightly capped. The quill-like shreds lose strength with age, so the supply has to be renewed each year. The odor of the tightly curling tubes is slight, the taste puckery and bitterish. When powdered, the bark becomes a light grayish brown.

Although some Indians smoked it, the main use among the tribes and the pioneers was to take 2 well-crushed ounces, cover them in a quart of bubbling water, steep an hour until cold, strain, then drink a 1½-ounce jigger of the tea at a time until the stomach or other cramps disappeared. Women afraid of miscarriage often took a tablespoon of the extract three times daily for five or six weeks before the expected event. It was also used to offset nervousness, weakness, to treat uterine infections, painful menstruation, as a kidney stimulant, and even for asthma.

STAGHORN SUMAC (*Rhus typhina*)

Family: Cashew (Anacardiaceae)

Common Names: Sumac, Sumach, Velvet Sumac, Smooth Sumac, Sleek Sumac, Sleek Sumach, Hairy Sumac, Shining Sumac, Winged Sumac, Scarlet Sumac, Fragrant Sumac, Sweet-Scented Sumac, Dwarf Sumac, Virginia Sumac, Upland Sumac, Mountain Sumac, French Sumac, French Sumach, German Sumach, Sugar Sumac, Lemonade Tree, Lemonade Berry, Vinegar Tree.

Characteristics: The large, stout, and velvety twigs of the staghorn sumac look so much like the branched and fuzzy antlers of a buck deer when in velvet that the quickly rising tree is readily recognizable. As if that weren't enough, you've only to cut one of these twigs, and a white, sticky, gelatinous sap will ooze onto your knife blade and at once change to black. Furthermore, all these shrubs and small trees with red berries are edible and harmless. It is the sumacs with white or somewhat yellowish, and incidently sagging, berries that are poisonous—poison ivy, poison oak, poison sumac.

The bark of the harmless members of the cashew family is smooth. The picturesque, often striped, smooth wood, orange to greenish in color, is so distinctive that it is frequently used commercially for such things as portrait frames and napkin-ring holders.

Even the fruits are rapidly recognizable. They start with small, tawny, and somewhat greenish flowers, the males and females growing on separate medicinals. The male clusters are many times about a foot long, and they are spreading. The smaller, denser, feminine panicles are tinier, forming compact fruit bunches that are made up of small, single-seeded, berrylike drupes which mature early in the fall and, startlingly crimson, stay on the shrubs or trees throughout the winter months. They are covered with bright scarlet hairs, pleasantly sharp to the taste with malic acid, the same substance that flavors grapes.

The staghorn sumac is one of a closely allied species whose red, noninjurious berries, sweetened, provide an agreeable beverage known to many a boy as Indian lemonade and to backwoods housewives as a substitute for lemon juice or vinegar. Both these uses are especially successful if the mature fruit, whose malic acid is very soluble in water, is used before the first rains, when it matures in the summer or early fall.

Area: The readily recognizable sumacs with their harmless red fruit thrive throughout southern Canada and the United States in such moist, sunny, open locations as meadows, pastures, and the edges of fruit and nut tree and agricultural farms, as well as beside roads, fences, stone walls, and the unshaded borders of brooks, rivers, and other bodies of water.

Uses: The milky, gummy juice, changing to a characteristic black on the knife blade, was injected into tooth cavities, where it was said to ease pain. The hardened juice, being comprised largely of tannic and gallic acids, was made into an ointment said to be effective in healing scratches, cuts, wounds, and even sores that had become infected. It was also put on moles and warts.

The bark was also used for healing by the Indians and early

©AJA

Staghorn Sumac (*Rhus typhina*)

settlers, as well as by the mountain men and by the pioneers heading westward in wagon trains. Steeped into a wash, it was used to coagulate the blood and stop bleeding. Both as a wash and made into an ointment, it was considered by many tribes to be especially effective for treating infections, burns, scalds, and even for such relative trivialities as redness from too long exposure to the sun.

More important, it was said to help intermittent fever and various vesicular skin diseases such as eczema, ringworm, shingles, and all the numerous virus ailments characterized by blisters on the skin and mucous membranes. Applied externally, it was often a last resort for pus-ridden sores, ulcers of long standing, and even gangrene. Tea steeped from the bark was resorted to by some Indians for helping cold symptoms.

The Ojibwas and other Indians living where the smooth sumac or scarlet sumac (*Rhus glabra*) grew—from the Maritime Provinces of southeastern Canada to Minnesota, south to Florida and Louisiana— found this species especially valuable medicinally. This sumac is similar to the staghorn sumac except that it is not velvety like the newly growing antlers of a male deer but, rather, completely smooth, with a palled whitish or azure bloom powdering the similarly plump twigs.

The Obijwas made a tea from the roots to coagulate the blood and check bleeding. The Creeks did the same thing and turned to the decoction to check dysentery. The root of this same species served a number of other tribes externally to produce heat and redness of the skin, as for aching joints and rheumatism.

The early blossoms were steeped in boiling water which, once it had cooled, was used as a wash for irritated eyes. The inner bark, the cambium, of the twigs and trunk was steeped in boiling water to provide an astringent. When one was passing blood with his stools, an Indian practice was to boil the ripe berries of this particular sumac and give the infusion to the patient. A gargle for sore throats was also prepared the same way. The same sort of brew was given to hemorrhaging women.

The root bark of the *R. glabra* was similarly used. In fact, the berries, leaves, and bark of this medicinal are still turned to in some backwoods localities for similar purposes. The leaves, for instance, are boiled, especially in the springtime, as a general tonic. This decoction was used, too, for venereal diseases. The leaves were used fresh and mashed as poultices. The bright red berries of this species were among those of the sumacs that were collected by the squaws in the fall and dried for winter use.

In all the red-berried sumacs the fruit that had dried on the plants was gathered for winter use. The Omahas, for instance, boiled it to make an astringent wash to stop bleeding after childbirth.

In Appalachia, the dried ripe fruit of the sumac is still considered a valuable source of astringent tannic acid, used for one thing as a gargle.

All in all, the sumacs had numerous uses. The root bark was not only used for diabetes, but also for both the young and aged who found restraining the evacuation processes difficult. The leaves are smoked in Appalachia to treat asthma. Preparations of the fruit are held to be useful in controlling accidental urination such as bed-wetting.

A number of tribes, particularly in the West, mixed the leaves and roots of the sumac with regular tobacco, half and half, in efforts, even then, to break the smoking habit. Some still assay the same treatment. The berries, steeped in vinegar, were given as a gargle for sore throats by the German settlers in the vicinity of Pennsylvania.

Root tea made from the staghorn sumac (*R. typhina*) was drunk for general indigestion and indisposition. The inner bark of this tree provided a tea for shrinking piles and for enemas to check internal bleeding. The berries of these and other sumacs were used in treatment of the yaws, an infectious contagious tropical disease marked by ulcerating lesions with later bone involvement.

Tea from the root bark of the staghorn sumac was considered particularly efficacious in stopping hemorrhaging in females who were unusually hirsute. The Catawabas brewed a tea of the berries of this tree and shrub for controlling the pain of stones and gravel in the bladder. Other Indians used such root bark to check bleeding, the berries for a tonic and digestion-improving tea, and the leaves for a gargle for sore throats. The Micmacs made a tea from this medicinal and inserted it into aching ears.

To make the so-called cooling sumac or Indian lemonade, separate any questionable fruit from a lavish handful of the mature red berries, mash the remainder just enough to break the skins, cover with bubbling water, and move from the heat to steep until the beverage is well colored. Strain through two thicknesses, preferably, of fine cloth to remove the fine hairs. Then sweeten to taste and serve hot or cold, depending on taste and circumstances. This is best achieved in the late summer or early autumn. Staghorn sumac fruit is pleasantly less acid than most of the other species.

Incidentally, as with everything else in this world (with my wife Vena it's pineapple), there will be a few who are allergic to the sumacs, and, of course, they should avoid it in all forms.

244

STINGING NETTLE (*Urtica*)

Family: Nettle (Urticaceae)

Common Names: Nettle, Ground Nettle, Forest Nettle, Slender Nettle, Dwarf Nettle, Great Nettle.

Characteristics: These perennials, notable for their stinging qualities which disappear, however, after they have been simmered slightly, are generally single-stalked greens that are among the first to appear in snowy regions in the springtime. Filled with chlorophyll, vitamin C, many indispensable trace minerals, and protein, nettles, being some 7 percent nitrogen on a dry-weight count, are wealthier in this essential plant food than some commercial fertilizers. Where they luxuriate, there is rich, fertile ground.

Area: Nettles grow across the northern portions of the continent, south through Canada and much of the United States.

Uses: Nettles can be amply cooked with only the water clinging to the plants when they are washed free of dust, and none of this should be wasted because of human-health reasons. In fact, a pleasant beverage is thus provided which the colonists believed helped the pains, aches, and twinges of those growing old. The entire food, one of the most palatable greens nature has to offer, was at one time thought to be a potent medicinal, good for a wide variety of ills—diabetes, fever marked by paroxysms of recurring chills and fever and perspiring, asthma, bronchitis, poor blood, consumption, bites and stings of poisonous pests, and even as a poison antidote. It was also believed valuable in weight-losing. Incidentally, only the tender tips of young plants or those not more than a foot tall should be used.

In addition to its high vitamin C content, which wards off scurvy, for which it is particularly valuable in the Far North after the long white winter, the stinging nettle is rich in vitamin A, which assists night vision, gives a sparkle to the eyes, and makes the hair more glossy. In this latter connection, applied several times daily as a hair tonic, it had the reputation of lessening falling hair, reducing dandruff, and helping bring about a generally healthy scalp.

The stalks, the stems of the leaves, and the leaves themselves bristle with a fine stinging fuzz in which formic acid is a major irritant. They are best gathered with knife or scissors and disposable paper bags, with one's hands protected by impermeable leather, rubber, or plastic gloves. Indians, not having these, counteracted the resulting itch both with crushed green dock leaves and with the rusty feltlike sheaths of young ferns.

245

Stinging Nettle (*Urtica*)

Slim, lengthy, branched, inconspicuous bunches of small verdant blossoms grow rather late in the summer in some localities, in angles between stalks and leaf stems.

The juice from the simmered greens was believed to kill and expel worms in children, to aid diarrhea, to help purify blood as a spring tonic, to increase the flow of urine, and to act as an astringent. Claims were made for its checking hemorrhaging of the lungs, bowels, and kidneys. Stirred into a small portion of honey, this decoction gained the reputation of helping to relieve asthma, of mitigating bronchitis, and of soothing coughs.

In efforts to stop nosebleeds, pressing a leaf against the root of the mouth with the tongue was said to be effective. Crushed nettles were also stuffed sparingly into the nostrils for the same reason.

Stinging nettles were widely used as an agent applied locally to produce superficial inflammation with the object of reducing inflammation in deeper adjacent regions. For instance, stinging the skin with nettles was used in treating arthritis. They were believed helpful in stanching wounds. Ground nettles were important to the nomadic Indians for treating numb feet. In all such cases, the innumerable little injections of formic acid may have been a helpful factor. Striking paralyzed limbs with nettles was credited many times with restoring healthier circulation and even movement. Neuralgia and rheumatism were also treated with heated poultices of the crushed leaves.

The flowers and seeds of stinging nettles were gathered and put in wine, then later drunk for ague. A sweetened preserve of the flowers and seeds was given for kidney stones. Wine in which nettle leaves had been soaked was also resorted to in some instances for starting menses.

Nettle roots were boiled and the decoction used as a mouthwash or gargle, as a bath for painful parts such as those caused by rheumatism, and for saturating compresses for application to both new wounds as well as old and festering sores. It was taken internally for jaundice. Mixed with honey and dry sugar, it was used to assist the expulsion of matter from the lungs and throat by causing coughing and expectorating, thereby also helping to cure wheezing and shortness of breath.

STONECROP (*Sedum*)

Family: Orpine (Crassulaceae)

Common Names: Stone Crop, Wild Stonecrop, Rosy-Flowered Stonecrop, Virginia Stonecrop, Rosecrown, Orpine, Red Orpine, Evergreen Orpine, Frog Plant, Prick Madam, Live-Long, Live-Forever, Aaron's Rod, Small Houseleek, Wall Pepper.

Characteristics: This wild medicinal is familiar to many a youngster—of which I was one—by the fact that one of its succulent, corpulent, green leaves, after being held between clean palms or pressed between a moist tongue and the hot roof of the mouth, can be inflated until it resembles a little frog's belly.

The unmistakable stout, oblong, green leaves climb in close cyclical whirls up 1- to 2-foot-high stalks which, in some species, are weak, prostrate, and spreading, as in the case of the *Sedum ternatum*. Wide, oval flower clusters of tiny individual blossoms, gradating from scarlet and dark red to creaminess, appear rather late in the season.

All parts of stonecrop are edible and usable medically, which makes it all the more interesting that the obese, rounded, or fingerlike and stringy, generally tuberous roots get to be threadlike and not easily chewed, once the plant flowers. But in the fall large quantities of newly maturing, sprightly, fresh white tubers can once again be dug.

Area: Favored in landscaping because of their showy clusters of prettily pointed petals, and frequently escaping from cultivated areas, the stonecrop is to be seen southward from Greenland. Some dozen species are to be found growing wild in the Rockies, while, thriving mostly in hill country, another grows from Massachusetts to Georgia, westward to the Great Lakes.

Uses: Indians and settlers, often troubled with warts, found the application of the insides of the parted leaves to be helpful. The bruised leaves were said to have a cooling effect on feverish patients. Applied externally, they were used to take the pain and soreness out of cankers, to help piles, and to assist in the treatment of scrofula—tuberculosis of the lymph glands especially in the neck, widely called the king's evil because of the former belief that it could be healed by a king's touch.

The jellylike exudation of the extremely juicy leaves was spread over persistent ulcers, burns and scalds, and pus-agitated sores of all kinds.

©AJA

Stonecrop (*Sedum*)

Internally, the juice was used for dropsy, for kidney stones, whose passage it was said to assist, as well as the inflammation resulting from them, and for troublesome nasal catarrh.

STRAWBERRY BLITE (*Chenopodium capitatum*)

Family: Goosefoot (Chenopodiaceae)

Common Names: Indian Strawberry, Strawberry Spinach, Indian Paint, Blite.

Characteristics: A member of the spinach and beet families, as well as the wild lamb's quarter, strawberry blite is easily recognizable when ripe because of its long masses of fleshy, red fruit which, soft and easily crushed, soon smudge the moccasins or boots of anyone rambling through the woods where they grow.

The actual flowers are tiny and of a greenish hue, petalless but with sepals, the modified leaves comprising a calyx. The pistils and the stamens are prominent, especially the latter, with generally five of the little pollen-producing stalks grouped around the pistils. The ovary bears two or three stigma-carrying styles. It is the swelling sepals which show up red and fleshy as the fruit they carry enlarges. The actual fruits are minute bladders, each with a single seed. These berrylike edible reproductive bodies occur between the leaves and stalks and at the ends of the stalks.

The succulent green leaves are lancelike, with undulating or roughly toothed rims.

Area: The strawberry blite, one of the most noticeable wild medicinals in newly burned clearings, on the edges of sandy pastures and meadows, in frequently rocky ground, and in damp valleys and bottomlands, grows across Canada from the Maritime Provinces to Alaska, southward to New England, the Great Lakes, and the midwestern states, being especially rich around our log cabin home in northeastern British Columbia just below the Yukon border.

Uses: The antiscorbutic young green leaves are far richer in vitamin C than spinach and are a fine source of calcium, iron, and potassium. The Indians made a decoction from the simmered leaves and washed it on rheumatic joints with the idea of easing and loosening them. The boiled leaves were also considered mildly laxative.

250

Strawberry Blite (*Chenopodium capitatum*)

The whole plants have been simmered, then mashed into a poultice to soothe aching teeth and bring down swellings. The rather tasteless fruit, nutritious both raw and cooked, furnished a person's system with rich vitamins and minerals.

STRAWBERRY TOMATO (*Physalis pruinosa*)

Family: Potato (Solanaceae)

Common Names: Husk Tomato, Bladder Tomato, Tomatillo, Ground Cherry, Mexican Ground Cherry, Poppers.

Characteristics: This cousin of that garden oddity, the Chinese lantern plant, has the same unusual and peculiar distinctiveness of being a small tomatolike rotundity boxed within a papery shell, not unlike a totally enclosed lighted lantern. The thin covering is really the enwrapping calyx, the thin outer formation of the leafy petals of the flower, which grow large enough to encase each of the golden red fruits that keep on sweetening and ripening in safety even after the whole drops to the ground.

The hairy perennial, spreading and sprawling several feet but hardly ever lifting higher than some 12 inches, has fuzzy, deeply green, fissured, and occasionally toothed heart-shaped leaves up to some 3 inches long.

Area: The strawberry tomato, grown commercially in some localities from which they readily escape, exists in southern Canada and many of the contiguous states.

Uses: The antiscorbutic strawberry tomato, pleasantly rich when raw in vitamins A and C and in sodium, phosphorus, calcium, iron, potassium, thiamine, riboflavin, and niacin, loses much of its vitamin C when canned for winter use but few of its other nutrients. The *P. alkekengi*, for example, has some 18,000 seeds per ounce and an emergence in from three or four weeks at temperatures between 65 and 75°F. The *P. pubesens* boasts approximately 35,000 seeds per ounce, which germinate in warm soil in from one to four weeks at 68 to 86°F.

A tea made from the simmered root was drunk by the Indians and pioneers for stomach trouble and, in stronger potions, was used in efforts to treat and heal open wounds. Except for crude surgery, more than one warrior and settler received no better or more effective treatment.

Strawberry Tomato (*Physalis pruinosa*)

SUGARBERRY (*Celtis laevigata*)

Family: Elm (Ulmaceae)

Common Names: Honeyberry, Sweetberry, Hackberry, Southern Hackberry, Western Hackberry, Desert Hackberry, Upland Hackberry, Thick-Leaved Hackberry, Rough-Leaved Hackberry, New-Leaf Hackberry, Georgia Hackberry, Mississippi Hackberry, Hack Tree, Net Leaf, Nettle Tree, Bastard Elm, Hoop Ash, Granjeno.

Characteristics: Shrubs and small trees, hackberries sometimes grow some 100 feet tall. Like the butternut and the black walnut, they have the unusual distinguishing trait of having their pith divided into naturally enclosed cavities. Splitting a twig longitudinally, you'll see the soft spongy interior as a series of white dividing walls, separating empty chambers.

Odd, too, is the fact that the generally even, grayish bark sometimes roughens with dark, hardening, wartlike protuberances that resemble bumps and raised corklike strips.

The spring flowers, less obvious because they are green, mature into round or egg-shaped, brownish orange but generally purple drupes—berrylike entities composed of thin, especially sweet pulp, each encasing a big round seed.

The sugarberry, generally flowering in April and May, disperses its seeds from October into the winter. *C. laevigata,* the sugarberry, has an average of 270 seeds per ounce, ranging from 230 to 360. The hackberry, *C. occidentalis,* averages 270 an ounce, ranging from 220 to 340. Most of these would germinate in the spring if sown the fall before. To improve the chances of germination, the Department of Agriculture recommends the stratification process of mixing the seed with moist sand, or sand and peat moss, and storing them at between 33 and 41°F as a substitute for the conditions of overwintering.

Area: The shrubs and trees range over a considerable proportion of the continent.

Uses: Sugarberries were regarded as being effective in urinary difficulties, especially inflammation of the mucous membranes which might otherwise lead to gravel and other concentrations of mineral salts, resulting in kidney stones.

A wash to arrest the growth of microorganisms in wounds and sores was said to have resulted from the boiling of the inner bark of the shrub or tree.

Sugarberry (*Celtis laevigata*)

SUNFLOWER (*Helianthus*)

Family: Composite (Compositae)

Common Names: Wild Sunflower, Common Sunflower, Giant Sunflower, Woodland Sunflower, Showy Sunflower, Pale-Leaved Wood Sunflower, Small Wood Sunflower, Ten-Rayed Sunflower, Ten-Petalled Sunflower, Thin-Leaved Sunflower, Thin-Leaf Sunflower, Aspen Sunflower, Saw-Toothed Sunflower, Stiff-Haired Sunflower, Little Sunflower, Weak Sunflower, Swamp Sunflower, Prairie Sunflower, Western Sunflower, Tall Sunflower, Marigold of Peru, Ox-Eye.

Characteristics: This medicinal, native to the Americas and now the state flower of Kansas, has a more realistic scientific name than most—*Helianthus,* two Greek nouns, the first of which, *helios,* means "sun" and the second, *anthus,* "flower." The showy yellow flowers not only look like a primitive reproduction of the sun, but they turn of their own accord toward this luminous celestial body's radiations.

The annuals and perennials are upright and most rhizomatous, many escaping from cultivation for their food and oil values. With up to a couple of dozen golden ray petals emanating from yellow and reddish purple to brown central disks where the seeds later mature, the often solitary terminal flowers become masses of gold in the summertime, from several to sometimes more than 15 feet high. The differing stems and leaves are mostly hairy.

The numerous species are difficult to isolate. They all have neutral ray flowers and flat and fertile disk blossoms which also bear chaff. The appendage crowning the ovary and functioning in the dispersal of the fruit consists of two scales which taper to a bristlelike point. The gland-dotted, smoothly rimmed, elongate lancelike, 2- to 6-inch-long, succulent, hairy leaves of the *Helianthus nuttallii,* for instance, mainly grow alternately. Up to some dozen feet high, these medicinals are among the biggest composites on this continent.

Sunflower seeds in the *H. annuus,* for instance, number about 650 to an ounce and take two to three weeks to germinate at 65 to 75°F.

Area: Sunflowers grow throughout southern Canada and the United States.

Uses: The sunflower seed is a health food, an hors d'oeuvre, an important sustenance, and a source of edible oil. The seeds and leaves have the qualities of both increasing the flow of urine and of promoting perspiring. The Indians and comers from the Old World long used them for bronchial and breathing difficulties. Boiled down in water in

256

Sunflower (*Helianthus*)

uncovered containers and strengthened with honey, the seeds were used to clear the throat and lungs of phlegm. Besides being useful as a diuretic, the seeds were credited with helping rejuvenate the prostate gland.

A tea made by adding a handful of the seeds to a container of bubbling water, and the whole seeped for ten minutes, was one of the fly controls in the early days.

Many a pioneer suffering with arthritis or with other aches and pains of the joints and muscles tried warm baths in which fresh or dried blossoms were combined.

Not only were the flower stems considered antimalarial, but it was believed that a sunflower growing by a cabin or teepee would guard the occupants against the disease.

Ojibwas were among the Indians using the crushed roots as poultices on bruises and other contusions and as a means of drawing blisters. Heated, these were also applied to arthritic joints.

The seeds soaked in whiskey, gin, or brandy were said to act as a gentle laxative.

Snakebites were first sucked to extract as much of the poison as possible, then soaked with a poultice of sunflower roots.

For the healing of burns and scalds, a poultice was made of the saw-toothed sunflower, *H. grosseserratus*. The Pimas extracted a bitter tea from sunflower leaves and administered it sparingly by small sips to feverish patients, spacing the medicine conservatively until hopefully the fever broke. A similar decoction was also utilized as a wash for arthritis.

A tea extracted from the flower heads of the *H. annuus* or common sunflower was taken internally in the West for lung difficulties. In the East it was the roots of the woodland sunflower, *H. strumosus* that were so used. Poultices made from the thin-leaved sunflower, *H. decapetalus,* were resorted to in some areas for sores that had been troubling for a long time.

SWEET RUSH (*Acorus*)

Family: Arum (Araceae)

Common Names: Sweet Grass, Sweet Root, Sweet Segg, Sweet Cane, Sweet Sedge, Sweet Rush, Sweet Flagroot, Sweet Cinnamon, Drug Sweetflag, Flagroot, Myrtle Flag, Sweet Myrtle, Calamus, Calamus Root, Bitter Pepper Root, Pine Root, Reed Acorus, Beewort.

Sweet Rush (*Acorus*)

Characteristics: The slim, slender, lean, stiff, bladelike, shiny, yellow-green leaves of the sweet rush, clasping one another tightly at the roots, generally beneath the surface, grow thinly up to about a yard high. The sweet rush, when crushed between the fingers, emits an aromatic fragrance in contrast to the somewhat similar but more darkly green blue flag, *Iris versicolor,* and the latter's other species which have no strong pleasant odor. Another distinctive difference between the two families is that the sweet rush rootstalk is agreeably gingery in smell and flavor, whereas those of the violently cathartic and emetic blue flag, with its poisonous *irisin,* are virtually odorless, with a harsh and offensive taste.

As if all this were not enough, the blue flag has a purple irislike flower. The sweet rush has a flower stalk, 2 or 3 inches long and with a clublike projection, appearing at an angle halfway up its leaf. This fingerlike, tapering spadix is crowded with tiny yellowish green flowers. The inner parts of this edible flag are sweet.

The roots are obese, horizontal, and bedecked with the shreds of the bottoms of older leaves, producing new leaves above stringy rootlets below, and they are distinguished by a gingery taste with, however, an odd soapy taste that, all in all, makes it even more distinctive.

Area: The sweet rush is found in swamps along the edges of streams, marshes, and wet places in southern Canada and the contiguous United States.

Uses: The bases of the leaves of the sweet rush are still candied in some parts of the country by being thinly sliced, briefly boiled in several changes of water, then placed in a bubbling syrup of 4 cups of sugar to every 2 cups of water and, often stirred, cooked until the majority of the sweetening has been assimilated. They are next drained, laid separately on something such as aluminum foil, immersed in sugar until they are completely dry, and then packed in closely sealed jars. This is and was believed to help digestion, relieve hoarseness, and serve as a tonic and body strengthener, giving especially swift energy. The stout rootstalks were also so used but first had to be tenderized over low heat for a few days—an easier matter with wood-burning stoves than with gas or electric.

In Appalachia the root is still chewed to rid the stomach of gas and the throat of phlegm. Throughout the country a root tea was made by simmering a tablespoon of this chopped part in 3 cups of water. One or 2 cups were sipped cold throughout the day for general digestive troubles and for acid stomachs.

The rootstalk was also considered to have a tranquilizing characteristic that, when it was chewed raw, sedated a pounding toothache until more lasting assistance could be secured. A small amount of the root, boiled, was used as a physic. The root was also crushed and pounded for brewing a tea for colic. Taken by the spoonful, the root was used, too, for concocting a cough medicine used even in cases of tuberculosis.

Some of the eastern Indians dried both the roots of the sweet rush and those of the wild sarsaparilla, *Aralia nudicaulis,* powdered them, and steeped them together for a cough medicine. The root of the sweet rush was also boiled and sipped in carefully prescribed doses for fever.

Singers and speakers sometimes chewed the raw root to clear the voice. If the entire upper respiratory system was clogged, as by a cold, a remedy once resorted to was to breathe in the smoke from the smoldering root.

In Appalachia the freshly cut, spicy leaves were and are sometimes still used as an insecticide. Sachets were hung or laid with clothes in an effort to keep away moths, and the leaves were spread on the floors of cabins so that their fresh spiciness when crushed by the feet would help ward off troublesome insects. Perhaps because of the agreeableness of its spicy aroma and tonic and pleasing taste, the sweet rush was also long thought of as exciting sexual desire.

TANSY (*Tanacetum vulgare*)

Family: Composite (Compositae)

Common Names: Common Tansy, Double Tansy, Bachelor's Buttons, Bitter Buttons, Golden Buttons, Yellow Buttons, English Cost, Ginger Plant, Stinking Willie, Scented Fern, Parsley Fern, Hind Heal, Hindheal.

Characteristics: The perennial tansy grows in clumps of erect, unbranched stems 2 to 3 feet high. It has pungent, strongly aromatic, fernlike foliage, some 4 inches wide and about 7 inches long, with jagged, toothed leaflets. Its flowers, green and inconspicuous, top the handsomely hardy plant and develop from July to September into clustering heads of flat, round, tubular, buttonlike, orangish yellow flowers that live several weeks and then dry into a dark golden beauty.

Area: Tansy grows throughout much of Canada and the United States.

261

Tansy (*Tanacetum vulgare*)

Uses: Tanacetin oil, distilled from tansy, has been used as an insect repellent. Taken internally in an effort to induce abortion, it has sometimes proved to be fatal. Toxic to man and animals when eaten, tansy concoctions taken internally had to be used sparingly and with great caution. The flowering tops were also employed to make a tea to promote menstruation.

In small doses the decoctions of the blossoms and leaves were used to kill and expel worms, as a tonic and narcotic both, as a stomachic to strengthen the digestive system and to increase appetite, for inducing perspiration on the dry skin of fever patients, to quiet hysteria, to assist convalescents in regaining strength, to encourage sleepiness, to help in kidney disturbances, to cleanse the lower intestines, for a number of female complaints, to help gallbladder sufferers, and even for jaundice.

It was also used as a substitute for pepper, in the making of the liqueur chartreuse, and sparingly, because of its strong aroma, to flavor such dishes as salads and omelets.

The plants were once hung in colonial kitchens to dry for such usages and also to help keep away insects. They were also strewn on floors for the latter reason.

Applied externally to sexual organs, tansy was reputed to aid fertility. Decoctions were applied to skin eruptions and sores. The tender young leaves, soaked in buttermilk for about ten days, provided a skin lotion. Infusions of the plant were used for bruises, sprains, sore muscles, arthritic conditions, as a bath to cool feverish patients, and as a general liniment.

Crushed leaves were used as poultices for everything from sprains and contusions to stomachache. They were bound around many an Indian head for headache. The Catawbas relied on the authoritatively aromatic tansy in steam baths for sore, bruised, and swollen feet, ankles, and lower legs.

TRUE WATERCRESS (*Nasturtium*)

Family: Mustard (Cruciferae)

Common Names: Watercress, Water Cress, Nasturtium, Water Nasturtium, Tall Nasturtium, Scurvy Grass.

Characteristics: True watercress, which, being a member of the mustard family, is pungently tasty, grows in thick beds in cold, flow-

True Watercress (*Nasturtium*)

ing water and in wet places—both slow and fast brooks including those which contain the fighting trout, in streams, small rills, springs, ponds, lakes, and even ditches. Make certain that you are just gathering the watercress, as it is also known, for the poisonous water hemlock—somewhat resembling the domestic carrot but with higher stems, whose lower stem stalks have three primary forkings—sometimes grows nearby. True watercress is easy to distinguish, however, as it creeps, freely rooting at the nodes or leaf joints, one incidentally hollow-stemmed string often having numerous, small, white, thready roots which should be left or replaced whenever feasible to encourage continuation.

Thickly growing if tiny true watercress has glossy, deeply green, smooth, undulatingly rimmed leaves with three to nine entities, the biggest of which are at the ends. The diminutive but still pungent, often unnoticed, milky blossoms, appearing from April to October, prosper in the familiar mustardlike crosses, many of them lifting from the intersections on a series of minute stalks connected with a longer stem. These mature into small, slim, seed-filled pods which, especially if they are not yet tough, are pleasantly peppery also.

Area: True watercress, where the habitat as described above is right, grows throughout the United States and Canada.

Uses: Unfortunately, even in sheer wilderness where the contamination may be from the wild animals, the spots where true watercress wavers and creeps can seldom be regarded as safe, and mere washing at home does not make it so. Therefore, to be entirely sure of purity the watercress should first be soaked ten minutes if the soaking liquid is warmish, and twice that long if it is very cold, in a quart of water purified either by one of the now usually expensive iodine-based water-purifying tablets or in the same amount of water in which eight drops of reasonably fresh 2½ percent tincture of iodine have been dropped.

The leaves and tender young stems are very rich in vitamins A and C, as well as containing vitamins B and B2. True watercress is also still used in numerous localities for kidney ailments and to increase the flow of urine, as well as for arthritis. Besides being crushed in water and drink in an effort to treat tuberculosis, it is also still believed useful by some for heart trouble. Its vitamins are said to help prevent hardening of the arteries by keeping the smaller blood vessels in healthy condition.

Some of the Indians resorted to this water nasturtium, as it is also called in some regions, because of its taste, for liver difficulties, and to cause gallstones to disperse or to disappear.

Its vitamins, enzymes, and such elements as iron, manganese, sulfur, calcium, and copper are said to enrich the blood, making it an excellent remedy for anemia and for many blood and skin difficulties.

It was said by some to cause abortion. A number of women ate it to ease labor pains. Although it had the reputation in some areas, when fresh, of ensuring temporary sterility, it has also been turned to as an aphrodisiac. The plant has been resorted to as a laxative— perhaps why some believe that it increases the appetite.

Some Europeans who came to the New World brought along the belief that watercress was good for deranged minds. It was also said to help children grow larger and taller. Old wives and grandmothers looked to it as a "blood thinner" and spring tonic after long hard winters.

U.S. Department of Agriculture scientists find that true watercress seeds number some 150,000 to an ounce and that they require anywhere from four days to two weeks to germinate at temperatures from 68 to 86°F.

TWINBERRY (*Mitchella repens*)

Family: Bedstraw (Rubiaceae)

Common Names: One Berry Checkerberry, Deerberry, Partridgeberry, Chequerberry, Foxbery, Chickenberry, Cowberry, Pigeon Berry, Teaberry, Stinking Berry, Snakeberry, Two-Eyed Berry, Two-Eyed Chequerberry, Checkerberry, Creepchequer Berry, Creeping Chequerberry, Squawberry, Squaw Plum, Squaw Vine, Partridge Vine, Hive Vine, Winter Clover, Running Box.

Characteristics: The distinguishing factor of the twinberry, as might be guessed by the name, is the fact that the fruit is a joined double berry. This evolves from a twin flower with a common base at the terminal of the stem, or in the angles between leaves and stalk. The four, sometimes three, petals of each, spreading at their tops, meet at the bottom to form a tiny long tube.

Each member of each pair of pleasant aromatic blossoms differs in that while one has a short pistil but long stamens, its companion has a long pistil and short stamens. The end result of these structures is that the bloom with the tall stamens nearly always fertilizes the one with the tall pistils, providing an inherent protection against a too

Twinberry (*Mitchella repens*)

intimate wedding and resulting in a continuingly rugged plant that has survived over the centuries.

The radiant red berries, each with a diameter of about ¼ inch, have an agreeable aromatic taste. Those not devoured by the birds and animals remain brightly on the plants all winter, until the following spring, when the light pink to milky white blossoms form in their unique manner once again.

The twinberry grows in trailing evergreen mats which are conspicuous, especially under the pines, in damp woods and on sandy hillocks throughout the year when not covered with snow. The plant creeps prostrate along the ground, anchoring itself with fresh roots wherever it branches. The shiny, roundish, evergreen leaves, duller beneath, each about ½ inch long, grow opposite to one another on stalks that thrust their way briefly skyward.

Area: Twinberries grow on this continent from Alaska to Quebec and the Maritimes, south to Florida and west to Colorado and Texas.

Uses: This creeping evergreen of the woods was regarded by the Indians as tonic, astringent, and diuretic. In fact, the entire plant was taken to increase the flow of urine; it was regarded by some of the tribes as particularly efficacious for this purpose as it had a less disagreeable effect on the digestion that some other such natural remedies. A common dosage was a teaspoonful of the vinelike stems to a cup of boiling water, taken a few sips at a time, 1 or 2 cold cupfuls a day.

The unique and astringent, almost tasteless berries were believed by the Indians and later by the colonists to be helpful in the control of diarrhea.

A tea made of 1 ounce of the dried plant steeped in a cup of water was taken in 4-ounce doses, the volume of a wineglass, for abnormal absence or supression of the menstrual discharge, for painful menstruation, and even for abnormally profuse menstrual flow— hence the name squaw vine. The same dosage, because of the way it increased the flow of urine, was also used even in pre-Columbian eras for dropsy, an abnormal accumulation of water in the body.

Some authorities of the day recommended that this tea be taken during the final month of pregnancy, then in larger doses as confinement neared and until the baby was delivered. The Iroquois and the Cherokees were among the tribes relying on this wild medicine to ease the pains and problems of pregnancy. In an effort to keep up the strength of the patient, the dried vines were sometimes combined with raspberry leaves in making this beverage.

WALNUT (*Juglans*)

Family: Walnut (Juglandaceae)

Common Names: Black Walnut, Common Black Walnut, Walnut Tree, American Walnut, Eastern Black Walnut, Texas Walnut, California Walnut, Nogal.

Characteristics: Particularly valuable for its wood, which is used for paneling and furniture, and for its nuts, the native walnut is a strong, straight, stately tree, averaging between 50 and 100 feet in height and sometimes soaring to as much as 150 feet, with a tightly knit trunk some 2 to 5 feet in diameter. Nogales, where Arizona borders Mexico, has taken its name from the Spanish word for walnuts, *nogal*. The dark brown, nearly black bark is divided into rounded dullish ridges by deep, slim furrows.

The stems are topped with a single leaf, the other alternative leaflets growing opposite one another, some dozen to twenty-two a branch. They give off a distinctive spicy odor when crushed between the fingers. Sharply tipped and finely toothed, formed something like slim arrowheads, they vary from a few to 2 dozen inches in length. Green, with often a yellow tinge on top, they are more lightly colored and generally hairy beneath.

Frequently mistaken for its close relative the butternut, walnuts have light tan pitch, whereas the butternut emits a dark brown, viscous substance. A hairy fringe is found about the leaf scars of the butternut, whereas none occurs on its cousin.

The roundish walnuts mature to from 1½ to about 3 inches in diameter by the time they are ready to drop from the broadly spreading branches about October, depending on the locality. Then the difficulty is getting off the thick, fleshy, warty, greenish husk—a job calling for waterproof gloves unless you don't mind staining your hands with a long-lasting brown dye. A knife is frequently used for the task, which the pioneers found easier if the damp walnuts were first spread in the sun until they became drier.

In turn, the at first wettish nuts underneath, each encased in its familiar sculptured bony shell, were also kept in the sunlight for a few days to dry and to lose some of their bitterness before being channeled open, or split into two halves with a thumbnail, to reveal their deeply indented, definitely delectable, four-celled nuts.

Area: Half of the world's dozen species of *Juglans* are native to the United States. They grow throughout a large part of the East and into the prairie states. A pair of different walnuts exists in California and

269

Walnut (*Juglans*)

another pair, growing up to more than a mile in altitude, elsewhere in the Southwest. Many walnuts are planted as shade trees.

Uses: Walnut meats boast a rugged 628 calories per 100 grams, as revealed by U.S. Department of Agriculture tests, which have shown this portion to have over 20 beneficial grams of protein, over 59 of fat, and almost 15 of carbohydrates. The same healthily edible volume was found to harbor phosphorus, 460 milligrams of potassium, 300 international units of the eye-benefiting vitamin A, 22 milligrams of thiamine, 0.7 of niacin, and 0.11 of riboflavin.

The Apaches used the juice of the hulls to divest their horses and cattle of such parasites as lice. It was also believed effective in ridding any wounds of maggots. Dogs were wormed with 1 or 2 tablespoonfuls. For humans, the same long-lasting juice was rubbed into graying hair to make it brown. Aside from this cosmetic use, the juice was thought helpful for passing intestinal worms in human beings and for treating ulcers, boils, carbuncles, syphilis, as well as ringworm and fungus infections. It was also believed to be a medicine for diphtheria. The same juice of the green husks was simmered with honey for use as a soothing gargle and cough syrup, as well as for irritated stomachs.

The depressant characteristic of the crushed green hulls was long ago evidenced by their now illegal and unsporting use, except in survival situations, in stupefying fish for easy catching by hand, their use then for eating not being at all impaired.

The bark of the trees was both boiled and steeped in bubbling water to make a wash that the Indians believed lessened the aches and pains of arthritis. This bark is very astringent.

The inner bark of the tree, the cambium which lies between the outer bark and the wood, was boiled for use as a physic, its immediacy depending on its strength. The inner bark of the root was also so used, especially for dysentery where it seemed to work mainly as a cleansing laxative. It was also gathered in the fall and so used as a cathartic. Furthermore, it was regarded as a remedy when, as was fashionable in colonial America, one felt "liverish."

A leaf infusion is still used in Appalachia both as an astringent and as a remedy against bedbugs.

The oil extracted from the ripe kernels—by boiling them in water, skimming the oil from the top, and then drying the nuts for eating— was adjudged good for colic. It was also believed that it helped in the expelling of tapeworms. This oil used to be recommended as a palliative for various skin troubles.

Some frontiersmen used to take the bark from a black walnut twig, char it in the campfire, and then apply it in water to draw the poison out of a snakebite.

When walnut meats became old, oily, and unpleasant to eat, they were utilized in an effort to heal boils, carbuncles, and even festering gangrene. These very astringent kernels, crushed in honey, were also believed efficacious in helping earache as well as inflammations of the ears.

The young green leaves, distilled with water, which was then applied by saturated compresses, were considered to be a cure for running ulcers and sores.

WILD ALLSPICE (*Benzoin*)

Family: Laurel (Lauraceae)

Common Names: Spicewood, Spicebush, Common Spicebush, Allspice Bush, Spiceberry, Downy Spice, Feverbush, Feverwood, Benjamin Bush, Souther, *Lindera benzoin*.

Characteristics: This is a deciduous shrub that grows to more than 15 feet in height, easily recognizable because of the spicy aroma of its bark, leaves, flowers, and bright-red berrylike drupes. Preferring stream banks, rich flood plains, spring-fed ravines, and damp woodlands, two species are native to this country, often forming thickets sought by the birds and by the distinctive spicebush butterfly.

Emerald green above, a lighter jade beneath, the leaves are simple, alternate, prominently veined, narrowly ovate with pointed tips and wedge-shaped bases, smooth, evenly rimmed, and on the average about 4 inches long. They oxidize to a rich gold in the autumn.

Topaz-yellow flowers, small and jewellike, appear before the leaves in the springtime, clustering at points where the subsidiary parts originate or center and making one think of a perfumed lady. They develop into one-seeded, oval, intensely ruby, berrylike drupes, usually slightly less than ½ inch long.

Area: One of the aromatic species ranges from Maine to southern Ontario, Michigan, Iowa, and Kansas, south to Texas and Florida. A like but downier type is more common in the southern states.

Uses: Decoctions of the bark were mainly used, although those made from the fruit and leaves also had their advocates. Even today in

272

Wild Allspice (*Benzoin*)

Appalachia, the bark is still relied on to treat coughs, dysentery, and cold symptoms, while it is considered by many backwoods families as being effective in destroying or expelling parasitic worms.

The Indians believed the wild allspice a good tonic, a stimulant, and medicine for inducing perspiration as in cases involving fever. Teas made from it were said to promote better circulation of the blood.

The ripe fruit, dried and powdered, was regarded by the colonists even as far back as the Revolution as a healthful replacement for allspice, while during the War Between the States the Southerners in particular relied on the young leaves, bark, and twigs, a handful simmered for ten to fifteen minutes in 4 cups of water, as a pleasant and actually stimulating tea substitute.

If one is in the woods and out of ready, safely drinkable water, chewing a scrap of the young aromatic bark will relieve that parched feeling.

WILD APPLE (*Malus*) (*Pyrus*)

Family: Rose (Rosaceae)

Common Names: Common Apple, Wild Crab, Wild Sweet Crab, Fragrant Crab, Garland Crab, American Crab Apple, Wild Crab Apple, Southern Crab Apple, Narrow-Leaf Crab Apple, Prairie Crab Apple, Lance-Leaved Crab Apple, Iowa Crab Apple, Oregon Crab Apple, Siberian Crab Apple, Biltmore Crab Apple, Wilding Tree.

Characteristics: All know the apple. The roundness of your wild greenish yellow discovery may be no more than an inch wide, sour and hard too, but not many fruits are so rapidly gathered, and the sourness and solidity combine to make some of the most delectable medicines you have yet encountered. Wild apple blossoms certainly rank among the most lovely in the forest. Their aroma and that of the maturing fruit have an engaging provocativeness seldom approached by the commercial perfumers of the world.

Seeds of the apple, *Malus domestica*—many of which became wild by various means including the thousands of seed-dispersing miles traveled by Johnny Appleseed (actually pioneer minister John Chapman, who spent much of his life walking through early Indian country between New England and Missouri, planting apple seeds and seedlings in likely locations)—number between 600 and 1,000 per ounce, need between 75 and 100 after-ripening days for germination, and then grow into annuals in about a month at optimum temperatures.

274

Wild Apple (*Malus*) (*Pyrus*)

The crab apple, *M. pumila*, yields approximately 1,000 seeds per ounce, which ideally need about seventy-five so-called after-ripening days for germination, then grow into annuals within about a month at optimum temperatures.

The seeds were also sown in the wilderness by birds, by settlers, including those on wagon trains who threw cores aside, and by such animals as deer. Incidentally, one should avoid crab apple seeds, as their content of poisonous hydrocyanic acid is, if volatile, high. The seeds of both these trees as a whole remain alive some two to three years.

The American crab apple, *M. coronaria*, for example, becomes a bushy shrub or an about 15- to 20-foot-high tree with alternate saw-toothed, sometimes lobed, often ovate leaves. A quintet each of petals and sepals, plus many stamens, all appear to stem from the top of the ovary, the latter becoming the fruit which remains crowned by the withered stamens and sepals. The somewhat waxy, yellowish green, 1- to 1½-inch-wide, fragrant wild crab apple—growing in thickets, open woods, and along trails and roads from New York to Missouri and Iowa, south in the uplands to South Carolina, Georgia, and Kansas—ripen in October and November.

Area: Wild apples grow from the Panhandle of Alaska across southern Canada, south throughout most of the United States.

Uses: College surveys have shown that apple-eating students were healthier than the apple-skipping remainder, having fewer upper-respiratory infections and tension-caused ailments. Whole apples, with 8 percent core and stem refuse and 84.8 water content included, proved in a 230-gram whole fruit in U.S. Department of Agriculture tests to have 123 calories of food energy, 15 milligrams of calcium, 0.6 of iron, 2 of sodium, 233 of potassium, 190 international units of vitamin A, 106 milligrams thiamine, 0.04 of riboflavin, 0.2 of niacin, and 8 of scurvy-preventing ascorbutic acid.

Smallpox was formerly treated by the Indians with wild crab apples. The wild apples were also thought to enrich the blood. Their malic, tartaric, and ascorbutic acids were considered to neutralize the by-products of arthritis and gout, as well as to stimulate the liver and the digestive processes. In fact, constipation was said to be lessened by the ingestion of raw whole apples mornings and nights. On the other hand, steeping the skin in bubbling water and drinking it by the half cupful every hour for as long as necessary was an old palliative for diarrhea. Natural cider was believed to help prevent the formation of kidney stones.

Brewing tea from wild apple bark was an old-time remedy believed useful for a long line of ailments. It was used, for instance, to induce perspiration to break fevers, as well as to bring on menstruation. It was also recommended for stomach trouble, dysentery, bladder gravel, toothache, and as a wash for insect bites. It was also commended for kidney, liver, digestive, and spleen difficulties and as a relief for general nausea.

Whenever it was possible to eat it raw and unpeeled, the wild apple was said to be best for health this way, with perhaps one's reassuring himself by Henry David Thoreau's philosophy, "Every Wild Apple shrub excites our expectation thus; somewhat as every wild child, it is, perhaps, a prince in disguise."

WILD CHERRY (*Prunus*)

Family: Rose (Rosaceae)

Common Names: Choke Cherry, Common Chokecherry, Black Chokecherry, Eastern Chokecherry, Western Chokecherry, Virginiana, Virginia Cherry, Virginia Prune-Bark, Stone Fruit, Cerisier, Coke, Serotina, Whicky Chery, Whicky Cherry, Cabinet Cherry, Black Choke, Blackchoke, Black Cherry, Wild Black Cherry, Sweet Black Cherry, Virginia Prune Bark, Rum Cherry, Whiskey Cherry, Pin Cherry, Wild Red Cherry, Fire Cherry, Bird Cherry, Capuli.

Characteristics: The youngster-loved chokecherry grows both as a bushy shrub and as a tree seldom higher than 22 feet, its branches bending with clusters of darkening red or blackish purple berrylike drupes which pucker the mouth but are nevertheless prized by many people, especially children. The pulp enshrouds a big stone, all maturing from white flowers. The elliptic, toothed, and sharply tipped leaves, about 1 to 4 inches long and half as wide, are brighter green at the top.

The rum cherry becomes a large, timber-valuable tree characterized throughout the year by a rough, unevenly cracking, scaly black bark on the older medicinals, reddish to greenish olive on the younger and there further distinguished by long, horizontal pores which appear more like white lines. It has an almondlike aroma, its flowers sagging in conelike spikes and its also much-sought, one-seeded drupes ripening in late summer and early fall to purplish black.

Wild Cherry (*Prunus*)

The pin cherry, the sole early and light-red wild cherry in the northern part of the continent, also bears tastefully sour drupes with one seed apiece, this fruit in flat and round clusters emanating from single spots. Seen usually in clearings, it dies when other forest growth shades it. The almondlike scent is still prevalent. Generally a small tree, it does not often grow more than a couple of dozen feet high.

The fruit of all these medicinals is pea-sized.

Area: Wild cherries grow throughout North America.

Uses: It should be noted that the pleasant, bitter, almondlike aroma of these medicinals is due to the presence of small amounts of hydrocyanic acid which, although highly volatile, can be highly poisonous and even fatal. This acid is particularly strong in the inner bark, seeds, and leaves. Despite this, the Indians and therefore the settlers often used some of these in their palliatives and their foods, and the huge amounts of fruit devoured never seemed to hurt any of us youngsters.

For instance, the Apaches, for one, ground the entire fruit, pit and all, and pressed the meal into small, hard, dark biscuitlike cakes which were stored and reconstituted on the trail by boiling, thus both softening and driving off the readily vaporizing prussic acid with heat.

In Appalachia today in some of the more remote localities the inner bark or cambium is still used as a flavoring agent in cooking, and a tea made from it is utilized for coughs, cold symptoms, as an expectorant, and for cholera.

Teas made from the bark, leaves, and dried roots of the wild cherries were also used for lung difficulties and for cold symptoms. The drupes were sometimes made into a wine, imbibed, among other reasons, to treat dysentery.

The dried and pulverized bark was scattered over open sores. It was smoked for headache and was another of the innumerable cold remedies which even then were always the subject of experiments. The bark was steeped to treat anything from measles to stomach trouble, and it was given to women in labor in an effort to relieve their pain. The infusion was also taken for worms, for tuberculosis, as a sedative, and for some of the fevers. Indians boiled the inner bark and gave an enema with it for hemorrhoids. As has been already indicated, a tea brewed from the inner bark seemed to help control nervousness and to allay spasms of the digestive tract.

The dried and soaked bark of the twigs in particular was believed successful in providing a stimulating medicine for helping a patient to cough up matter from the lungs and throat. Wild cherry brews were also turned to in quantity by the multitudes who lived in dusty, dry lands. And gum exuding from the trees was candied and given to those suffering with kidney stones. Infusions made from it were thought to be useful for treating whooping cough, as well as for bronchitis.

Even babies plagued with stomach upsets were quieted with soaked bits broken from the Indians' hard wild cherry biscuitlike cakes made for winter and trail rations.

Ulcers were dusted with the powdered inner bark. Hot infusions of the bark and root proved stimulating to weary travelers. The roots were dug in the fall to provide a steaming tea before meals to restore appetite and to assist digestion.

Rum cherries got their name from the New England practice, popular in the famous triangle trade, of being simmered in water, strained, sweetened with an equal bulk of sugar of one sort or another, and then poured in by taste to rum and other brandies both to soften the biting taste and for the even more profit-conscious result of thriftily stretching the alcoholic beverages in what proved to be a tasty manner. They were also crushed, then fermented with sugar to make what was considered to be a medically effective wine.

When Captain Meriwether Lewis fell ill with fever and abdominal cramps on the Lewis and Clark expedition, he was on his feet the next day after being dosed with chokecherry twigs simmered in water.

A mouthwash and gargle which seemed particularly effective with cankers, used and spat out, was made by boiling the bark of the roots. Also, a bit of root bark was sometimes held against a canker for long periods of time. In the region of the head, sore eyes were treated with the steam of boiling wild cherry cambium, also used upon cooling as an eyewash. The same treatment was turned to for snow blindness which, of course, is an inflammation and not blindness at all and can be caused merely by the sun shining through a tent or tepee.

Strong wild cherry bark tea even found its advocates as a liniment for sore muscles and for joints paining both from overexertion and from arthritis. A more diluted tea was used for jaundice. It was also drunk for nausea.

Incidentally, stored inner bark, preferably kept covered in a cool and dark place, was believed to lose its effectiveness within a year.

WILD CLOVER (*Trifolium*)

Family: Pea (Leguminosae)

Common Names: Common Clover, Common Red Clover, Red Clover, Purple Clover, Purple Prairie Clover, White Clover, White Sweet Clover, Yellow Clover, Yellow Sweet Clover, Strawberry Clover, Sweet Clover, Prairie Clover, Meadow Clover, White Prairie Clover, Foothill Clover, Ditch Clover, Longstalk Clover, Broadleaved Clover, Pinpoint Clover, Bighead Clover, Clammy Clover, Hop Clover, Low Hop-Clover, Smaller Hop-Clover, Large Hop Clover, Buffalo Clover, Rabbitfoot Clover, Cow Clover, Tomcat Clover, Tick Clover, Beggar's Ticks, Tick Trefoil, Clever Grass, Trefoil, Bee-Bread, Four-leaf Clover.

Characteristics: There are a number of different species of this plant on this continent, but everyone knows the common varieties, mainly those with red, white, and occasionally yellow bloosoms—everyone, that is, who has ever successfully sought as a youngster the so-called lucky four-leaved oddities among the vast stretches of trefoil masses of green foliage or who has sucked honey from one of the individual minute tubelike flowers forming the fragrant heads.

Red clover, *T. pratense,* is the official flower of the New England State of Vermont. It is a biennial or perennial legume with long-stemmed, trifoliate leaves, each ordinarily with three oval-shaped leaflets. The globular to ovate flower heads are dense and roseate.

White clover, *T. repens,* is selected by many a home owner for his lawn, as, being a low, white-flowered, creeping perennial with glabrous runners and usually long-stemmed leaves, it does not need constant mowing. Bread made from its seed-replete dried flowers, being healthful and nourishing, has saved peoples from starvation.

Too, clover is widely known as an important food crop for all kinds of livestock at every time of the year, whether green or dry. It attracts large numbers of bumblebees, which serve to fertilize it, the genus not being successful in Australia until bees were brought in, too.

Areas: Clovers, some of them going wild from introduced species, prosper in all sorts of conditions and soils throughout much of the United States and Canada.

Uses: The red clovers, known by a number of different common names, depending on the locality, are regarded as antispasmodics, good for nervous indigestion and allied troubles. The flowers have been used therapeutically also as an expectorant, sedative, and for healing wounds and sores.

Wild Clover (*Trifolium*)

An ointment was made from them for spreading over ulcers, and a poultice made by crushing a handful of blossoms and steeping them in a small amount of water for four hours, then putting the mixture on while it was still warm. It is also soothing to irritated mucous membranes, and therefore is used for coughs. For youngsters, rashes were washed with a strong decoction of the flowers and water.

In fact, a syrup was made for whooping cough by simmering 2 ounces of blossoms to a quart of thick sticky solution of sugar and water, straining and then sipping this several times daily, especially when the coughing became particularly irritating.

The dried and ground flowers of the red clover were, according to the *U.S. Dispensatory,* used in some antiasthma cigarettes. Tea brewed from the flowers was also used to improve sluggish appetites, regulate digestive functions, and to treat liver ailments.

The blossoms of both the red and white clovers had the reputation of being blood purifiers and a strong tea steeped from them individually was applied externally to boils, ulcers, and other skin disorders. They were also drunk to cleanse the system and were furthermore taken as alternatives.

Some of the Indians ate the tender young leaves, especially raw but also sparingly simmered to prevent and cure scurvy, characterized by such symptoms as roughening of the skin, congestion about the hair follicles, large bruiselike areas of hemorrhaging, pain in the joints and muscles, and often swelling of the joints.

WILD GERANIUM (*Geranium maculatum*)

Family: Geranium (Geraniaceae)

Common Names: Geranium, Spotted Geranium, Scented Geranium, Pink Geranium, Sticky Geranium, Cranesbill Geranium, Cranesbill, Sticky Western Cranesbill, Common Cran's Bill, Wild Cranesbill, Wild Crane's Bill, Spotted Crane's Bill, Storkbill, Stork Bill, Heron's Bill, Alum Root, Alumroot, Wild Alum Root, Alum Bloom, Astringent Root, Chocolate Flower, Crowfoot, Dove's Foot, American Kind, American Tormentil, Tormentil, Herb Robert, Old Maid's Nightcap, Old-Maid's Nightcap, Shameface.

Characteristics: The wild geranium, in some regions about a foot high, also at times reaches a height of about 2 feet. It is erect, grayish green, usually unbranched, and hairy. The leaves, light green

Wild Geranium (*Geranium maculatum*)

with paler spots, some 3 to 6 inches wide and characterized by gland-tipped hairs, are deeply parted into three or five toothed divisions, each again cleft. They become an unforgettable red before dying.

The symmetrical rose-purple, pale or violet-purple, often pink or white flowers, appearing from April to June, are borne in loose clusters some 1 to 1½ inches high. They are pretty much standardized with five sepals, five petals, ten stamens in two rows, and a red-tipped pistil with a five-chambered ovary and five-cleft style. These styles, elongating to about an inch, form a beak to the fruit; *Geranium* is derived from a Greek word meaning "heron" or "crane." The five-celled fruit clusters, each with one seed, curl abruptly open when ripe and snap the seeds a yard or so away.

The rootstock is 2 to 3 inches long usually, rough, knotty, fibrous, thick, with numerous branches and with scars indicating the presence of stems of former years. When dry, it has a somewhat purplish hue internally.

Area: Wild geraniums, which grow from Newfoundland to Georgia, west to Manitoba, Kentucky, and Tennessee in the East and in the West from South Dakota to British Columbia, southward into Nevada and California, flourish throughout much of North America's Temperate Zone.

Uses: Wild geraniums were said to be the Indians' strongest astringent, the green solution made from the powdered roots and water being especially valuable for dysentery and for internal hemorrhaging. It was also favored for drying up such sores as slowly healing ulcers. Crushed geranium roots were favored for poultices for such ailments as protruding piles and for arthritis, overexercised joints, sore feet, ruptures, and the like.

A tea steeped from the roots was perhaps the most widely used birth control substance taken internally, the drinker being thought to be safe from pregnancy for at least a year.

Household geraniums, incidentally, are members of the same family but are of a different, also large species known as *Pelargoniums*.

Root tea from the wild geranium was considered effective for delicate stomachs, neuralgia, as a diuretic, and for compresses kept damp for burns, for bleeding wounds, infectious sores, and piles.

When dried, the roots could be ground into a purplish brown, generally chocolate-colored powder, an average dose for diarrhea, dysentery, cholera, and the like being 15 grains. Infusions of the dried leaves, too, were held to be valuable as mouthwashes for sore throats, cankers, sore and even ulcerated gums, and pyorrhea. Held in the mouth, it was said to lower the pain level of a toothache or a sore tooth. A similarly used mouthwash was also prepared by boiling a portion of root. It was also claimed to be good for sore jaws.

Indians, followed by the settlers, used the powdered dried root to stem bleeding and, since it was also regarded as an antiseptic, to help heal wounds of all sorts. The Cherokees chewed the fiber of the root and blew it into the mouths of children suffering from thrush. They also combined wild geranium and wild grape, *Vitis cordifolia,* roots in making a wash for the same purpose.

Some also used the dried rhizomes as a tonic as well as an astringent. This was also utilized in an effort to reduce swellings and also for gonorrhea, gleets, and agues.

Ordinarily, the leaves and roots were harvested in the spring just before the wild geranium sprang into bloom and again in the late summer.

WILD HORSERADISH (*Armoracia*)

Family: Mustard (Cruciferae)

Common Names: Horseradish, Horse-Radish, Sting Nose, Red Cole.

Characteristics: The flowers of four white petals arranged in a crosslike formation mark the wild horseradish as another member of the mustard or *Cruciferae* family. If they did not, the pungency of the roots soon would. This medicinal is a perennial that has escaped to damp regions from the log cabins and other shelters around which it was originally planted by settlers, mostly English, when this continent was first colonized, and is not to be seen in the more primitive areas.

The majority of the leaves rise from the roots on long, robust, plump, furrowed stems and are generally ½ foot in width by about twice that length, with undulating, widely toothed rims. Slimmer, noticeably smaller, green leaves angle upward immediately from the smooth stalks that are topped by clusters of the small white blossoms which produce seeds only rarely and then up to about half a dozen in each half of the widely scattered ovoid pods.

It is the instantly ardent root with its pleasantly pungent, burning, fiery taste that is the immediate identifier. These roots are usually about 1 foot in length and anywhere from 1 to 2 inches in

Wild Horseradish (*Armoracia*)

diameter, suddenly dividing at the terminus. The roots are distinctively white.

Area: Originally brought from Europe and planted in their yards by the early settlers, the wild horseradish has spread from the mother plants in moist places, particularly along streams, throughout much of the northeastern United States and southeastern Canada.

Uses: The raw white roots of the wild horseradish are so ruggedly peppery that their pungency is quelled to a certain extent by their being grated and blended with a little vinegar or, better, lemon juice.

Being so extraordinarily rich in the antiscorbutic vitamin C, the unlikely root saved numerous scurvy-plagued individuals who were deficient in this vitamin because of nonfresh, salt-preserved rations. The immediacy of its cure was regarded by many as miraculous, and there was the added benefit that this vital nutritive was present in the root the year around, even when it was dug from frozen ground beneath the snows.

Other uses soon manifested themselves, and many an early doctor relegated the fiery parts to a state of importance as a stimulant, diuretic, expectorant, vermicide, rubefacient, and diaphoretic.

The roots seemed to increase the flow of urine, thus being held valuable in the treatment of dropsy when the abnormal accumulation of serous fluid in the connective tissues and serous cavities of the body was due to too scanty urination. Furthermore, it was not only believed to help prevent the formation of kidney stones and gravel if taken regularly, but also to cause the expulsion of such calculi already in the body.

It was thought to be valuable in the treatment of colds and allied symptoms because of any value there may be to vitamin C in such circumstances, animation of the nervous system, raising of the activity of the perspiration glands, the easing of congestion and the help this gives in expelling phlegm, and its action in perhaps helping to cure sore throat and hawking. A tablespoon each of lemon juice and grated horseradish allowed to steep for half an hour in one fourth of a cup of water, drained so as to get just liquid, and this last added to half a cup of honey, will apparently help to soothe a hoarse throat if sipped by the teaspoonful once an hour until the harshness and any accompanying tickle has disappeared. For all uses the fresh root is, incidentally, much more potent than the dried.

In the old days, and in some parts of America at present, if a child or adult seemed to lack appetite, the mother or grandmother often steeped a tablespoon of the grated root in 3 cups of water and portioned it out cold, a few sips at a time, 1 or 2 cupfuls every twenty-four hours, until the sluggishness had disappeared.

The fresh leaves, also valuable as an antiscorbutic when eaten raw or simmered only until tender in a small amount of water and then eaten, juice and all, were applied locally where neuralgia was acting up.

The pounded root sometimes took the place of the more severe mustard plaster externally, heating and reddening the skin where arthritic or overexercised joints were aching, where gout or sciatica were paining, or where the liver or spleen were swollen. It was similarly used for chilblains when this inflammatory swelling and soreness was the result of overexposure of the hands, feet, legs, et cetera, to the cold.

Mixed with milk, the grated roots were believed useful in curing rashes and other minor skin ailments.

Indians, this time learning from the newcomers to the New World, used wild horseradish tea to treat both ague and cholera. Some of the tribes softened a large leaf on a hot stone by the campfire, folded it in two, and fastened it to the hollow of a hurt or aching foot. They used the root as a stimulant, and the tea made from it for stomach upsets and to increase the flow of urine.

No one was ever known to relish the root, once it had been cooked, by the way.

WILD LICORICE (*Glycyrrhiza glabra*)

Family: Pea (Leguminosae)

Common Names: Licorice, American Licorice, Amalillo, Sweet Wood.

Characteristics: Wild licorice is a tall, erect, shrublike, weedy-looking perennial, 1 to some 5 feet tall, with prickly, sharp, fast-clinging, hooklike spined, brown burrlike, seed-filled pods that grow from thick clusters of pale yellow to greenish white flowers, each some ¼ inch long, on an elongated axis that bears its blossoms on short stems in succession toward its apex. These flower stalks lift from the angles at the spot where the leaves grow from the main stems, which spread widely at their bases.

The leaves themselves are distinctive, growing in pairs of about

289

© AJA

Wild Licorice (*Glycyrrhiza glabra*)

five to nineteen leaflets, with one at the tip, each dark-green entity. Some of them are gummy beneath, up to 1 inch in length.

The herb lifts from an underground stem or rhizome that is dark or grayish brown, and longitudinally creased, with a sweetish yellow interior. Commercial licorice has been obtained from these rootstocks with their glycyrrhizin and sugar.

Area: Wild licorice is found on the prairies and throughout the East, Midwest, and Southwest from Alaska and central Canada southward toward Mexico and the Gulf of Mexico.

Uses: Wild licorice is used medically as a gentle laxative and as a demulcent capable of soothing and protecting an abraded or irritated mucuous membrane, the dried rootstock being boiled to provide these in the form of a pleasant tea. This is still used in some regions in treating childhood fevers. The roots were fermented, along with water, and taken internally for stomachache and blood diseases, even hopefully for syphilis.

An oil was obtained from the root which was dropped into an aching ear or tried for deafness. A hormone in the root was said to be efficacious for blood disorders, psoriasis, and asthma. An extract from the roots has long been used in cough remedies, both for hoarseness and to bring up phlegm. Bits of the rootstock have been chewed for the same reasons, as well as for bronchial complaints. Also, the sweet mucilaginous properties of these have long made them popular for keeping in the mouth in hot, windy, dusty, dry lands. It was also supposed to help kidney functions.

Cholera was one of the ailments frequently treated with steam baths and cathartics, followed by wild rice, *Zizania*, gruels, and wild licorice tea. To this was often added a bit of dried jack-in-the-pulpit, *Arisaema triphyllum,* included, too, when the decoction was given for coughs.

Wild licorice was also utilized to care for stomach ulcers, arthritis, and paining muscles and joints. With women, a rhizomic extraction was tried to induce menstrual flow, as well as to help fever in nursing mothers and to ease in the expulsion of afterbirth.

In sarsaparillalike concoctions, it was a standby of the old-time medicine man. Too, roots were crushed or chewed and made into poultices for wounds of all sorts and for such sores as ulcers.

Prepared at home as a tea, a common prescription was a tablespoonful of the dried and often powdered root steeped for an hour in a pint of originally boiling water, strained, and sipped when cold during the day.

WILD ONION (*Allium*)

Family: Lily (Liliaceae)

Common Names: Nodding Onion, Nodding Wild Onion, Sickle-Leaved Onion, Swamp Onion, Marsh Onion, Tree Onion, Shortstyle Onion, Sierra Onion, Sierra Garlic, Wild Garlic, Eastern Wild Garlic, Meadow Garlic, Field Garlic, Siberian Garlic, Wild Chive, Wild Leak.

Characteristics: The one thing to watch out for is to use only those plants and bulbs that have the familiar odor and flavor of the onion family. None are poisonous. However, some domestic and wild plants, and bulbs especially, have an onionlike *appearance* only and are among the most insidious poisons in the plant world although, because of familiarity with them as flowers, you and children particularly may regard them as edible. Beware of them and keep them out of youngsters' reach as much as possible—admittedly a difficult thing to do in gardens. But try to drill into them the fact that all parts of such plants should be left strictly alone, and keep them out of reach when they are not in the ground.

The typical wild onion has slim, awllike, often hollow leaves similar to those of the vegetable garden species. Underground, it is a layered bulb with a distinctive odor and taste. Flowers appear at the tops of otherwise naked stems.

There are, as always, exceptions. With the *Allium canadense* or eastern wild garlic or meadow garlic, bulbs grow at the top. When Père Jacques Marquette, seventeenth-century Jesuit missionary and explorer went from Wisconsin in 1674 to the present vicinity of Chicago, he and his party existed mainly on wild onions, likely this species. In the Menominee language, the word *Cigaga-Wuni* (to spell it phonetically) was the name of the wild leek, *A. tricoccum,* or skunk place, the first part of which name was given this region where so many of these plants thrived and were also probably eaten by the Marquette party.

The continent-crossing expedition of Rogers and Clark was introduced to the wild medicinals by the Indians, there being some fifty varieties in the Rocky Mountain region alone.

Area: These numerous, pungent members of the lily family—the wild onions, leeks, chives, scallions, shallots, and garlics—grow throughout North America except in the land of the permafrost in the Arctic and Far North. The withered stems and seedpods of a number of the varieties stick up above the winter snows and indicate the presence of usable bulbs in the ground below.

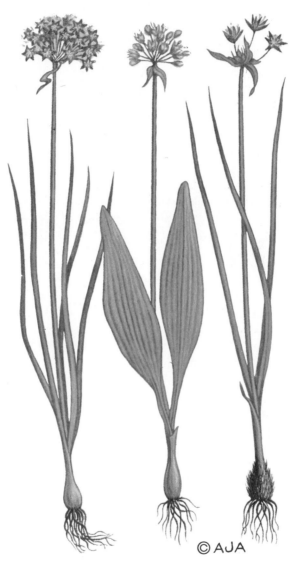

Wild Onion (*Allium*)

Uses: For centuries, according to no less an authority than the U.S. Department of Agriculture, a medicinal oil has been extracted from the *A. sativum*, or wild garlic, and has been used to treat such ailments as bronchitis. The crushed bulbs were made into a poultice applied to the chest of those suffering from pneumonia.

The old people among the Indians and the settlers were brought up making cough syrups by cooking the sliced bulbs and dissolving the juice into some sweetness which might well have been maple sugar. Such syrup was used to treat cold symptoms and to help such afflicted children drift off to sleep. The same syrup was also used to attack hives.

Incidentally, the odor which is repellent to many people after someone has been eating garlic and the like can easily be eradicated. Just brushing the teeth, tongue, and gums thoroughly, so that no bits of the medicinal remains, will leave a fresh-smelling mouth.

These wild medicinals have long been what often seemed to be a miraculous cure for scurvy. When Maximilian, Prince of Wied, was weak with the vitamin deficiency at Fort Clark in 1834, it was the Indians who got the green leaves and bulbs of wild garlic (*A. reticulatum*), which cured him when his plight seemed hopeless. On Major Stephen Long's large expedition to the Rockies in 1819 and 1820, 300 of his men were laid low with scurvy, a third of them fatally, and it was likely the wild garlic brought in by the Indians which saved the remainder. On General George Crook's so-called Starvation March down the Yellowstone River in 1876, wild onions were credited with helping the men avoid scurvy.

The Cheyennes were among the Indians crushing the bulbs and stems of wild garlic, applying this as a poultice to carbuncles and boils, and then, when the sore burst or was opened, washing out the pus with a strong tea simmered from the same medicinal.

The Dakotas and the Winnebagos were among the Indians who crushed the wild onion and applied it to bee, wasp, hornet, and other insect bites with what was said to have been marked success in reducing the swelling and pain. Some Indians used it in an effort to draw the poison out of snakebites.

Many of the early Americans, both Indians and pioneers, simmered the juice of the wild onion family down to a heavy syrup which was used for coughs, tickling throats, and other cold symptoms. Some of the Indians and settlers used the juice expressed from roasted wild onions and wild garlic for infants with croup. Wild onion poultices are so used in parts of Appalachia today. The juice was also dropped into the ear to relieve aching and the ringing noise that individuals sometimes notice.

Crushed members of the family were applied to scalds and burns, even those caused from too much exposure to ultraviolet rays, as well as to sores and even unsightly blemishes. It was also said to help digestion, to keep away disease germs in some instances, and to aid piles and hemorrhoids. The Indians and sourdoughs moistened clean, heavily steam-sterilized sphagnum moss, which covers thousands of miles of our continental North, with wild onion juice diluted with sterile water for antiseptic applications to wounds and suppurating sores.

The meadow garlic, *A. canadense,* has been used to rid the digestive system of gas, to increase the flow of urine, and to help patients relieve their respiratory systems of phlegm. Other members of the wild onion family have also been so utilized.

Water in which sliced or crushed wild onions had been steeped for at least twelve hours was drunk on empty stomachs to rid the system of worms.

WILD PLUM (*Prunus*)

Family: Rose (Rosaceae)

Common Names: American Wild Plum, Wild Red Plum, Wild Yellow Plum, Wild Goose Plum, Canada Plum, California Plum, Sierra Plum, Beach Plum, Flatwoods Plum, Chichasaw Plum, Bullace Plum, Munson Plum, Porter Plum, Sand Plum, Hog Plum, Horse Plum, August Plum, Thorny Plum, Thornless Plum, Sloe Plum, Allegheny Sloe, Sloe, Indian Cherry, Mountain Cherry, Graves.

Characteristics: Cousins of the wild cherries, wild plum shrubs and small trees can be distinguished from them by a number of individual characteristics. The fruits are fleshier. They have flatter stones, whereas those of the wild cherries are spherical. The fruit is covered with a powdery white bloom. A line circles their long axis. A number of the wild plums have branchlets that are pointed, becoming spined, whereas none of the wild cherries are so defended. Another difference is that the plums' twigs lack terminal buds.

The beach plum (*P. maritima*), for example, looks like a bush more commonly than a tree, and as some of these sucker readily from their deep, rough, far-ranging roots, it frequently thrives in thickets

Wild Plum (*Prunus*)

of rambling shrubs up to about a man's height. Ovoid leaves, fuzzy below, have sharply tooth rims in place of thorns. The habitat is often the sand dunes, as in Massachusetts. Numerous white flowers emerge before the leaves.

The plums, generally differing between a half to an inch in width, range in hue from yellow and red to blue and blackish purple. Because they rely on insects to pollinate them, the weather has a great effect both on the flights and on the development of the pollen ducts, several years often passing between fruit production, especially during the all too common bleak, chill, misty, and darkly rainy springs.

Area: Over a dozen wild plums enhance the United States and southern provinces of the Dominion of Canada: the Canada or horse plum (*P. nigra*) from Alberta to Newfoundland, south to New England and by the St. Lawrence River and the Great Lakes to Wisconsin; the wild goose plum, *P. hortulana,* from Kansas to West Virginia, south to Mississippi and Texas; the wild, yellow, or red plum (*P. americana*), from New England through Pennsylvania and the Mississippi Valley to Montana, Oklahoma, New Mexico, Texas, then over to Florida; Allegheny sloe or porter's plum (*P. alleghaniensis*), from Pennsylvania to Connecticut; the sand plum (*P. watsoni*), from Kansas to Nebraska; the Chickasaw plum (*P. augustifolia*), from Florida to Newfoundland, west to Texas, Indiana, and Kansas; the California, Pacific, or sierra plum (*P. subcordata*), from southern Oregon to northern California; the beach plum (*P. maritima*), from Nova Scotia and New Brunswick to Virginia and inland to the Great Lakes.

Uses: Wild plums are antiscorbutic, astringent, and acidulous. The bark of the trees and bushes was considered to act as an antispasmodic and a remedy for nervous indigestion, as well as being slightly sedative. The Ojibwas were among the tribes both steeping and boiling the roots to destroy or rid their digestive tracts of worms.

The Indians, and later the newcomers from the Old World, used tea brewed from the roots of the Pacific plum, *P. subcordata,* in particular for difficulties with the urinary system. They made a mouthwash, believed useful, too, when there was an overabundance of mucus, by simmering the leaves. Gum found on the medicinals, sometimes combined with the leaf tea, was believed to cause both kidney stones and gallstones to dissolve.

For abraded parts of the skin and mucous membrane, bark cut and scraped from the roots of the wild plum, *P. americana,* especially, was simmered and used as a wash considered to be both solacing and healing. This was also used for a mouthwash, being thought especially efficacious in the cure of cankers. It was believed to be an effective gargle as well.

WILD ROSE (*Rosa*)

Family: Rose (Rosaceae)

Common Names: Rose, Red Rose, Common Wild Rose, California Wild Rose, Wood Rose, Rock Rose, Moss Rose, Pasture Rose, Arkansas Rose, Japanese Rose, Fendler Rose, Ash-Leaved Rose, Multiflora Rose, Cinnamon Rose, Prickly Rose, Climbing Rose, Nutka Rose, Wild Brier, Sweetbrier, Brier Hip, Neeches.

Characteristics: The wild roses most of us so pleasantly recognize are shrubs, in addition to vines, from a few inches to some dozen feet high with spined, subdivided stems. The generally somewhat pink blossoms, occasionally more whitish or scarlet, are usually an aromatic one or several inches in diameter, generally unfurling on branchlets diverging from more aged stalks. The leaves, which are commonly compound, are angularly toothed.

The rose family interbreeds and varies so diversely, as one can be well aware of by the numerous domesticated types in home gardens and in the flower markets, that it is fortunate that all are edible and usable medically. The differences in scents, hues, and variously sized shapes add only to the excitement of coming upon a different species. They often grow up beyond the timberline.

The flowers, which in the wild species are often only a fragrant ring of five wide petals, evolve into red to orange seedpods measuring up to a plump inch in diameter, commonly known as haws or hips, which are roundly smooth and bunching to a very noticeable, withering, five-leaved topknot. This most important fruit, with its interior of vitamin-replete seeds, adheres staunchly and valuably to the wild rose throughout the winter, well into the springtime, when the vital plants begin to blossom afresh.

Area: These brambled beauties flourish from the farthest reaches of Alaska and the fog-bound Aleutians, past Hudson Bay to the northern Atlantic shores, southward through the Dominion of Canada and the United States and down into Mexico, prospering wherever the ground is adequately damp.

Wild Rose (*Rosa*)

Uses: The Indians of North America availed themselves of the many and varied medicinal uses of wild roses well before the beginning of recorded history. For instance, they even recognized the happily soothing and relaxing psychological value of breathing in roses' sweetness. The flowers, soaked overnight in rainwater, were used to bathe sore eyes. The essence was applied to aching foreheads to ease discomfort there.

The cooled petals were taken internally to abate fevers. They were steeped in water to make a tea which was added as a sweetening and restorative agent to broths for the ill and convalescent and, combined with mint, taken internally for relaxation and sleep.

For the very critical influenzas of the early days, as well as for diarrhea with which blood was passed, tablespoonful doses of the strong tea were prescribed. For bladder disabilities, especially common in the dusty interior of the continent, this wild rose tea was resorted to as a pleasant palliative. The dried petals, with their high vitamin C content, were also blown into sore throats to coat and soothe the inflamed parts.

The tinctured petals of the rock rose in particular, covered and steeped in cold alcohol for several days until the tincture was tinged a deep purplish red, were given sparingly by some physicians of the late eighteen hundreds for diarrhea, inflammation of the eyeball, and even for venereal diseases.

The Indians and pioneers combined the pure white lard from rendered black bear fat, as well as other edible greases, with the crushed and ground petals for mouth sores, as well as to use for eczema every few hours until the inflammation and itching had eased. The dried and powdered petals were stirred into cool water for heartburn. The powder was applied directly to fever sores and blisters.

Teas brewed from the redder of the wild roses, the brighter the better, were relied upon by some of the Indians and colonists to increase the stamina of the heart. Wild rose petals, being astringent, were candied into soft preserves, believed to soothe coughing. The flowers were simmered and the decoction pressed into service as a gargle, later drunk, for sore throats. It was also dropped into infected ears.

Cooled and sweetened with honey or maple sugar, it was resorted to for controlling fever. Many an Indian and settler gathered the flowers when they were at their sweetest and dried them, then kept them carefully cool and covered for usage during the long cold winters.

Tea steeped from the scrubbed roots of the wild rose was believed by some tribes to be very effective for coughs. Rocky Mountain Indians in particular imbibed a tea concocted from the roots for fever and for other cold symptoms. Such a tea was credited with being mild enough, used in carefully administered small portions, to be given to children suffering with one or another of the flu viruses and for abnormal discharges of the bowels in which blood was passed. Decoctions, in which the properties of the roots were extracted by boiling, were sipped for stomach and liver disorders, as well as for failing urination.

The cleaned live roots, mashed between two smooth stones, were applied to scratches, cuts, wounds of various sorts, and sores. The dried and powdered roots were also so utilized. The inner bark of the root was applied to boils that had either burst or had been lanced.

Some Indians, wounded by accident or battle, allowed these injuries first to cleanse themselves by bleeding, then applied powdered or shaved rose stems to them. After the localized enlargement and the pain had subsided, a final covering of rose leaves was said to leave little or no mark from the hurt. The inner bark of the stems, either dry or wet and sometimes heated, was also occasionally initially applied.

Too, wild rose leaves were employed externally, especially to the forehead, to soothe an overagitated Indian or colonist and to bring rest and sleep.

One reason why rose hips became such an important wild medicine in North American was that, although neither the Indians or the settlers knew it, they contain more of the all-vital vitamin C than do even oranges. They were boiled to make a syrup that seemed to give relief from itching on any part of the body.

In fact, the whole haw with the seeds was mashed and thought to relieve trouble with the lower intestines, especially for those individuals suffering from piles. Also, the entire crushed haws were relied on by numerous women to control inordinate menstruation. Even the red skins of the fruit were sought to settle queasy stomachs.

Because the evasive antiscorbutic is lost with heat and age, the best way the Indians could get it during the winter months was by plucking and eating the withered haws directly from the plants to which they adhere until the fresh blossoms arrive. Dried and powdered, they were not so effective; so the best thing the women could find to do with them when they gathered them at their plumpest was to make a puree, preserve, or extract from them and use this in other foods with which it blended agreeably.

Rose-hip tea, made the regular way or, best, by leaving a handful of the haws in cool water overnight, was a relished and healthful beverage. Those with tuberculosis were among those seeking it.

Even the seeds are extremely rich in vitamin E. They were included in most of the wild rose hip prescriptions, of course, but the seeds simmered by themselves provided a liniment sought for external, as well as internal, use for muscular pains and the pangs of arthritis. By themselves they were also believed to be effective for lower intestinal troubles and for troublesome piles.

The whole wild rose plant, all well washed and cut into bits, was soaked in brandy, which was then used sparingly, because of the effect of the alcoholic content, for syphilis.

Even the fungus galls that appeared on some wild rose plants had their uses, being crushed while fresh and applied as poultices to boils, both to bring them to a head and, once they had burst, to relieve the inflammation, pain, and redness, and to help dry them up with as little remaining mark as possible.

WILD STRAWBERRY (*Fragaria*)

Family: Rose (Rosaceae)

Common Names: Strawberry, Scarlet Strawberry, Field Strawberry, Mountain Strawberry, Yukon Strawberry, California Strawberry, Virginia Strawberry, Wood Strawberry, European Wood Strawberry, Beach Strawberry, White Strawberry, Earth Mulberry.

Characteristics: It is appropriate that the wild strawberry is a member of the rose family, for no more fragrant or delicious berry is known to mankind. In fact, nothing comes even remotely close to this wild, tiny, sweet tidbit that is well known to anyone who has ever seen a domestic strawberry growing, as the wilderness variety is only a miniaturization, infinitely more delectable then the domestic. Proving that good things really do come in small packages is the fact that the only drawback to the wild strawberry is its comparative minuteness, although one can sit in the middle of a wild patch and soon eat his sweet and satisfying fill.

The largest wild strawberries I have ever encountered have been about an inch long, found in southeastern Alaska, the Aleutians, the Seward Peninsula, and around the Gulf of Alaska—the *F. chiloensis*. Yet in the interior of the forty-ninth state and along the Yukon River are to be found the more usual tiny delicacies.

Wild Strawberry (*Fragaria*)

To be accurate, the so-called fruits are actually the diminutive surface seeds, the pleasurable part being really the embellishing delection that is the fruit receptacle. This is usually the well-known red in color except in the case of the white strawberry, likewise delightfully sweet, that is to be found in and around Pennsylvania, West Virginia, and New York.

Everything begins with the perfumed five-petaled blossom, with its five sharply tipped leaflike sepals and another quintet, the bracts—the leaflike reproductive spore holders at the bottom of the floral cluster. About two dozen stamens extend in a thick circle around the seed containers of each flower, adhering so tightly that they remain when the white petals dry and shrivel.

Most important medicinally are the deeply green, vitamin-rich leaves, taller than the fruit, whose stems lift immediately from the roots and are composed of a trio of robustly toothed leaflets, defensively equipped with somewhat gentle bristles.

Area: Wild strawberries enhance the far northern territories of the Dominion of Canada across to our forty-ninth state, then move south to Mexico, prospering throughout the continent with the exception of the dry regions.

Uses: The ragged and poverty-ridden minutemen and other heroes of the American Revolution were in many cases saved from scurvy, as well as being stimulated and revived, by tea made from the fresh green foliage of the wild strawberry, still verdant even when found beneath the snows of Valley Forge and elsewhere in the thirteen independence-seeking colonies.

These soldiers were merely reenacting the practices of the earlier colonists, who turned to this wild antiscorbutic when their gums started getting soft, their bodies weak, and their unhealed sores lingering. The best way to get the most minerals and vitamins from these leaves, outside of eating them raw, is to tip boiling water over a handful of the fresh green foliage in the evening and let the decoction steep overnight. When it is drunk, cold, a fresh batch can be started.

The wild strawberries themselves were thought to be effective against gout, bladder gravel, other kidney difficulties, and even intestinal worms. In cases of fever, backwoods housewives sought to bring down the temperature by a pleasantly cool and refreshing beverage prepared by squeezing wild strawberries into cold water.

The Indians ate wild strawberries for colds before vitamin C was known—devoured them to increase the flow of urine, to bring down what they knew as hard swellings, in lotion form for ulcers on and about the reproductive organs, for heart trouble, mashed as paste to remove tartar and clean the teeth, for toothache, and as an astringest and refrigerant. (As far as the fruit's being effective in tooth care there may be no connection, but I have always eaten wild strawberries the year around, in winter in the form of jam, and I have never had a toothache or lost a tooth.)

Juice from fresh wild strawberries was mixed with water and used to bathe hot, reddened eyes. The juice was also squeezed into badly inflamed and matter-exuding ulcers, with what were said to be often healing effects. It was also said to relieve sunburn.

Some Indian nations, passing along their lore to the later arrivals in this New World, made bitters from wild strawberry roots, particularly as a tonic and hoped-for blood purifier after the long cold winters. One recipe called for a handful of roots placed in a large earthenware container, covered with bubbling water, steeped all night, and then in the morning brought to a boil for four hours before being strained and bottled. A common dose was 2 tablespoons both upon rising and upon retiring. This was also used to increase the urine flow, to quell bloody diarrhea and excessive menstruation, and for jaundice. Some hopefuls even regarded it as a remedy for gonorrhea, used both internally and externally. Stronger infusions were said to help liver and kidney pain.

A tea made from ½ ounce of dried leaves and a cup of boiling water was believed effective for diarrhea in children, as well as for kidney trouble, and as a mild astringent. Adults used it too. The fresh-leaf tea was used for eczema, both internally and externally, as well as for relieving stomach trouble.

A number of so-called authorities, even today, praise the effectiveness of fresh strawberry-leaf tea as a beverage more healthful than either store-purchased tea or coffee.

WILD TEA (*Myrica*) (*Comptonia*)

Family: Sweet Gale (Myricaceae)

Common Names: Sweet Fern, Fern Bush, Meadow Fern, Spleen Fern, Shrubby Fern, Spleenwort Bush, Spleenwort Fern, Shrubby-Sweet Fern, Ferngate, Ferngale, Sweet Bush, Canadian Sweetgale, Sweetgale, Sweet Gale, Sweet Ferry.

Characteristics: Wild tea is a fernlike, perennial bush with a woody stalk and leaves, growing about 4 feet high, sweet-smelling and multibranched. The small limbs are lightly hairy. The aromatic

Wild Tea (*Myrica*) (*Comptonia*)

leaves grow alternately, 3 to 6 inches long, linear, and deeply cleft. It produces fuzzy pistillate flowers—that is, blossoms with the ovule-bearing organs of the seed plants, consisting of the ovaries with their appendages but no stamens—in catkins.

These are followed by brown, gleaming burrs about a quarter of an inch across from which—if one does not mind staining his thumbnail yellow with a nearly indelible resinous oil—will yield tender, tasty nutlets, particularly in the early summer while they are still tender.

The fragrant leaves were among those used during the American Revolution, and before, as a substitute for store tea with its taint of an English tax in the view of the patriots. A teaspoon of the dried leaves steeped for each cup of bubbling water produced a very agreeable beverage. If used directly from the plant, the amount of leaves was just doubled.

Area: Wild tea prefers open sterile woodlands, pastures, meadows, clearings, dry woods, nearly or entirely treeless upland slopes from New Brunswick and the other Maritime Provinces to Saskatchewan, south to Minnesota and through the Appalachians to North Carolina, Georgia, and Tennessee.

Uses: The beverages, both potent and delicate, brewed from the pleasantly fragrant leaves of the fernlike wild tea were used in a number of ways by the Indians and settlers. They were taken internally and also used as a wash for poison ivy rashes, blisters, and sores. In fact, it was believed that, if the wash were used for these soon enough after exposure, it would dissolve and wash away the irritating substances and prevent the trouble which was transferred not only by direct contact with the irritant but indirectly as from the fur of dogs and cats which had passed through an ivy bed.

A strong enough leaf tea was believed to ease both stomach and abdominal cramps and diarrhea. The complete perennial, so brewed, provided a remedy for paroxysms of acute abdominal pain, perhaps localized and caused by spasms, obstruction, or twisting of the colon. Care had to be taken, of course, not to be misled by appendicitis, characterized by extreme sensitivity in the right lower abdomen and in the early days hopefully treated instead by cold compresses.

Such tea drunk at childbirth was believed to help physically in the delivery of the baby. Supplies of frost-wilted leaves were gathered in the fall, dried, and kept throughout the cold months for all such purposes.

It was also drunk for a stimulating effect especially by convalescents weakened by fever, and its aromatic pleasantness was used to make such early remedies as cough medicines taste better. It was one of the many arthritis treatments, both as a beverage and for hot moist applications to ease pain in the afflicted part. In this regard, the leaves were simmered by the Indians for providing a hot moist poultice to be held against the cheek to ease the agony of a toothache.

Also used as a closet and drawer scent and moth-repellent, the aromatic shrub was said to repel mosquitoes and other winged biters when spread damply over the dwindling coals of a campfire or smoked by someone on the go.

No less an authority than the *U.S. Dispensatory* stated that a decoction of the medicinal be used to treat diarrhea, while other authorities recognized its value with difficulties arising from poison ivy and the like.

WILLOW (*Salix*)

Family: Willow (Salicaceae)

Common Names: White Willow, European White Willow, Snow Willow, Black Willow, Pussy Willow, Swamp Willow, Blue Willow, Shining Willow, Canada Willow, Quebec Willow, Prairie Willow, Tall Prairie Willow, Coastal Plain Willow, Weeping Willow, Drummond's Willow, Glaucous Willow, Glossy Willow, Crack Willow, Sandbar Willow, Silky Willow.

Characteristics: The above is only a sampling of the names, for some 200 to 300 willows grow throughout the world, depending on which school of thought the botantist who is doing the counting follows; at least a third of them grow in this country. They range from large attractive trees, to shrubs and bushes, to small shoots in the Arctic and mountains, which are important for many times being at first spring source of vitamin C and, incidentally, of plant food, Being seen most frequently near water, they also grow in lofty stony country.

Particularly when some species become snowy with the widely known pussy willows, which I've seen growing from beaver houses on still-frozen ponds, it is not hard to recognize them, especially as most varieties have narrow and long smooth or toothed leaves, or oblong lancelike leaves, with short stems. Partly because they are the first growth to leaf in the springtime, they are the favorite browse of moose and other members of the deer family.

Willow (*Salix*)

To pick a few individual species, the black willow, *S. nigra,* is the largest American willow, stretching 50 and sometimes nearly 100 feet high in damp bottomlands and along water, although some remain bushes. The branches are reddish, smooth, brittle where they leave the trunks, which lift largely in clumps. The fruits are narrow, vaselike, closed receptacles containing innumerable silky tufted seeds which run approximately 150,000 to the ounce, one reason why they are so widely spread through New Brunswick west to Ontario and South Dakota, south to Texas.

The sandbar willow (*S. interior*), on the other hand, is a shrub from some 1 to nearly 3 yards tall, growing in thickets on sand and gravel along streams and other spots where there is often flooding. Again, the branchlets are reddish and mostly smooth. The characteristic willow leaves are narrowly lancelike, sharp-tipped at either end, and smoothly green on both sides and sometimes silky silver, growing on extremely short stalks. They grow from the Maritimes to gold-panning Alaska, south to Maryland and New Mexico.

Area: As can be surmised, the willow family grows in quantity in Canada and the United States from the Arctic to Mexico.

Uses: The bitterness in the leaves and the thin inner bark of the majority of the willows comes from salicylic acid, which gives the common aspirin its own bitterness, making this general species one of natures's most important natural gifts to mankind. The North American Indians soon discovered that tea decocted and steeped from the cambium of the majority of the willows (a very few of the shoots turn out to be sweet when eaten for nourishment and vitamin C—a fact which makes them more palatable but less important medically) was important for arthritis and for reducing fever and many pains—this centuries before the isolation and marketing of the drug aspirin. In fact, the willow's name of *Salix* comes from salicylic acid.

The ashes of burned willow twigs were blended with water and used for gonorrhea. Willow roots were powdered with stones and turned to in an effort to dry up sores resulting from syphilis. The settlers joined the Indians in using potent teas brewed from the thin cambium or inner bark of the bitter willows to treat venereal diseases.

The dried and powdered bitter bark, astringent and detergent, was applied to the navels of newly born babies. It was utilized to stop severe bleeding, as were the crushed young green leaves, the bark, and the seeds, also stuffed up the nostrils to stop bad nosebleeds. These were also used for toothache, the salicin in them here being the important component. They were steeped in water or wine as a dandruff controller and preventative.

Some tribes turned to the simmered bark and roots of the black willow, *S. nigra*, for weakness and lack of vigor that they attributed to poor blood. The inner bark of the black willow was brewed into a strong tea for keeping moist compresses over ulcers and gangrene.

The Mohicans were among the Indians soaking the inner bark of the red willow (*S. lucida*), to get bile out of the stomach and allow vomiting. The Chickasaws used the roots this way and for nosebleeds, as well as in small amounts for headache. Some of the Indians of New England used a weaker solution of the scraped bark of the red willow for cold symptoms and smoked the scraped and cut cambium for asthma. Other Indians, the settlers following, steeped the bark of the Red Willow and imbibed it for headache and lumbago.

To fend off fevers, the Creeks washed themselves in a boiled solution of the roots. Some crushed the bark and bandaged it around the head to ease headaches. The Ojibwas turned to the inner bark for external use on wounds and sores; other tribes to check bleeding—a use also made of the root bark of the pussy willow, *S. discolor*, as well as other willows. Some bands utilized root tea in an enema for severe diarrhea.

As if all this were not enough, the roots were used to kill and expel worms. Willow tea was used by the drop to relieve inflamed eyes.

The settlers soon adopted the Indian practice of steeping willow roots for spring tonic, adjudged all the better for being bitter. And some tried many of the tribes' use of pussy willow catkins as an aphrodisiac.

WITCH HAZEL (*Hamamelis virginiana*)

Family: Witch Hazel (Hamamelidaceae)

Common Names: Common Witch Hazel, Wych Hazel, Southern Witch Hazel, Eastern Witch Hazel, White Hazel, Snapping Hazel, Snapping Hazel-Nut, Hamamelia, Spotted Alder, Striped Alder, Tobacco Wood, Wood Tobacco, Winterbloom, Pistachio, Long Boughs.

Characteristics: The plant has nothing to do with witches. The usual name is derived from an Old English word meaning "pliable" and related to "weak," not exactly a comedown when one considers that although the medicine is an official drug, there has never been

Witch Hazel (*Hamamelis virginiana*)

any complete agreement as to its efficiency despite the fact that the public buys it by the millions of gallons.

Witch hazel is a crooked tree or shrub, usually 8 to 15 feet tall, although it sometimes reaches 25 feet in height. The twisting stem and long, forking branches with brown, smooth bark are characteristic, as is the balsamic fragrance of the bruised parts. It produces new shoots from the base. A peculiar feature, except in the spring-flowering species, is the late appearance of the threadlike, yellow flowers, their not appearing until late in the autumn or in the early winter after the leaves, smooth above and paler and smooth or almost so beneath, have fallen.

As for the urnlike, downy seed capsule, this does not mature until the following season, when it bursts open, scattering the shining, hard, black seeds with great force and to a considerable distance. These grow from a two-celled ovary, composed of a pair of pistils united below, forming a double-beaked, two-celled woody capsule, the one ovule suspended from the apex of each chamber becoming a bony entity. There are eight stamens, half of them perfect and the other half scalelike and sterile.

The twigs are mostly hairy, bearing the fruits in long clusters. The leaves are simple, 3 to 5 inches long, thick, scalloped along their margins, with an obtuse apex and curved to a tapering base, roundish to round-oval, borne on short stalks. Both the twigs and the buds are rough with a rusty or tawny pubescence.

Area: Used in landscaping and growing in moist light woods and along rocky banks and streams throughout most of the United States except in the Far West, this North American plant thrives especially from the Maritimes and Quebec to Florida, westward to Minnesota and Texas.

Uses: The twigs, leaves, and bark are all used to prepare witch hazel extract, which has been used for everything from shaving lotions and vaginal douches to treating contusions, sprains, insect bites, and piles. The fresh leaves especially contain a high concentration of tannin which make them very astringent. Indians taught the settlers to apply them to bruises and swellings.

The tannin, gallic acid, and the volatile oils are strongly hemostatic, and therefore a tea steeped from the leaves and bark has long been considered effective for bleeding in the stomach, as for ulcers, and in an enema for inwardly bleeding piles. The Iroquois also used a tea made from the steeped leaves, sweetened to taste with maple sugar, as both a pleasant and beneficial tea with meals. One recipe for the tea was a teaspoonful of the granulated or finely chopped leaves and bark added to a cup of bubbling water and steeped for five minutes. It was believed, incidentally, that the oils were more potent if the components were gathered in the late autumn and winter.

Compresses and bandages, kept wet with witch hazel, were applied to varicose veins and to burns, rashes, skin irritations, and infections. A small amount of alcohol was often added if available, and a steam extract from the twigs was what was often used. Cold compresses were also used for headaches and for sore and inflamed eyes. A decoction prepared from the inner bark was considered by many Indians as being especially efficacious for bathing the eyes.

The entire moistened herb was spread over hot rocks in enclosed places and water poured atop it for steam baths, which were believed to bring about speedy relief from feverish colds, catarrh, coughing, and abnormally heavy phlegm discharges.

The extract was used in massages for overexertion and muscular strain, for arthritis, and for general conditioning. It was applied manually, sometimes with a bit of moistened cotton, to insect bites, hemorrhoids, scalds, burns, and swellings.

Witch hazel was also relied upon as a rinse and gargle for irritated throats, sore gums, cankers, and general mouth irritations.

When one was traveling where water was scant, he often chewed the bark, which was first bitter and astringent but left a pleasantly lingering sweetish, pungent taste.

YARROW (*Achillea millefolium*)

Family: Composite (Compositae)

Common Names: Common Yarrow, Milfoil, Knight's Milfoil, Milfoil Thousand-Leaf, Soldier's Woundwort, Soldier's Wound-Wort, Bloodwort, Sanguinary, Nosebleed, Devil's Plaything, Green Arrow, Thousand-Leaf, Thousand-Seal, Thousand-Leaved Clover, Gordaldo, Gordoloba, Cammock, Old Man's Pepper, Carpenter Grass, Carpenter's Grass, Dog Daisy, Woolly Yarrow.

Characteristics: Once smelled, the aromatically lacy foliage and flat-topped terminal flowers of the yarrow will ever after be recognized. The almost always white blossoms are very rarely yellow and even more occasionally purple. They are small, developing in spring

314

Yarrow (*Achillea millefolium*)

and summer into sometimes convex clusters. The complex leaves are made up of very small entities on small stems branching off of single stalks. Growing alternately, they are also many times clustered at the bottom of the usually less than 3-foot-high central stems. Finely dissected, they are linear to narrow-spatulate or lanceolate. The foliage as a whole often seems grayish from numerous small hairs.

Gathered in the late summer or early fall, many still scent the cabins where they are hung high to dry for later use.

Yarrow is widely known in England as tansy, an entirely different important medicinal plant here in the New World (covered elsewhere in this volume).

Area: The fragrant lacy and distinctive plants grow from coast to coast over most of Canada and the United States.

Uses: Yarrow roots are still the traditionally used local anesthetic of many of the western Indians, as revealed by two cases recorded by the Research Service of the U.S. Department of Agriculture.

One involved a Nevada Indian who was suffering acutely from a deep thigh wound in which foreign substances had entered the cut. Fresh, scrubbed yarrow roots were crushed to a soft spongy mass and applied gently to the spot. Within half an hour the anesthetic had so dulled the pain that it was possible to expand and clean the wound. The second concerned a deeply sunk splinter that, following soaking in a solution of yarrow roots, was similarly opened and removed. This was accomplished by members of the family.

Not only fresh poultices, but washes in which the leaves and stems were also sometimes boiled were used in similar cases after battles and accidents. The entire plant was often reduced to a paste, spread over newly set fractures, and bound in place with fresh dandelion leaves or sterilized cloths.

The yarrow had the additional quality of acting as a coagulant and therefore was used for everything from a gashed toe to a spear-torn side. The leaves of the yarrow, steeped in water, thus became in numerous regions the most commonly employed herb to stem the flow of blood. They were even soaked and stuffed up the nostrils to quell nosebleed.

Yarrow poultices were resorted to for common bruises and abrasions. In cases of burns and scalds, yarrow was crushed as between two smooth rocks, combined with water, and spread over the injury before perhaps wild onions were bruised, salted, and applied both in an effort to withdraw the heat and to prevent blistering.

The styptic characteristics of the yarrow were resorted to for all kinds of nicks and cuts, even those from the pioneer's razor. The leaves were even reported to heal inflammations, eczema, rashes, infections, and the like.

Yarrow tea was applied to sore nipples. Boiled yarrow leaves were used as a wash for eyes irritated from dust, glare, and snow blindness. It was tried in eruptions such as those arising from measles and chicken pox. Swellings were bathed in the tea, as were regions irritated by poison ivy and poison oak and by general itching. It was a natural wash for fevers.

Bits from freshly cut yarrow roots were inserted in aching tooth cavities. It was even believed that the constant chewing of yarrow root or continual applications of root tea would kill the nerve of an ulcerated tooth.

Indians suffering from the gout took decoctions of yarrow. It was turned to for sciatica. It was resorted to for neuralgia. The Chicakasaws took an infusion of yarrow for cramps in the neck. It was given warm as a soothing agent in cases of hysteria. It was used to combat tuberculosis.

Yarrow was even used in attempted abortions. Dr. Charles F. Millspaugh reported in his 1892 book on *Medicinal Plants* that the use of yarrow was no more limited to the Indians than the age-old practice of abortion elsewhere in the world. The dosage suggested was 10 drops or more of the oil of the herb. The doctor recorded that yarrow was "one of the most frequently used abortives among ignorant people— not so dangerous generally as that following the use of nutmeg but very often serious." Too, yarrow tea, made from fresh leaves, was widely favored for suppressed menstruation.

Some of the tribes resorted to a yarrow poultice for spider bites, and, of course, after the sucking of the wound, it was used for poisonous snakebites.

The leaves of the yarrow were also favored for fevers. Hot yarrow tea, made from the dried leaves, was sought to induce perspiring, regarded as effective in breaking a fever. This was also used for chills. The feverish patient was bathed, too, in cold yarrow tea.

If one was constantly troubled by the necessity of getting up at night to urinate, tea made from either the fresh or dried flowers temporarily stopped the annoyance. Strong yarrow flower tea was favored as a diuretic. Such a tea was also taken for worms.

A poultice of bruised yarrow leaves was laid or bound over the forehead for headaches.

A weak brew of the entire plant was pressed into service as an astringent gargle and mouthwash. It was believed to be successful as a vaginal douche for leukorrhea. Indians injected it as an enema for hemorrhoids. It was generally relied on to adjust malfunction of the kidney, liver, and the genitourinary systems. Even today, yarrow is steeped in an effort to help a diseased condition in the stomach and intestinal system.

A small amount of the roots or preferably the whole plant was steeped in a small amount of water as a tonic for someone who was run down. A chilled infusion was recommended for convalescents. It was, as might have been suspected, another of the spring tonics. Tea made from the plant was given twice daily as a blood builder following childbirth.

The entire plant, including the roots, was boiled and taken mornings and nights to help one retain his strength during a cold. In fact, the chewing of yarrow root was supposed to help break up a cold.

Yarrow baths were favored for arthritis, and a solution served as a favored liniment for overexerted joints and muscles.

Leaves were soaked and a wad of them pressed into an aching or infected ear. The juice dropped into the eys was believed to stop redness and inflammation.

The dried and powdered herb was steeped with plantain tea to stem internal bleeding.

Generally, the herb is an aromatic with diaphoretic and emmenagogue activity that seemed to work out well as a general vulnerary. Leaves of both the common yarrow (*A. millefolium*), and the woolly yarrow (*A. lanulosaw*), were picked for numerous difficulties with the reproductive organs.

An ointment for wounds was made by blending yarrow leaves with a pure edible lard such as those made from wild-animal fat.

YUCCA (*Yucca*)

Family: Lily (Liliaceae)

Common Names: Datil Yucca, Broad-Leaved Yucca, Spanish Bayonet, Spanish Dagger, Dagger Plant, Date Fruit, Datil, Soap Weed, Soapweed, Small Soapweed, Bear Grass, Joshua Tree, Our Lord's Candle, Adam's Needle, Eve's Darning Needle.

Characteristics: Not really a cactus, the yucca nevertheless grows in desert and desertlike areas and includes the well-known Joshua